# SHAKESPEARE FOR ONE

*Men*

### THE COMPLETE
### MONOLOGUES AND
### AUDITION PIECES

*edited by*

## DOUGLAS NEWELL

**Heinemann**
A division of Reed Elsevier Inc.
361 Hanover Street
Portsmouth, NH 03801–3912
www.heinemanndrama.com

*Offices and agents throughout the world*

**Library of Congress Cataloging-in-Publication Data**
Shakespeare, William, 1564–1616.
  [Plays. Selections]
    Shakespeare for one : men : the complete monologues and audition
pieces / [edited by Douglas Newell].
        p. cm.
      ISBN 0-325-00488-9 (alk. paper)
        1. Acting—Auditions.   2. Men—Drama.   3. Monologues.
I. Newell, Douglas.   II. Title.

PR2771 .N48 2002
822.3′3—dc21                                    2002009730

Editor: Lisa A. Barnett
Production: Vicki Kasabian
Cover design: Jenny Jensen Greenleaf
Typesetter: TechBooks
Manufacturing: Steve Bernier

Printed in the United States of America on acid-free paper
06  05  04  03  02  DA  1  2  3  4  5

For Ralphie . . . who graciously overlooked the fact
that I had but two legs.

# CONTENTS

# ACKNOWLEDGMENTS

What would eventually become *Shakespeare for One* was born in a stuffy L.A. basin bungalow, yanked kicking and screaming from the keyboard of a solitary, out-of-work actor searching desperately for a purpose in life. Which is not to say that it wasn't a hoot or that there wasn't a little help along the way.

To Gene Openshaw, an old friend who does so many things so extraordinarily well, I owe heartfelt thanks for providing suggestions, advice, and enthusiasm back when WillyBook routinely tottered near the abyss.

For the loan of his computer to a penniless thespian, I thank John Brady; for nobly taking the heat when I was so tardy in returning that computer, I thank John's son and my chum through thick and thin, Peter Brady.

And finally, for her unwavering support and her inexplicable faith that I would indeed see this quixotic journey through to the very end, I offer both love and gratitude to my true companion, Patty Conroy.

# INTRODUCTION

## Overview

Each chapter covers one of Shakespeare's thirty-seven plays and starts off with a thumbnail sketch of the story's key developments. Plot details not directly related to the featured monologues are omitted.

Following the synopsis is an abridged cast of characters, listing only those persons who somehow play a role in one or more speeches.

Preceding each monologue is its act, scene, and line number in the play; a description of its physical setting; and a brief account of the action or circumstances that have led to the moment at hand.

Line numbers appearing along the side of each monologue refer to the explanatory notes following that speech.

At the back of the book you will find a guide to the pronunciation of character and location names, as well as other information that might be useful in choosing particular monologues.

## The Chosen Few

It only makes sense that one of the first issues to be tackled in putting together a comprehensive collection of monologues is exactly what constitutes a monologue. With *Shakespeare for One*, it wasn't long before a few basic qualifications had emerged:

- First off, the speech had to have some semblance of proper structure; which is to say, it needed a more-or-less functional beginning, middle, and end.
- In addition, the selection being considered could require neither wholesale editing nor the presence of another actor in order for it to work logically or dramatically.
- What's more, it was decided that all monologues should have an estimated

running time of at least one minute; any shorter and they would rarely be of use in the classroom or as an audition piece.

With such minimal guidelines in place, an initial pass through Shakespeare's canon resulted in an unruly collection of nearly 450 eligible monologues. After several rounds of culling, a far more manageable assortment of speeches finally emerged from the pack: 175 solid solos for the male actor, every one suitable for audition or classroom use.

Most, but not all, of the also-rans had one or more flaws that rendered them unacceptable for the purposes of this project. For example, a few contenders had the requisite length and structure but, alas, were woefully lackluster affairs whose chief attribute was to wax expository.

Then too, some otherwise promising speeches had to be eliminated because nothing even resembling a serviceable entry and/or exit line could be found. Many more candidates were dismissed because, once removed from their proper context, they retained little to offer in the way of theatrical thrills—no action, no intrigue, nothing.

On the other hand, there were those monologues that, while arguably deficient in one way or another, still seemed all too likeable to simply dismiss out of hand. Wherever such flawed gems popped up, they were duly noted in a list of "Alternates" appearing at chapter's end. Anyone seeking even more options than those presented in *Shakespeare for One* is encouraged to turn to the plays themselves and look into a few of these outtakes.

## On Editing Shakespeare

From the very inception of this project there existed an ideal to steadfastly resist altering Shakespeare's text in any appreciable way. It was a fine ideal indeed—and more than a little impractical.

Before long it became clear that unless minor modifications were permitted here and there, a wealth of potentially outstanding material would have to be discarded. Such waste seemed self-defeating, to say the least. After all, *Shakespeare for One* is intended for the actor, not the scholar; it is designed to be used, not studied. And although safeguarding the integrity of both text and annotation has always been a top priority, there is no intention here to offer up this volume as the latest and greatest arbiter of Shakespearean polemics.

Thus, irony reared its impish head, and the hands-off rule of editing was itself amended. But only grudgingly, and only a little. Observe . . .

- Once in a while it was necessary to shuffle one or more parts of a given speech in order to include all relevant text; entry (4) from *Julius Caesar*, for example, deftly employs such benign sleight of hand.
- Occasionally, for the sake of clarity or cohesiveness, a bit of another character's line was appropriated for inclusion in the featured monologue. Hamlet's encounter with the ghost in entry (3) becomes workable for the solo actor only by doing just that.
- When dealing with verse, a character's own fragmented lines were often linked together in order to keep intact both meter and intended meaning.
- Finally, on very rare occasion it was deemed necessary to add an extraneous word or two to the original text. This sort of liberty was not taken lightly. Rather, it was the last resort of an editor in dire need of a transition, and all such renegade words are clearly marked by brackets.

Yet even with all this regrettable (but necessary) mucking about, the fact remains that fewer than one in ten monologues from *Shakespeare for One* was altered from its standard form in any appreciable way.

Other than the above-mentioned bracketing of extraneous words, no special attention was drawn to departures from the original text. The intention here was not to conceal any rampant editorial license, but merely to facilitate use of the material. The less cluttered a script, the easier it is to work with. Since act, scene, and line information is provided for every entry, it's a simple matter to examine the source text as traditionally presented, should some question arise regarding the piece's integrity.

As to judging where to begin and end each selection, the optimal start and stop points for each speech were usually pretty evident. Keep in mind, though, that the entry and exit lines furnished in *Shakespeare for One* might not be the best available for every conceivable set of circumstances. Feel free to experiment. The idea was to present each entry as completely as possible, thereby allowing each user the opportunity to do their own fine-tuning.

Finally, there is the question of Shakespeare's glorious linguistic idiosyncrasies. Shakespeare would hardly be Shakespeare, of course, without curious constructions such as *to't* and *i'th'*, or compressed verbs like *wond'red* and *o'erwhelm*. And since a prime function of such contractions is to sustain the meter of verse, it seemed far preferable to keep them as they traditionally appear rather than resort to some sort of misbegotten modernization.

As to whether or not an extra syllable here or there really matters all that much, well, that's a call for each individual actor to make. It's true that fiddling about with Shakespeare is an endeavor fraught with peril, but the history of theatre is thick with it nonetheless. Fortunately, most situations encountered by the student or auditioning actor are likely to allow for a good deal of flexibility.

## Defining Terms

Acting is tricky. Acting Shakespeare is really tricky. Yet even Shakespeare's most daunting and inscrutable passages can be successfully navigated if one is properly prepared for the journey.

An essential element of that preparation is comprehending precisely what, at each and every moment, the author is getting at. There's no denying that Shakespeare's work is marvelously (and oft times maddeningly) elliptical. Even so, solutions are available to most of the tangled webs he weaves. With its comprehensive approach to annotation, *Shakespeare for One* aims to provide the befuddled actor with as many of those solutions as possible.

The definitions and explanations presented in *Shakespeare for One* are based on information gathered from a variety of authoritative sources. In those rare instances when even the collective wisdom of scholars past and present has failed to yield a solution, a consensus best guess, marked with a question mark (?), is offered instead.

## Setting the Scene

It goes without saying that the plot-related comments found at the beginning of each chapter and preceding each entry are not offered as stand-ins for actually reading the play. Instead, they are asked to perform two narrowly defined roles: one, set the scene a bit for the uninitiated so they don't have to read an entire play just to test-drive its monologues; and two, gently jog the memories of those who might know a given play, but can't quite recall the particulars leading up to the entry at hand.

Should there come a time when more specific plot or character details are required, any of several titles sitting in your local bookstore will do the trick just fine. In fact, the ideal companion piece to *Shakespeare for One* (if you'll permit a bit of cross-promotion) is an outstanding compilation of information and advice entitled *A Guide to Scenes and Monologues from Shakespeare and His Contemporaries*, also published by Heinemann.

But be forewarned that even the best of study guides cannot provide the actor with everything he or she will need in the way of background material. The only way an actor can be fully prepared and can thoroughly appreciate both character and context is to know the source material.

Hamlet got one thing right, anyway: the play *is* the thing.

# ALL'S WELL THAT ENDS WELL

When Bertram ventures off to Paris with his companion Parolles, Helena is devastated. Though she's long adored the young Count, the lowborn Helena has always believed him to be unattainable. But things start looking up when, shortly after her own arrival in Paris, Helena cures the King of France of a serious ailment, and by way of reward is granted her one true wish—to have Bertram for her husband.

Though Bertram is duty-bound to do his king's bidding, he clearly resents having to wed Helena. Not long after the wedding ceremony, he spurns his bride and marches off to the wars.

Some time later, Helena learns that her wayward husband is in Florence courting another woman. Before long Helena has concocted an intricate scheme to insure that Bertram is hers once and for all. After a few unexpected twists and turns, her plan eventually succeeds: Bertram at last sees the error of his ways, he professes to Helena his undying love, and just as promised . . . all's well that ends well.

**KING OF FRANCE**
**BERTRAM,** Count of Rossillion
**PAROLLES,** a follower of Bertram

**COUNTESS OF ROSSILLION,** mother to Bertram
**HELENA,** a gentlewoman raised by the Countess

(1)                     **PAROLLES**                    [I.1.126]

SCENE: The Count of Rossillion's palace

*{Evidently in the mood to flex his rhetorical muscles, Parolles provides Helena with a few of his self-serving ideas on the subject of female chastity.}*

1    It is not politic in the commonwealth of nature to preserve virginity. Loss of virginity is rational increase, and there was never virgin got till virginity was first lost. That you were made of is metal to make virgins. Virginity, by being once lost may be ten times found; by being ever kept, it is ever lost. 'Tis too cold a
5    companion; 'tis against the rule of nature. To speak on the part of virginity is to accuse your mothers, which is most infallible disobedience. He that hangs himself is a virgin; virginity murders itself, and should be buried in highways out of all sanctified limit, as a desperate offendress against nature. Virginity breeds mites, much like a cheese; consumes itself to the very paring, and so
10   dies with feeding his own stomach. Besides, virginity is peevish, proud, idle, made of self-love, which is the most inhibited sin in the canon. Keep it not; you cannot choose but lose by 't. Out with 't! Within t' one year it will make itself two, which is a goodly increase, and the principal itself not much the worse. 'Tis a commodity will lose the gloss with lying; the longer kept, the less worth.
15   Off with 't while 'tis vendible; answer the time of request. Virginity, like an old courtier, wears her cap out of fashion; richly suited, but unsuitable, just like the brooch and the toothpick, which wear not now. Your date is better in your pie and your porridge than in your cheek; and your virginity, your old virginity, is like one of our French wither'd pears; it looks ill, it eats drily. Marry, 'tis a
20   wither'd pear; it was formerly better, marry, yet 'tis a wither'd pear. Will you anything with it?

**1 politic** expedient, advisable   **2 is rational increase** i.e., results in a reasonable gain   **got** begotten   **3 That** that which   **metal** substance
**4 may ... found** i.e., may produce ten more virgins in its place   **6 accuse your mothers** charge your mothers with a wrongdoing   **infallible** certain
**7 is a virgin** i.e., is the same as a virgin (in that virginity is, in Parolles's view, a sort of suicide)   **7–8 buried ... limit** (Custom dictated that suicide victims be buried at highway crossroads rather than in sanctified ground.)
**8 desperate** reckless   **9 paring** i.e., skin   **10 his** its   **idle** useless, unprofitable   **11 inhibited** prohibited   **canon** laws of the Church (There is a likely allusion here to the Seven Deadly Sins, of which pride—or "self-love"—is the first.)   **12 Out with 't** lend it out—while charging interest to do so   **t' one** the one, a single   **13 principal** original investment (here, the former virgin)   **14 will** that will   **gloss** luster of newness   **lying** lying unused or unsold (with a play on lying on one's backside)   **15 vendible** in demand   **answer ... request** respond now while there is a demand
**16 richly ... unsuitable** fine fare, but unfashionable   **17 wear not now**

are not now in style (At one time the wearing of brooches as hat ornaments and the conspicuous use of toothpicks were both fashionable affectations.) **17–18 Your . . . cheek** i.e., a date serves one better as a cooking ingredient than as a symbol of one's withered cheek   **19 ill** unappetizing **eats drily** tastes dry **Marry** indeed, to be sure   **20 Will you** will you do

(2)                    KING OF FRANCE                    [II.iii.108]

SCENE: The King of France's palace

*{Against all odds, the King has been cured by Helena of a life-threatening ailment. To show his appreciation, the King grants Helena the right to take for her husband whichever unmarried man of the realm she desires. Predictably enough, she opts for Bertram, a young man she's long adored. And just as predictably, Bertram balks at the arrangement, whereupon a rejuvenated King vents his royal wrath upon the lad.}*

| | |
|---|---:|
| Know'st thou not, Bertram, what she has done for me? | 1 |
| She has raised me from my sickly bed. | |
| 'Tis only title thou disdain'st in her, the which | |
| I can build up. Strange is it that our bloods, | |
| Of color, weight, and heat, pour'd all together, | 5 |
| Would quite confound distinction, yet stands off | |
| In differences so mighty. If she be | |
| All that is virtuous—save what thou dislik'st, | |
| A poor physician's daughter—thou dislik'st | |
| Of virtue for the name. But do not so. | 10 |
| From the lowest place when virtuous things proceed, | |
| The place is dignified by th' doer's deed. | |
| Where great additions swell 's, and virtue none, | |
| It is a dropsied honor. Good alone | |
| Is good without a name; vileness is so; | 15 |
| The property by what it is should go, | |
| Not by the title. She is young, wise, fair; | |
| In these to nature she's immediate heir, | |
| And these breed honor. That is honor's scorn | |
| Which challenges itself as honor's born | 20 |
| And is not like the sire. Honors thrive | |
| When rather from our acts we them derive | |
| Than our foregoers. The mere word's a slave, | |
| Debosh'd on every tomb, on every grave | |
| A lying trophy, and as oft is dumb | 25 |

Where dust and damn'd oblivion is the tomb
Of honor'd bones indeed. What should be said?
If thou canst like this creature as a maid,
I can create the rest. Virtue and she
30    Is her own dower; honor and wealth from me.
Here, take her hand, [and] check thy contempt;
Obey our will, which travails in thy good;
Believe not thy disdain, but presently
Do thine own fortunes that obedient right
35    Which both thy duty owes and our power claims,
Or I will throw thee from my care forever
Into the staggers and the careless lapse
Of youth and ignorance; both my revenge and hate
Loosing upon thee, in the name of justice,
40    Without all terms of pity. Speak thine answer.

**2 sickly bed** sickbed   **3 the which** which   **6 stands off** stand apart
**7 differences** (social) distinctions   **8 save** except   **11 proceed** come forth
**13 great additions swell 's** pretentious titles inflate us (i.e., our self-pride)
**14 dropsied** swollen   **alone** in and of itself   **15 is so** i.e., is what it is,
irrespective of its name (in the same way that good is good)
**16–17 property ... title** the quality should be judged for what it is, not for
its name   **18 these ... heir** these are her natural attributes
**20–21 challenges ... sire** lays claim to an honorable title, yet fails to behave
honorably   **23 foregoers** predecessors   **24 Debosh'd** debauched,
corrupted   **25 trophy** memorial   **dumb** silent   **30 dower** dowry   **32 our**
my (the king is employing the royal plural)   **travails in** toils for
**33 presently** immediately   **34 Do ... right** do your own fortunes justice
by rendering that obedience   **37 staggers** (1) giddy, wild conduct (2)
bewilderment   **careless lapse** reckless decline, precipitous fall (in morality)
**39 Loosing** giving vent to, discharging   **40 all ... pity** any form of mercy

**ALTERNATE**
King of France   [V.iii.32–70]

# ANTONY AND CLEOPATRA

Even the considerable charms of Cleopatra cannot detain Antony when word of his wife's death and the threat of an impending civil war compels his return to Rome. Once he's back home, Antony smoothes over a little trouble with his fellow triumvir, Octavius, by marrying Octavius's sister, Octavia. The peace proves short-lived, however, when Antony abandons Rome and his new wife in favor of a return to Egypt and its beguiling Queen of the Nile. War between Antony and Caesar soon follows.

After an initial triumph, Antony's military fortunes soon turn sour when his navy deserts him. Disheartened by defeat, and under the false impression that Cleopatra has died, Antony mortally wounds himself. A short time later he expires in his beloved's arms.

For her part, Cleopatra decides to end things on her own terms rather than succumb to a fate as Octavius's war prize. With loyal attendants by her side, Egypt's queen applies a poisonous snake to her breast and dies.

**MARK ANTONY,** a Roman triumvir
**OCTAVIUS CAESAR,** a Roman triumvir
**EROS,** friend to Antony

**CLEOPATRA,** Queen of Egypt
**OCTAVIA,** sister to Caesar, wife to Antony
**CHARMIAN,** attendant to Cleopatra
**IRAS,** attendant to Cleopatra

(1)                    **ANTONY**                    [IV.xii.9]

SCENE: A battlefield outside Alexandria

*{Antony's navy has suddenly deserted him in favor of Octavius Caesar. He immediately concludes that Cleopatra must have betrayed him, and is somehow behind this unfortunate development.}*

| | |
|---|---|
| 1 | All is lost! |
| | This foul Egyptian hath betrayed me. |
| | My fleet hath yielded to the foe, and yonder |
| | They cast their caps up and carouse together |
| 5 | Like friends long lost. Triple-turn'd whore! 'Tis thou |
| | Hast sold me to this novice, and my heart |
| | Makes only wars on thee. |
| | O sun, thy uprise shall I see no more. |
| | Fortune and Antony part here; even here |
| 10 | Do we shake hands. All come to this? The hearts |
| | That spaniel'd me at heels, to whom I gave |
| | Their wishes, do discandy; melt their sweets |
| | On blossoming Caesar; and this pine is bark'd, |
| | That overtopp'd them all. Betray'd I am. |
| 15 | O this false soul of Egypt! This grave charm, |
| | Whose eye beck'd forth my wars and call'd them home, |
| | Whose bosom was my crownet, my chief end, |
| | Like a right gipsy, hath at fast and loose |
| | Beguil'd me to the very heart of loss. |
| 20 | [*Enter Cleopatra.*] Ah, thou spell! Avaunt! |
| | Vanish, or I shall give thee thy deserving, |
| | And blemish Caesar's triumph. Let him take thee, |
| | And hoist thee up to the shouting plebeians! |
| | Follow his chariot, like the greatest spot |
| 25 | Of all thy sex; most monster-like, be shown |
| | For poor'st diminutives, for dolts, and let |
| | Patient Octavia plough thy visage up |
| | With her prepar'd nails. [*Cleopatra exits.*] 'Tis well th' art gone, |
| | If it be well to live; but better 'twere |
| 30 | Thou fell'st into my fury, for one death |
| | Might have prevented many. Eros, Ho! |
| | The shirt of Nessus is upon me. Teach me, |
| | Alcides, thou mine ancestor, thy rage. |
| | Let me lodge Lichas on the horns o' th' moon, |
| 35 | And with those hands, that grasp'd the heaviest club, |
| | Subdue my worthiest self. The witch shall die. |
| | To the young Roman boy she hath sold me, and I fall |
| | Under this plot. She dies for it. Eros, ho! |

**4 cast...up** (Throwing one's cap in the air could express either joy or a concession to defeat.)   **5 Triple-turn'd** three-times unfaithful (referring to her trysts with Julius Caesar, Cneius Pompey, and Antony himself)   **6 novice** i.e., Octavius Caesar   **11 spaniel'd** followed me devotedly, like a spaniel **at heels** at my heels   **12 discandy** melt away, dissolve   **13 bark'd** stripped of its bark (and thus killed)   **15 grave charm** deadly sorceress   **16 beck'd** beckoned **wars** warring   **17 crownet** coronet   **18 right** outright, true **fast and loose** a game of deception commonly associated with gypsies **20 Avaunt** be gone   **24 Follow his chariot** i.e., in a position of disgrace as part of Caesar's triumphal procession through the streets of Rome **spot** stain, blemish   **26 diminutives, dolts** pejorative terms referring to the common folk viewing the procession   **27 Octavia** Antony's wife and Caesar's sister **plough** plow   **28 prepar'd** i.e., sharpened **30–31 Thou...many** (The precise meaning of this passage is not clear. Antony may be suggesting that, had Cleopatra fallen earlier into his disfavor, this whole war and its many casualties might have been avoided.) **32–34 The...moon** (Hercules, AKA "Alcides," mortally wounded the centaur Nessus with a poisoned arrow. Before dying, however, Nessus managed to trick Hercules into wearing his blood-soaked shirt. The remnants of poison still in the garment induced such agony in Hercules that, in a fit of rage, he threw his servant Lichas high into the air.)

(2)                           ANTONY                    [IV.xiv.55]

SCENE: A field near Cleopatra's palace

*{Under the mistaken impression that Cleopatra has died by her own hand, Antony has resolved to follow in her footsteps. Now all that remains is to convince his dear friend Eros to lend a bit of assistance.}*

Since Cleopatra died,                                                    1
I have liv'd in such dishonor that the gods
Detest my baseness. I, that with my sword
Quarter'd the world, and o'er green Neptune's back
With ships made cities, condemn myself to lack              5
The courage of a woman—less noble mind
Than she which by her death our Caesar tells
"I am conqueror of myself." Thou art sworn, Eros,
That, when the exigent should come, which now
Is come indeed, when I should see behind me              10
Th' inevitable prosecution of
Disgrace and horror, that, on my command,
Thou then wouldst kill me. Do 't; the time is come.

Thou strik'st not me, 'tis Caesar thou defeat'st.
15   Put color in thy cheek, Eros.
Wouldst thou be window'd in great Rome and see
Thy master thus with pleach'd arms, bending down
His corrigible neck, his face subdu'd
To penetrative shame, whilst the wheel'd seat
20   Of fortunate Caesar, drawn before him, branded
His baseness that ensued?
Come then; for with a wound I must be cur'd.
Draw that thy honest sword, which thou hast worn
Most useful for thy country. Do it at once;
25   Or thy precedent services are all
But accidents unpurpos'd. Draw, and come.

**5 With ... cities** i.e., commanded flotillas so immense and tightly packed that they looked like floating cities  **to lack** for lacking   **9 exigent should come** need should arise   **11 inevitable** inescapable  **prosecution** pursuit   **16 window'd** placed near a window   **17 pleach'd** folded   **18 corrigible** submissive   **19 penetrative** deeply piercing, penetrating
**20–21 branded ... ensued** made obvious, as with a brand, the shame of he who followed   **23 honest** honorable   **25 precedent** past, former
**26 accidents unpurpos'd** pointless actions

ALTERNATES
Enobarbus   [II.ii.186–239]
Antony       [III.xiii.105–131]

# AS YOU LIKE IT

Orlando, fearing for his life and fed up with his brother Oliver's neglectful guardianship, decides to seek his fortune elsewhere. Accompanied by his old friend and servant Adam, he arrives in the Forest of Arden and joins the company of Duke Senior, who's been living in banishment since his evil brother Frederick usurped his title.

When Orlando's beloved Rosalind is likewise banished by Frederick, she disguises herself as a boy and, accompanied by her cousin Celia and Touchstone the fool, she strikes out in search of her father, Duke Senior. When she and Orlando happen to meet in the forest, Rosalind decides to have some fun with the fact that he cannot see through her disguise by offering to school the lovesick lad on the finer points of romance.

Elsewhere in the forest, Silvius the shepherd is having no luck at all in wooing the affections of a local maiden named Phebe. After Rosalind overhears Phebe's heartless rebuff of poor Silvius, she steps in to severely upbraid the maid for her cruelty—and, by doing so, induces Phebe to fall in love with her.

Eventually, everything turns out swell: Rosalind drops her disguise and reunites with Orlando, Phebe makes up with Silvius, a repentant Oliver shows up just in time to pair off with Celia, a similarly reformed Frederick restores to Duke Senior his rightful position, and even Touchstone finds love as marriage and merriment abound.

**DUKE SENIOR,** living in banishment
**DUKE FREDERICK,** brother to Duke Senior
**AMIENS,** lord attending on Duke Senior
**JAQUES,** lord attending on Duke Senior
**OLIVER,** eldest son of the late Sir Rowland de Boys
**ORLANDO,** brother to Oliver, in love with Rosalind
**ADAM,** servant to Oliver, companion to Orlando
**TOUCHSTONE,** a professional fool
**SILVIUS,** a shepherd, in love with Phebe
**WILLIAM,** a country fellow, in love with Audrey
**FIRST LORD,** lord attending on Duke Senior

**ROSALIND,** daughter to Duke Senior
**CELIA,** daughter to Duke Frederick, cousin to Rosalind
**PHEBE,** a shepherdess
**AUDREY,** a country girl

(1)                          ORLANDO                          [I.i.i]

SCENE: An orchard near Oliver's house

*{Orlando considers his unfortunate lot in life. Lending a sympathetic ear is old Adam, who is both Orlando's confidant and servant to Orlando's dastardly brother, Oliver.}*

1    As I remember, Adam, it was upon this fashion bequeath'd me by will but poor
     a thousand crowns, and, as thou say'st, charg'd my brother, on his blessing, to
     breed me well; and there begins my sadness. My brother Jaques he keeps at
     school, and report speaks goldenly of his profit. For my part, he keeps me
5    rustically at home, or, to speak more properly, stays me here at home unkept;
     for call you that keeping for a gentleman of my birth, that differs not from the
     stalling of an ox? His horses are bred better; for, besides that they are fair with
     their feeding, they are taught their manage, and to that end riders dearly hir'd.
     But I, his brother, gain nothing under him but growth, for the which his animals
10   on his dunghills are as much bound to him as I. Besides this nothing that he
     so plentifully gives me, the something that nature gave me his countenance
     seems to take from me. He lets me feed with his hinds, bars me the place of a
     brother, and as much as in him lies, mines my gentility with my education. This
     is it, Adam, that grieves me; and the spirit of my father, which I think is within
15   me, begins to mutiny against this servitude. I will no longer endure it, though
     yet I know no wise remedy how to avoid it.

**1 bequeath'd me** (By implication, Orlando refers here to the actions of his father.)   **but poor** merely   **2 on his blessing** on (pain of losing) his blessing   **3–4 keeps at school** maintains at the university   **4 profit** success, progress   **5 rustically** like a peasant   **properly** accurately   **stays** detains   **unkept** improperly cared for   **7 fair with** in fine condition from   **8 manage** paces and movements of a trained horse   **dearly** at great expense   **11 countenance** behavior, (lack of) regard   **12 hinds** farm workers   **bars me** deprives me of   **13 in him lies** he is able   **mines** undermines   **education** (lack of proper) education

(2)                    DUKE SENIOR                    [II.i.i]

SCENE: The Forest of Arden

*{Some time back, Duke Senior was stripped of both title and lavish lifestyle*
*by his usurping brother, Duke Frederick. Since then he's been forced to lead a*
*considerably more Spartan existence out here in the woods. As this gentle lecture*
*to a few of his companions demonstrates, however, the Duke has accepted his*
*fate with grace and good cheer.}*

| | |
|---|---:|
| Now, my co-mates and brothers in exile, | 1 |
| Hath not old custom made this life more sweet | |
| Than that of painted pomp? Are not these woods | |
| More free from peril than the envious court? | |
| Here feel we not the penalty of Adam, | 5 |
| The seasons' difference, as the icy fang | |
| And churlish chiding of the winter's wind, | |
| Which, when it bites and blows upon my body, | |
| Even till I shrink with cold, I smile and say | |
| "This is no flattery; these are counselors | 10 |
| That feelingly persuade me what I am." | |
| Sweet are the uses of adversity, | |
| Which, like the toad, ugly and venomous, | |
| Wears yet a precious jewel in his head; | |
| And this our life, exempt from public haunt, | 15 |
| Finds tongues in trees, books in the running brooks, | |
| Sermons in stones, and good in everything. | |
| Come, shall we go and kill us venison? | |
| And yet it irks me the poor dappled fools, | |
| Being native burghers of this desert city, | 20 |
| Should in their own confines with forked heads | |
| Have their round haunches gor'd. | |

**3 painted** insincere, artificial   **4 envious** malicious, hateful   **5 feel we not**
we do not feel too harshly **penalty of Adam** i.e., the loss of innocence and
the change of seasons ("seasons' difference") from summer to winter (In the
Garden of Eden weather was spring-like all year round.)   **7 churlish** harsh
**11 feelingly** through my own feelings and sensations   **12 uses** advantages
**14 Wears...head** (Refers to the toadstone, a jewel or similar object that
was often worn as a charm and thought, as well, to be in a toad's head.)
**15 exempt** cut off **public haunt** the society of humans   **19 fools**
innocent creatures   **20 burghers** inhabitants   **desert** deserted, uninhabited
(by humans)   **21 forked heads** barbed arrowheads

(3)                            **FIRST LORD**                        [II.1.25]

SCENE: The Forest of Arden

*{A member of Duke Senior's band provides the Duke and his boys a bittersweet account of something he's just witnessed.}*

1     Indeed, my lord,
     The melancholy Jaques grieves at that,
     And, in that kind, swears you do more usurp
     Than doth your brother that hath banish'd you.
5     Today my Lord of Amiens and myself
     Did steal behind him as he lay along
     Under an oak whose antique root peeps out
     Upon the brook that brawls along this wood,
     To the which place a poor sequest'red stag,
10    That from the hunter's aim had ta'en a hurt,
     Did come to languish; and indeed, my lord,
     The wretched animal heav'd forth such groans
     That their discharge did stretch his leathern coat
     Almost to bursting, and the big round tears
15    Cours'd one another down his innocent nose
     In piteous chase; and thus the hairy fool,
     Much marked of the melancholy Jaques,
     Stood on th' extremest verge of the swift brook,
     Augmenting it with tears.
20    "Poor dear," quoth he, "thou mak'st a testament
     As worldlings do, giving thy sum of more
     To that which had too much." Then, being there alone,
     Left and abandoned of his velvet friends:
     "'Tis right," quoth he, "thus misery doth part
25    The flux of company." Anon a careless herd,
     Full of the pasture, jumps along by him
     And never stays to greet him. "Ay," quoth Jaques,
     "Sweep on, you fat and greasy citizens;
     'Tis just the fashion. Wherefore do you look
30    Upon that poor and broken bankrupt there?"
     Thus most invectively he pierceth through
     The body of the country, city, court,
     Yea, and of this our life, swearing that we
     Are mere usurpers, tyrants, and what's worse,
35    To fright the animals and to kill them up
     In their assign'd and native dwelling-place.
     [Thus] did [we] leave him in this contemplation,
     Weeping and commenting upon the sobbing deer.

**2 at that** i.e., the hunting of deer (He is responding to the sentiments uttered by Duke Senior at the end of the preceding entry.)  **3 kind** fashion, manner   **4 banish'd you** (see preceding entry)   **6 along** stretched out **7 antique** ancient   **8 brawls** noisily moves   **9 sequest'red** separated, (i.e., cut off from the herd)   **15 Cours'd** pursued   **16 fool** (used here as a term of endearment)   **17 Much marked of** closely watched by **18 extremest verge** very edge   **20 testament** bequest   **21 worldlings** humans, mortals   **21–22 giving...which** giving even more to that which already   **23 of** by  **velvet** prosperous (Velvet garments were often worn by the rich; here, there is also an allusion to the velvet found on a deer's antlers.)   **24 part** depart from   **25 flux of company** continuous flow of people, crowd  **Anon** soon  **careless** carefree   **26 Full...pasture** well fed **him** (referring to the wounded stag)   **28 greasy** a term of general contempt (with a play on the oily nature of venison)   **31 most invectively** with such abusive language   **34 what's** whatever may be   **35 up** off

(4)                         ADAM                    [II.III.2]

SCENE: Before Oliver's house

*{Orlando has just beaten Oliver's champion wrestler, and big brother has not taken kindly to the setback. Good soul that he is, Adam intercepts an unsuspecting Orlando just as he is about to enter Oliver's house.}*

What, my young master? O my gentle master,                              1
O my sweet master, O you memory
Of old Sir Rowland! Why, what make you here?
Why are you virtuous? Why do people love you?
And wherefore are you gentle, strong, and valiant?                      5
Why would you be so fond to overcome
The bonny priser of the humorous Duke?
Your praise is come too swiftly home before you.
Know you not, master, to some kind of men
Their graces serve them but as enemies?                                10
No more do yours. Your virtues, gentle master,
Are sanctified and holy traitors to you.
O, what a world is this, when what is comely
Envenoms him that bears it! Unhappy youth,
Come not within these doors! Within this roof                          15
The enemy of all your graces lives.
Your brother—no, no brother; yet the son—
Yet not the son, I will not call him son

Of him I was about to call his father—
20    Hath heard your praises, and this night he means
To burn the lodging where you use to lie
And you within it. If he fail of that,
He will have other means to cut you off.
I overheard him and his practices.
25    This is no place, this house is but a butchery;
Abhor it, fear it, do not enter it.
I have five hundred crowns,
The thrifty hire I sav'd under your father,
Which I did store to be my foster-nurse
30    When service should in my old limbs lie lame,
And unregarded age in corners thrown.
Take that, and He that doth the ravens feed,
Yea, providently caters for the sparrow,
Be comfort to my age! Here is the gold; [*Gives gold.*]
35    All this I give you. Let me be your servant.
Though I look old, yet I am strong and lusty,
For in my youth I never did apply
Hot and rebellious liquors in my blood,
Nor did not with unbashful forehead woo
40    The means of weakness and debility;
Therefore my age is as a lusty winter,
Frosty, but kindly. Let me go with you.
I'll do the service of a younger man
In all your business, and I will follow thee
45    To the last gasp, with truth and loyalty.
From seventeen years till now almost fourscore
Here lived I, but now live here no more.
At seventeen years many their fortunes seek,
But at fourscore it is too late a week;
50    Yet fortune cannot recompense me better
Than to die well and not my master's debtor.

**2 memory** memorial, reminder   **3 Sir Rowland** i.e., Sir Rowland de Boys, deceased father to Oliver and Orlando   **make you** are you doing   **6 fond** foolish   **7 bonny priser** stout prize fighter   **humorous** moody, in bad humor   **10 graces** virtues   **11 more** better   **14 Envenoms** poisons **Unhappy** unfortunate   **21 use to lie** make a habit of sleeping **24 practices** schemes, plots   **25 place** dwelling place, home   **butchery** slaughterhouse   **28 thrifty ... sav'd** money I thriftily saved out of my wages **30 service ... lame** the ability to perform my duties as a servant is hampered by my aged limbs   **31 unregarded** disrespected, ignored **thrown** be thrown   **32–33 He ... sparrow** (alludes to various biblical passages, e.g., Luke 12:24)   **36 lusty** vigorous   **38 Hot** fiery, strong **rebellious** unhealthful   **39 unbashful forehead** brazen demeanor

**42 kindly** pleasant   **49 too ... week** too late a time (the phrase being roughly equivalent to "too late in the game")   **51 well** happy, at rest

(5)                    JAQUES                    [II.vii.12]

SCENE: The Forest of Arden

*{Jaques displays his rather eccentric ways in this oration before Duke Senior and company.}*

| | |
|---|---|
| A fool, a fool! I met a fool i' th' forest, | 1 |
| A motley fool. A miserable world! | |
| As I do live by food, I met a fool, | |
| Who laid him down and bask'd him in the sun, | |
| And rail'd on Lady Fortune in good terms, | 5 |
| In good set terms, and yet a motley fool. | |
| "Good morrow, fool," quoth I. "No, sir," quoth he, | |
| "Call me not fool till heaven hath sent me fortune." | |
| And then he drew a dial from his poke, | |
| And, looking on it with lack-luster eye, | 10 |
| Says very wisely, "It is ten o'clock. | |
| Thus we may see," quoth he, "how the world wags. | |
| 'Tis but an hour ago since it was nine, | |
| And after one hour more 'twill be eleven; | |
| And so, from hour to hour, we ripe and ripe, | 15 |
| And then, from hour to hour, we rot and rot; | |
| And thereby hangs a tale." When I did hear | |
| The motley fool thus moral on the time, | |
| My lungs began to crow like chanticleer, | |
| That fools should be so deep-contemplative, | 20 |
| And I did laugh sans intermission | |
| An hour by his dial. O noble fool! | |
| A worthy fool! One that hath been a courtier, | |
| And says, if ladies be but young and fair, | |
| They have the gift to know it. And in his brain, | 25 |
| Which is as dry as the remainder biscuit | |
| After a voyage, he hath strange places cramm'd | |
| With observation, the which he vents | |
| In mangled forms. O that I were a fool! | |
| I am ambitious for a motley coat, | 30 |
| Provided that you weed your better judgments | |
| Of all opinion that grows rank in them | |
| That I am wise. I must have liberty | |

Withal, as large a charter as the wind,
35    To blow on whom I please, for so fools have.
And they that are most galled with my folly,
They most must laugh. And why, sir, must they so?
The "why" is plain as way to parish church:
He that a fool doth very wisely hit
40    Doth very foolishly, although he smart,
Not to seem senseless of the bob. If not,
The wise man's folly is anatomiz'd
Even by the squand'ring glances of the fool.
Invest me in my motley; give me leave
45    To speak my mind, and I will through and through
Cleanse the foul body of th' infected world,
If they will patiently receive my medicine.

**1 fool** (it was Touchstone he encountered)    **2 motley** wearing motley
(Motley is a woolen fabric of mixed colors that was typically worn by the
professional jester.)    **6 set** forthright, outspoken    **8 heaven...fortune**
(alludes to the proverb "Fortune favors fools")    **9 dial** pocket sundial    **poke**
pocket    **12 wags** proceeds    **15 ripe** ripen, age    **18 moral** moralize
**19 crow** roar, whoop (with laughter)    **chanticleer** (a) rooster    **21 sans**
**intermission** without stopping    **26 dry** (Dryness of the brain was
considered instrumental in having a good memory.)    **remainder** left over
**30 ambitious** eager, desirous    **32 rank** wild    **34 Withal** also    **charter**
acknowledged right, privilege    **36 galled with** annoyed with, victimized by
**38 way...church** i.e., an obvious and well-marked path    **39–41 He...**
**bob** he who is the target of a fool's witticism behaves foolishly if he does not
ignore the barb, even though he may well be stinging from the attack    **41 If**
**not** otherwise    **42 anatomiz'd** dissected, fully revealed    **43 squand'ring**
**glances** random barbs    **44 Invest me in** furnish me    **47 they** i.e., the
populace

(6)                          JAQUES                          [II.VII.139]

SCENE: The Forest of Arden

*{As he is wont to do (see previous entry), Jaques indulges in a spot of philoso-*
*phizing for the benefit of Duke Senior. This time, however, it is the more*
*contemplative side of his nature that Jaques reveals.}*

1    All the world's a stage,
And all the men and women merely players.
They have their exits and their entrances,

And one man in his time plays many parts,
His acts being seven ages. At first the infant,                5
Mewling and puking in the nurse's arms.
Then the whining schoolboy, with his satchel
And shining morning face, creeping like snail
Unwillingly to school. And then the lover,
Sighing like furnace, with a woeful ballad                     10
Made to his mistress' eyebrow. Then a soldier,
Full of strange oaths and bearded like the pard,
Jealous in honor, sudden and quick in quarrel,
Seeking the bubble reputation
Even in the cannon's mouth. And then the justice,              15
In fair round belly with good capon lin'd,
With eyes severe and beard of formal cut,
Full of wise saws and modern instances;
And so he plays his part. The sixth age shifts
Into the lean and slipper'd pantaloon,                         20
With spectacles on nose and pouch on side,
His youthful hose, well sav'd, a world too wide
For his shrunk shank; and his big manly voice,
Turning again toward childish treble, pipes
And whistles in his sound. Last scene of all,                  25
That ends this strange eventful history,
Is second childishness and mere oblivion,
Sans teeth, sans eyes, sans taste, sans everything.

**6 Mewling** whimpering   **8 morning** bright, rosy   **10 Sighing like
furnace** i.e., releasing sighs like a furnace spews smoke   **11 Made to**
i.e., addressing the beauty of   **12 strange** new, unfamiliar   **bearded...pard**
with a mustache as long as a leopard's whiskers   **13 Jealous in honor**
overly protective of his honor   **sudden** rash   **14 bubble** worthless, empty
**16 capon** (Likely refers to the common practice of bribing judges with the
gift of a capon.)   **18 saws** sayings   **modern instances** trite examples
**20 pantaloon** a foolish and enfeebled old man, as per the classic caricature
found in Italian comedies   **22 sav'd** preserved   **25 his** its   **27 childishness**
childhood   **mere** utter   **28 Sans** without

(7)                        TOUCHSTONE                        [V.i.30]

SCENE: The Forest of Arden

*{Touchstone has fallen hard and fast for a country maid named Audrey. When
William, Audrey's former beau, happens upon the scene, Touchstone lets him
have it.}*

1    I do now remember a saying, "The fool doth think he is wise, but the wise man
     knows himself to be a fool." The heathen philosopher, when he had a desire to
     eat a grape, would open his lips when he put it into his mouth, meaning thereby
     that grapes were made to eat and lips to open. Learn this of me: to have, is to
5    have; for it is a figure in rhetoric that drink, being pour'd out of a cup into a
     glass, by filling the one doth empty the other; for all your writers do consent
     that ipse is he. Now, you are not ipse, for I am he; he, sir, that must marry
     this woman. Therefore, you clown, abandon—which is in the vulgar leave—
     the society—which in the boorish is company—of this female—which in the
10   common is woman; which together is, abandon the society of this female, or,
     clown, thou perishest; or, to thy better understanding, diest; or, to wit, I will
     kill thee, make thee away, translate thy life into death, thy liberty into bondage.
     I will deal in poison with thee, or in bastinado, or in steel; I will bandy with
     thee in faction; I will o'errun thee with policy; I will kill thee a hundred and
15   fifty ways. Therefore tremble, and depart.

**2–3 heathen...open** (Touchstone begins this attempt to intimidate and
befuddle his rival with a little quasi-philosophy. What sense there is here
probably is inspired by the sight of William with his mouth agape, staring at
Touchstone in utter bewilderment. Touchstone's point—if indeed he has
one—seems to be that Audrey (represented by the grape) is a treat which is
no longer available for William's lips to enjoy.)  **5–6 drink...other**
i.e., Audrey has changed hands from one to another, the one's loss being the
other's gain  **6 writers** philosophers  **consent** agree in opinion  **7 ipse** "he
himself" in Latin  **8 in the vulgar** put familiarly  **9 boorish** (speech of)
peasants  **9–10 in the common** as usually put  **12 translate** transform
**13 bastinado** thrashing with a stick or cudgel  **steel** swords  **bandy**
contend, battle  **14 in faction** belligerently  **o'errun** overwhelm  **policy**
cunning


(8)                          TOUCHSTONE                        [V.IV.43]

SCENE: The Forest of Arden

*{When Touchstone's credentials as a courtier come into question, he is quick to
put forth an admirable defense.}*

1    If any man doubt that [I have] been a courtier, let him put me to my purgation.
     I have trod a measure; I have flatt'red a lady; I have been politic with my friend,
     smooth with mine enemy; I have undone three tailors; I have had four quarrels,
     and like to have fought one, that was ta'en up thus: We met, and found the
5    quarrel was upon the seventh cause; upon a lie seven times remov'd, as thus,
     sir: I did dislike the cut of a certain courtier's beard. He sent me word, if I

said his beard was not cut well, he was in the mind it was: this is call'd the
Retort Courteous. If I sent him word again it was not well cut, he would send
me word he cut it to please himself: this is call'd Quip Modest. If again, it
was not well cut, he disabled my judgment: this is call'd the Reply Churlish. If     10
again, it was not well cut, he would answer I spake not true: this is call'd the
Reproof Valiant. If again, it was not well cut, he would say I lie: this is call'd
the Countercheck Quarrelsome. And so to the Lie Circumstantial and the Lie
Direct. I durst go no further than the Lie Circumstantial, nor he durst not
give me the Lie Direct; and so we measur'd swords and parted. I will name     15
you in order now the degrees of the lie: The first, the Retort Courteous;
the second, the Quip Modest; the third, the Reply Churlish; the fourth, the
Reproof Valiant; the fifth, the Countercheck Quarrelsome; the sixth, the Lie
with Circumstance; the seventh, the Lie Direct. All these you may avoid but the
Lie Direct; and you may avoid that too, with an If. I knew when seven justices     20
could not take up a quarrel, but when the parties were met themselves, one
of them thought but of an If, as, "If you said so, then I said so"; and they shook
hands and swore brothers. Your If is the only peacemaker; much virtue in If.

**1 put…purgation** challenge me to clear myself (of the accusation that I am
lying)   **2 measure** slow and stately dance   **politic** diplomatic   **3 smooth**
superficially agreeable   **undone** ruined, bankrupted (by running up huge bills
and then refusing to pay them)   **4 like to have** nearly   **ta'en up** settled
amicably   **6 dislike** express my dislike of   **9 Modest** moderate
**10 disabled** slighted, belittled   **13 Countercheck** rebuke, contradiction
**Circumstantial** indirect   **14 durst** dared   **15 measur'd swords** (i.e., as
if preparing for a duel)   **21 take up** settle   **23 swore brothers** became
sworn brothers (i.e., pledged their loyalty to each other)

ALTERNATE
Oliver   [I.i.137–173]

# THE COMEDY OF ERRORS

Twenty-three years ago, there was a ship that foundered in a storm. Among the ship's passengers tossed into the raging sea were a merchant, his wife, their twin baby boys (both named Antipholus), and another set of infant twins (both named Dromio) being raised by them.

Fortunately, everyone was rescued; unfortunately, not by the same rescue parties. As things turned out, the merchant, one Antipholus, and one Dromio were taken to Syracuse, while the merchant's wife, the other Antipholus, and the other Dromio ended up in the city of Ephesus.

After turning eighteen, the pair of twins from Syracuse set out in search of their long-lost brothers, and five years into their quest finally arrive in Ephesus. Because no one realizes that there are now two Antipholuses and two Dromios in town, a series of mistaken identifications and general mayhem ensue. Eventually, of course, everything is set right and the long-separated families are reunited.

**ANTIPHOLUS OF EPHESUS,** twin brother to Antipholus of Syracuse

**ANTIPHOLUS OF SYRACUSE,** twin brother to Antipholus of Ephesus, in love with Luciana

**DROMIO OF EPHESUS,** twin brother to Dromio of Syracuse, servant to Antipholus of Ephesus

**DROMIO OF SYRACUSE,** twin brother to Dromio of Ephesus, servant to Antipholus of Syracuse

**ADRIANA,** wife to Antipholus of Ephesus

**LUCIANA,** sister to Adriana

(1)                **ANTIPHOLUS OF SYRACUSE**                [III.ii.29]

SCENE: Before the house of Antipholus of Ephesus

*{There's a great deal that Antipholus fails to understand about Luciana: why she steadfastly resists his honorable intentions, why she insists that he's married to her sister Adriana, and especially, why she claims to already know him. One thing that's perfectly clear to him, however, is that the maid is irresistible.}*

Sweet Mistress—what your name is else, I know not,                 1
Nor by what wonder you do hit of mine—
Less in your knowledge and your grace you show not
Than our earth's wonder, more than earth divine.
Teach me, dear creature, how to think and speak;                   5
Lay open to my earthy-gross conceit,
Smoth'red in errors, feeble, shallow, weak,
The folded meaning of your words' deceit.
Against my soul's pure truth why labor you
To make it wander in an unknown field?                            10
Are you a god? Would you create me new?
Transform me then, and to your pow'r I'll yield.
But if that I am I, then well I know
Your weeping sister is no wife of mine,
Nor to her bed no homage do I owe.                                15
Far more, far more to you do I decline.
O, train me not, sweet mermaid, with thy note,
To drown me in thy sister's flood of tears!
Sing, siren, for thyself and I will dote.
Spread o'er the silver waves thy golden hairs,                    20
And as a bed I'll take them and there lie,
And in that glorious supposition think
He gains by death that hath such means to die.
Let Love, being light, be drowned if she sink!

**2 hit of** hit on, guess   **4 earth's wonder** (Commonly thought to be an allusion to Queen Elizabeth, who may well have attended an early performance of this play.)   **6 Lay open** reveal   **earthy-gross conceit** unrefined intellect   **8 folded** hidden   **deceit** confusing and apparently misleading meaning   **14 weeping sister** (Refers to Adriana's reaction when Antipholus claimed he did not know her; see II.ii.109)   **16 decline** incline, feel drawn   **17 train** entice, enchant   **note** song   **18 To** only to   **21 as...them** I'll pretend they are a bed   **22 supposition** notion, imagination   **23 death, die** (These words were often intended as allusions to sexual climax.)   **24 light** weightless (and therefore buoyant)   **be...sink** (offered frivolously, assured as Antipholus is that Love cannot possibly sink)

(2)                    **ANTIPHOLUS OF EPHESUS**                    [V.1.214]

SCENE: A street in Ephesus

*{Perhaps more than anyone else, Antipholus of Ephesus has been victimized by the misidentification and mayhem running rampant in his home town. With everyone but the other Antipholus and Dromio in attendance, he lays out for the Duke the details of his whole trying ordeal.}*

| | |
|---|---|
| 1 | My liege, I am advised what I say; |
| | Neither disturbed with the effect of wine, |
| | Nor heady-rash, provok'd with raging ire, |
| | Albeit my wrongs might make one wiser mad. |
| 5 | This woman lock'd me out this day from dinner. |
| | That goldsmith there, were he not pack'd with her, |
| | Could witness it, for he was with me then; |
| | Who parted with me to go fetch a chain, |
| | Promising to bring it to the Porpentine, |
| 10 | Where Balthazar and I did dine together. |
| | Our dinner done, and he not coming thither, |
| | I went to seek him. In the street I met him, |
| | And in his company that gentleman. |
| | There did this perjur'd goldsmith swear me down |
| 15 | That I this day of him receiv'd the chain, |
| | Which, God he knows, I saw not; for the which |
| | He did arrest me with an officer. |
| | I did obey, and sent my peasant home |
| | For certain ducats; he with none return'd. |
| 20 | Then fairly I bespoke the officer |
| | To go in person with me to my house. |
| | By th' way we met |
| | My wife, her sister, and a rabble more |
| | Of vile confederates. Along with them |
| 25 | They brought one Pinch, a hungry lean-fac'd villain, |
| | A mere anatomy, a mountebank, |
| | A threadbare juggler and a fortune-teller, |
| | A needy, hollow-ey'd, sharp-looking wretch, |
| | A living dead man. This pernicious slave, |
| 30 | Forsooth, took on him as a conjurer, |
| | And, gazing in mine eyes, feeling my pulse, |
| | And with no face, as 'twere, outfacing me, |
| | Cries out, I was possess'd. Then all together |
| | They fell upon me, bound me, bore me thence |
| 35 | And in a dark and dankish vault at home |
| | There left me and my man, both bound together, |

Till, gnawing with my teeth my bonds in sunder,
I gain'd my freedom and immediately
Ran hither to your Grace; whom I beseech
To give me ample satisfaction                                                 40
For these deep shames and great indignities.

**1 advised** well aware of   **2 disturbed** deranged, disoriented
**3 heady-rash** overhasty   **4 one wiser** one who was wiser   **5 This
woman** (referring to Adriana)   **6 goldsmith** (referring to Angelo the
goldsmith)   **pack'd** in league   **7 witness** testify to   **8 parted with**
departed from   **9 Porpentine** (Antipholus and Angelo agreed to meet at
the Porpentine Inn; see III.i.116.)   **10 Balthazar** a local merchant and friend
to Antipholus   **13 that gentleman** (referring to the "Second Merchant,"
who is among the many gathered here)   **14 swear me down** i.e., compel
me to acknowledge   **18 peasant** servant   **19 certain ducats** (referring to
the purse of ducats, or gold coins, that he instructed Dromio to retrieve; see
IV.i.105)   **20 fairly** courteously   **bespoke** requested   **25 lean-fac'd**
menacing-looking   **26 anatomy** skeleton   **mountebank** charlatan, quack
**27 juggler** trickster, con artist   **28 sharp-looking** hungry-looking
**30 Forsooth** truly   **took...as** took on the role of   **32 no...'twere** a face
so thin and pale that it seemed almost nonexistent   **outfacing me** staring
me down   **34 fell upon** assailed, swarmed   **thence** from there, away
**35 vault** cellar   **36 man** manservant   **37 in sunder** asunder, in two
**41 deep** grievous

**ALTERNATE**
Balthazar   [III.i.85–106]

# CORIOLANUS

Though roundly criticized for his arrogance and lack of compassion in a time of famine, Coriolanus is nonetheless the man the people turn to when Rome comes under the threat of an attack by the Volscian army. His courageous leadership brings victory to the Romans, for which he is duly praised. But his contemptuous ways soon incite the masses (and some jealous tribunes) against him, and before long he is banished.

Looking to exact some revenge, Coriolanus offers to join his former enemy, the Volscian general Aufidius, in an assault upon Rome. Only a last-minute plea by Coriolanus's mother, Volumnia, persuades Coriolanus to preempt the attack and instead arrange a truce between the two armies.

When he too grows jealous of Coriolanus's rising popularity, Aufidius decries the Roman's efforts for peace as a betrayal of the Volscian people. Aufidius's propaganda soon bears fruit: Coriolanus is ultimately murdered at the behest of a mob and at the hands of Aufidius's assassins.

**CORIOLANUS,** known also as Caius Marcius, a Roman statesman and general
**MENENIUS AGRIPPA,** friend to Coriolanus
**TULLUS AUFIDIUS,** general of the Volscians

**VOLUMNIA,** mother to Coriolanus

(1)                    **MENENIUS**                    [I.1.65]

SCENE: A street in Rome

*{The rabble is roused. With their city ravaged by famine, the common folk of Rome stand convinced that their hardships have been needlessly compounded by callousness on the part of the authorities. Menenius, sensing that the mob before him is poised and ready for rebellion, steps forward to try and nip a potential riot in the bud.}*

I tell you, friends, most charitable care                                    1
Have the patricians of you. For your wants,
Your suffering in this dearth, you may as well
Strike at the heaven with your staves as lift them
Against the Roman state, whose course will on                                5
The way it takes, cracking ten thousand curbs
Of more strong link asunder than can ever
Appear in your impediment. For the dearth,
The gods, not the patricians, make it, and
Your knees to them, not arms, must help. Alack,                              10
You are transported by calamity
Thither where more attends you, and you slander
The helms o' th' state, who care for you like fathers,
When you curse them as enemies. Either you must
Confess yourselves wondrous malicious,                                       15
Or be accus'd of folly. I shall tell you
A pretty tale. It may be you have heard it,
But since it serves my purpose, I will venture
To stale 't a little more.
There was a time when all the body's members                                20
Rebell'd against the belly, thus accus'd it:
That only like a gulf it did remain
I' th' midst o' th' body, idle and unactive,
Still cupboarding the viand, never bearing
Like labor with the rest, where th' other instruments                       25
Did see and hear, devise, instruct, walk, feel,
And, mutually participate, did minister
Unto the appetite and affection common
Of the whole body. The belly answer'd
With a kind of smile, which ne'er came from the lungs—                       30
For, look you, I may make the belly smile
As well as speak—it tauntingly replied
To th' discontented members, the mutinous parts
That envied his receipt; even so most fitly

35      As you malign our senators for that
        They are not such as you. Note me this,
        Your most grave belly was deliberate,
        Not rash like his accusers, and thus answered:
        "True is it, my incorporate friends," quoth he,
40      "That I receive the general food at first
        Which you do live upon; and fit it is,
        Because I am the store-house and the shop
        Of the whole body. But, if you do remember,
        I send it through the rivers of your blood,
45      Even to the court, the heart, to th' seat o' th' brain;
        And, through the cranks and offices of man,
        The strongest nerves and small inferior veins
        From me receive that natural competency
        Whereby they live. And though that all at once"—
50      You, my good friends, this says the belly, mark me—
        "Though all at once cannot
        See what I do deliver out to each,
        Yet I can make my audit up, that all
        From me do back receive the flour of all,
55      And leave me but the bran." What say you to 't?
        The senators of Rome are this good belly,
        And you the mutinous members. For examine
        Their counsels and their cares, disgest things rightly
        Touching the weal o' th' common, you shall find
60      No public benefit which you receive
        But it proceeds or comes from them to you
        And no way from yourselves. What do you think?

**2 For** as for   **3 dearth** famine   **4 staves** staffs   **5 on** continue on
**6 curbs** chains   **8 your impediment** your opposition (to the Roman state)
**11 transported** carried away   **12 attends** awaits   **13 helms** helmsmen
**15 wondrous** amazingly   **19 stale 't ... more** tell it again (thereby making
it more stale)   **20 members** parts   **22 gulf** deep pit   **24 Still** always
**cupboarding** hoarding   **25 Like** equal   **where** whereas   **instruments**
organs (of the body)   **27 participate** cooperating   **28 appetite ...**
**common** common desires and inclinations   **30 lungs** (The lungs were once
thought to be the source of laughter.)   **34 his receipt** that which it received
**fitly** appropriately   **35 for that** because   **37 Your** this
**grave** contemplative, earnest   **39 incorporate** being of the same body
**40 I ... first** i.e., I am first to receive all of the body's nourishment   **45 th'**
**seat ... brain** the throne that is the brain   **46 cranks and offices** winding
paths and remote household rooms   **47 nerves** the body's principal stores
of strength and stamina, i.e., muscles   **48 competency** supply (of needed
elements)   **53 my audit up** i.e., an accurate accounting   **55 bran** chaff,

worthless remainders   **57 For** for if you   **58 disgest** digest   **59 Touching**
concerning   **weal o' th' common** public welfare   **you** and you

(2)                                    CORIOLANUS                            [I.1.164]

SCENE: A street in Rome

*{Menenius's game attempt at appeasement notwithstanding (see preceding en-*
*try), Rome's citizens continue to grouse that Coriolanus is "chief enemy to the*
*people." Their main bone of contention is Coriolanus's refusal to provide them*
*with cheap corn in this time of widespread famine. Never one to shy away from*
*a challenge, Coriolanus arrives on the scene and meets the mob head on.}*

| | |
|---|---:|
| What's the matter, you dissentious rogues, | 1 |
| That, rubbing the poor itch of your opinion, | |
| Make yourselves scabs? What would you have, you curs, | |
| That like nor peace nor war? The one affrights you, | |
| The other makes you proud. He that trusts to you, | 5 |
| Where he should find you lions, finds you hares; | |
| Where foxes, geese. You are no surer, no, | |
| Than is the coal of fire upon the ice, | |
| Or hailstone in the sun. Your virtue is | |
| To make him worthy whose offense subdues him | 10 |
| And curse that justice did it. Who deserves greatness | |
| Deserves your hate; and your affections are | |
| A sick man's appetite, who desires most that | |
| Which would increase his evil. He that depends | |
| Upon your favors swims with fins of lead | 15 |
| And hews down oaks with rushes. Hang ye! Trust ye? | |
| With every minute you do change a mind, | |
| And call him noble that was now your hate, | |
| Him vile that was your garland. What's the matter, | |
| That in these several places of the city | 20 |
| You cry against the noble Senate, who, | |
| Under the gods, keep you in awe, which else | |
| Would feed on one another? What's your seeking? | |
| You sit by th' fire, and presume to know | |
| What's done i' th' Capitol; who's like to rise, | 25 |
| Who thrives and who declines; side factions, and give out | |
| Conjectural marriages, making parties strong | |
| And feebling such as stand not in your liking | |
| Below your cobbled shoes. You say there's grain enough? | |

30    Would the nobility lay aside their ruth
     And let me use my sword, I'd make a quarry
     With thousands of these quarter'd slaves, as high
     As I could pick my lance.

**1 dissentious** rebellious   **2 poor itch** i.e., shallowness, superficiality
**3 scabs** despicable scoundrels   **4 The one** i.e., war   **5 The other**
i.e., peace  **proud** smug   **7 surer** more reliable   **10 worthy** praiseworthy
**subdues him** has ruined him   **11 did it** i.e., punished him for his fault
**12 your affections are** i.e., being admired by you   **16 rushes** long-bladed
grass   **17 a** your   **18 now** just now   **19 garland** object or symbol of glory
and praise   **20 several** various   **22 which else** who otherwise
**23 seeking** demand   **25 like** likely   **26 side** take sides with  **give out**
declare   **27 marriages** i.e., political alliances  **making parties** pronouncing
certain parties   **28 feebling** declaring to be weak  **such as** i.e., other parties
that   **29 cobbled** mended   **30 ruth** compassion   **31 quarry** heap of dead
bodies   **32 quarter'd** slaughtered, hacked into quarters   **33 pick** throw

(3)                  **CORIOLANUS**              [IV.I.I]

SCENE: A street near Rome's border

*{Having been banished from Rome for what his enemies claimed were traitorous acts, an unusually subdued Coriolanus bids farewell to his mother, Volumnia.}*

1    Come, leave your tears; a brief farewell. The beast
     With many heads butts me away. Nay, Mother,
     Where is your ancient courage? You were us'd
     To say extremities was the trier of spirits;
5    That common chances common men could bear;
     That when the sea was calm all boats alike
     Show'd mastership in floating; fortune's blows
     When most struck home, being gentle wounded craves
     A noble cunning. You were us'd to load me
10   With precepts that would make invincible
     The heart that conn'd them. I prithee, mother,
     Resume that spirit when you were wont to say,
     If you had been the wife of Hercules,
     Six of his labors you'd have done, and sav'd
15   Your husband so much sweat. I'll do well yet.
     'Tis fond to wail inevitable strokes,
     As 'tis to laugh at 'em. My mother, you wot well
     My hazards still have been your solace; and
     Believe 't not lightly—though I go alone,

Like to a lonely dragon, that his fen 20
Makes fear'd and talk'd of more than seen—your son
Will or exceed the common or be caught
With cautelous baits and practice.
Bid me farewell, and smile. I pray you, come.
While I remain above the ground, you shall 25
Hear from me still, and never of me aught
But what is like me formerly. Give me
Thy hand. Come.

**1–2 beast … heads** i.e., crowd, multitude   **3 ancient** former
**4 extremities** times of extreme affliction   **7–9 fortune's … cunning**
i.e., when fortune's blows strike their hardest, bearing such misfortune like a
gentleman requires that one be both noble and cunning   **11 conn'd them**
learned them by heart   **prithee** pray thee, beg of you   **12 wont** accustomed
**16 'Tis** it is   **as fond** foolish   **wail** bewail, lament   **strokes** i.e., of fortune
**17 wot** know   **18 still have** have always   **20 fen** swamp (i.e., the dragon's
lair)   **22 Will … common** will either prove myself superior to the
common man   **23 cautelous** deceitful   **practice** treachery, trickery
**26 aught** anything

(4)                    CORIOLANUS                    [IV.v.65]

SCENE: A room in Aufidius's house

*{Bent on avenging his recent banishment from Rome, Coriolanus pays a visit
on his archenemy, Aufidius.}*

My name is Caius Marcius, who hath done 1
To thee particularly and to all the Volsces
Great hurt and mischief; thereto witness may
My surname, Coriolanus. The painful service,
The extreme dangers, and the drops of blood 5
Shed for my thankless country are requited
But with that surname—a good memory,
And witness of the malice and displeasure
Which thou shouldst bear me. Only that name remains.
The cruelty and envy of the people, 10
Permitted by our dastard nobles, who
Have all forsook me, hath devour'd the rest,
And suffer'd me by th' voice of slaves to be
Whoop'd out of Rome. Now this extremity
Hath brought me to thy hearth; not out of hope— 15
Mistake me not—to save my life, for if

I had fear'd death, of all the men i' th' world,
I would have 'voided thee; but in mere spite,
To be full quit of those my banishers,
20    Stand I before thee here. Then if thou hast
A heart of wreak in thee, that wilt revenge
Thine own particular wrongs, and stop those maims
Of shame seen through thy country, speed thee straight,
And make my misery serve thy turn. So use it
25    That my revengeful services may prove
As benefits to thee, for I will fight
Against my cank'red country with the spleen
Of all the under fiends. But if so be
Thou dar'st not this, and that to prove more fortunes
30    Th' art tir'd, then, in a word, I also am
Longer to live most weary, and present
My throat to thee and to thy ancient malice;
Which not to cut would show thee but a fool,
Since I have ever followed thee with hate,
35    Drawn tuns of blood out of thy country's breast,
And cannot live but to thy shame, unless
It be to do thee service.

**3–4 thereto ... surname** to that (fact) may my surname bear witness
**4 My surname, Coriolanus** (Coriolanus was formerly known as Caius
Marcius; the title of "Coriolanus" was bestowed upon him only after his
resounding victory at Corioles; see I.ix.62–65.) **painful** laborious
**7 memory** reminder   **11 dastard** treacherous, cowardly   **13 suffer'd**
allowed   **14 Hoop'd** driven away with taunts   **18 mere** pure   **19 full quit
of** settle accounts with   **21 wreak** vengeance   **22–23 maims Of shame**
disgraceful injuries   **23 through** throughout   **straight** without delay
**24 turn** purpose   **27 cank'red** corrupt, infected with evil   **spleen** malice,
rage   **28 under fiends** fiends of Hell   **so be** it be so that   **29 prove more
fortunes** further test your fortunes   **31 Longer ... weary** most weary of
living any longer   **32 ancient** long-standing   **35 tuns** barrels

(5)                              **AUFIDIUS**                              [IV.v.101]

SCENE: A room in Aufidius's house

*{Aufidius is no one's fool. When Coriolanus comes knocking to offer him assis-
tance in wreaking havoc upon Rome (see preceding entry), the Volscian general's
response is immediate and unequivocal.}*

O Marcius, Marcius!                                             1
Each word thou hast spoke hath weeded from my heart
A root of ancient envy. If Jupiter
Should from yond cloud speak divine things,
And say "'Tis true," I'd not believe them more                 5
Than thee, all noble Marcius. Here I clip
The anvil of my sword, and do contest
As hotly and as nobly with thy love
As ever in ambitious strength I did
Contend against thy valor. Know thou first,                   10
I lov'd the maid I married; never man
Sigh'd truer breath. But that I see thee here,
Thou noble thing, more dances my rapt heart
Than when I first my wedded mistress saw
Bestride my threshold. Why, thou Mars, I tell thee,           15
We have a power on foot; and I had purpose
Once more to hew thy target from thy brawn,
Or lose mine arm for 't. Thou hast beat me out
Twelve several times, and I have nightly since
Dreamt of encounters 'twixt thyself and me;                   20
We have been down together in my sleep,
Unbuckling helms, fisting each other's throat,
And wak'd half dead with nothing. Worthy Marcius,
Had we no other quarrel else to Rome but that
Thou art thence banish'd, we would muster all                 25
From twelve to seventy, and, pouring war
Into the bowels of ungrateful Rome,
Like a bold flood o'erbeat. O, come, go in,
And take our friendly senators by th' hands,
Who now are here, taking their leaves of me,                  30
Who am prepar'd against your territories,
Though not for Rome itself.
Therefore, most absolute sir, if thou wilt have
The leading of thine own revenges, take
Th' one half of my commission; and set down—                  35
As best thou art experienc'd, since thou know'st
Thy country's strength and weakness—thine own ways,
Whether to knock against the gates of Rome,
Or rudely visit them in parts remote,
To fright them ere destroy. But come in;                      40
Let me commend thee first to those that shall
Say yea to thy desires. A thousand welcomes!
And more a friend than e'er an enemy;
Yet, Marcius, that was much. Your hand. Most welcome!

**3 ancient envy** long-standing malice   **6 clip** embrace   **7 anvil** i.e., Coriolanus (upon whom Aufidius has wielded his sword in the way one would beat an anvil)   **13 dances** causes to dance   **15 Mars** god of war **16 power on foot** army standing ready in the field  **purpose** intended **17 target** shield  **brawn** brawny arm   **18 out** thoroughly   **19 several** different   **22 helms** helmets  **fisting** grasping   **23 wak'd** (then I have) awakened   **26 twelve to seventy** i.e., years of age   **28 o'erbeat** overwhelm (it)   **31 prepar'd** (for battle)   **33 absolute** excellent **34 leading** command, generalship   **35 my commission** the forces under my command  **set down** determine, decide upon   **39 rudely** with violence **40 ere destroy** before we utterly destroy (them)   **41 commend** present, introduce

ALTERNATES

Menenius   [II.i.47–96]
Cominius   [II.ii.82–122]

# CYMBELINE

Cymbeline simply would not stand for his daughter Imogen's secret marriage to Posthumus, and so he had the poor lad banished. Landing on his feet in Rome, Posthumus wagers with a local scoundrel named Iachimo that his beloved Imogen cannot be corrupted. Though Iachimo fails miserably in his attempt to seduce Imogen, he returns from Britain with enough misleading evidence to convince Posthumus otherwise.

Incensed by his wife's apparent betrayal, Posthumus dashes off a letter to Pisanio (his manservant back in Britain) that instructs him to murder Imogen. Pisanio, however, is unable to do his master's bidding. Instead, he persuades Imogen to make her way to Rome—for safety's sake, disguised as a boy—and set matters straight with her husband.

Pursuing Imogen into the countryside is Cymbeline's stepson, Cloten, who intends to forcibly return her to the fold. Along the way, however, he tangles with banished lord Belarius and his two sons, and is forthwith beheaded for his trouble.

Meanwhile, the war between Rome and Britain has escalated. Posthumus returns to Britain just in time to assist Belarius and his boys (who are actually Cymbeline's sons, kidnapped by Belarius when they were babies) in rallying the British forces. Before all is said and done, the Roman invaders are routed, Posthumus and Imogen are reunited, and there is peace once more in the British Isles.

CYMBELINE, King of Britain
CLOTEN, stepson to Cymbeline
POSTHUMUS, husband to Imogen
BELARIUS, a banished lord
IACHIMO, an Italian rogue
PISANIO, servant to Posthumus

IMOGEN, daughter to Cymbeline, wife to Posthumus
QUEEN, wife to Cymbeline

(1)                          IACHIMO                          [II.II.II]

SCENE: A room in Cymbeline's palace

*{Acting on a bet he made with Posthumus back in Italy, Iachimo arrived in
Britain aiming to seduce Posthumus's wife, Imogen. When the direct approach
failed to win her heart, Iachimo came up with an alternate plan: sneak into
Imogen's bedchamber and record the room's (and Imogen's) features in such
intimate detail that Posthumus will be forced to concede Iachimo's conquest.
Now, as the midnight hour approaches, the plot is afoot . . . Imogen is fast asleep
in her bed as Iachimo silently slinks from his hiding place.}*


| | |
|---|---|
| 1 | The crickets sing, and man's o'er-labor'd sense |
| | Repairs itself by rest. Our Tarquin thus |
| | Did softly press the rushes ere he waken'd |
| | The chastity he wounded. Cytherea, |
| 5 | How bravely thou becom'st thy bed, fresh lily, |
| | And whiter than the sheets! That I might touch! |
| | But kiss, one kiss! Rubies unparagon'd, |
| | How dearly they do 't! 'Tis her breathing that |
| | Perfumes the chamber thus. The flame o' th' taper |
| 10 | Bows toward her, and would under-peep her lids, |
| | To see th' enclosed lights, now canopied |
| | Under these windows, white and azure lac'd |
| | With blue of heaven's own tinct. But my design, |
| | To note the chamber. I will write all down: |
| 15 | [*He begins writing.*] |
| | Such and such pictures; there the window; such |
| | Th' adornment of her bed; the arras, figures, |
| | Why, such and such; and the contents o' th' story. |
| | Ah, but some natural notes about her body, |
| 20 | Above ten thousand meaner movables |
| | Would testify, t' enrich mine inventory. |
| | O sleep, thou ape of death, lie dull upon her, |
| | And be her sense but as a monument, |
| | Thus in a chapel lying! Come off, come off; |
| 25 | [*Takes off her bracelet.*] |
| | As slippery as the Gordian knot was hard! |
| | 'Tis mine; and this will witness outwardly, |
| | As strongly as the conscience does within, |
| | To th' madding of her lord. On her left breast |
| 30 | A mole cinque-spotted, like the crimson drops |
| | I' th' bottom of a cowslip. Here's a voucher, |

Stronger than ever law could make. This secret
Will force him to think I have pick'd the lock and ta'en
The treasure of her honor. No more. To what end?
Why should I write this down that's riveted,                          35
Screw'd to my memory? She hath been reading late
The tale of Tereus; here the leaf's turn'd down
Where Philomel gave up. I have enough.
To th' trunk again, and shut the spring of it.
Swift, swift, you dragons of the night, that dawning               40
May bare the raven's eye! I lodge in fear;
Though this a heavenly angel, hell is here.
[*A clock strikes as he goes into the trunk.*]
One, two, three. Time, time!

**I o'er-labor'd** over worked, greatly fatigued **sense** mind   **2 Our Tarquin**
the Roman, Tarquinus, who raped Lucrece   **3 press** step on   **rushes** plants
used as a carpet of sorts by scattering them over the bare floor
**4 Cytherea** Venus   **5 bravely** splendidly   **7 But kiss** just a kiss   **Rubies**
(referring to her lips)   **8 do 't** i.e., kiss each other   **10 would under-peep**
wishes to peek under   **11 lights** i.e., eyes   **12 windows** eyelids   **13 tinct**
color   **design** goal, intention   **17 arras** heavy curtain or tapestry   **figures**
carvings   **18 contents ... story** (referring to the scenes depicted on the
arras (?))   **19 notes** birthmarks   **20 Above** better than   **meaner**
**movables** more common items   **22 ape** impersonator   **dull** heavy
**23 sense** perception, awareness   **monument** statue that adorns a tomb
**26 Gordian knot** an intricate knot which Gordius, King of Phrygia, tied and
then defied anyone to undo   **27 witness** testify   **28 conscience**
consciousness   **29 madding** madness   **30 cinque-spotted** of five spots
**31 voucher** proof   **37 Tereus** mythical king who raped his sister-in-law
Philomela, and then cut out her tongue so she could not implicate him
**38 gave up** was forced to yield (to Tereus)   **39 of** on
**40 dragons ... night** (referring to the moon and stars)   **41 bare ... eye**
(It was thought that the raven always awoke at dawn.)

(2)                      POSTHUMUS                      [II.v.1]

SCENE: A house in Rome

*{Convinced that his wife has been unfaithful to him (see preceding entry),
Posthumus reflects upon the nature of woman.}*

Is there no way for men to be but women                                    1
Must be half-workers? We are all bastards,

And that most venerable man which I
Did call my father was I know not where
5    When I was stamp'd. Some coiner with his tools
Made me a counterfeit; yet my mother seem'd
The Dian of that time. So doth my wife
The nonpareil of this. O, vengeance, vengeance!
Me of my lawful pleasure she restrain'd
10    And pray'd me oft forbearance; did it with
A prudency so rosy the sweet view on 't
Might well have warm'd old Saturn, that I thought her
As chaste as unsunn'd snow. O, all the devils!
This yellow Iachimo, in an hour, was 't not?
15    Or less?—at first? Perchance he spoke not, but,
Like a full-acorn'd boar, a German one,
Cried "O!" and mounted; found no opposition
But what he look'd for should oppose and she
Should from encounter guard. Could I find out
20    The woman's part in me! For there's no motion
That tends to vice in man but I affirm
It is the woman's part. Be it lying, note it,
The woman's; flattering, hers; deceiving, hers;
Lust and rank thoughts, hers, hers; revenges, hers;
25    Ambitions, covetings, change of prides, disdain,
Nice longing, slanders, mutability,
All faults that have a name, nay, that hell knows,
Why, hers, in part or all, but rather all.
For even to vice
30    They are not constant, but are changing still;
One vice but of a minute old for one
Not half so old as that. I'll write against them,
Detest them, curse them. Yet 'tis greater skill
In a true hate to pray they have their will;
35    The very devils cannot plague them better.

**1 be** exist   **2 half-workers** partners (in procreation)   **5 stamp'd**
conceived   **7 Dian** Diana, goddess of chastity   **8 nonpareil** paragon
(of virtue)   **10 pray'd ... forbearance** often begged me to abstain
**11 prudency** modesty   **the** that the   **on 't** of it   **12 Saturn** in Roman
mythology, the father of Jupiter   **14 This ... hour** this sallow-complexioned
Iachimo had won her within an hour   **15 at first** right away
**16 full-acorn'd** full of acorns (acorns being a favorite food of boars)
**German** (In German, the word for acorn also means "penis.")   **18 But**
even though   **19 Could I** if only I could   **20 woman's** feminine   **motion**
inclination, impulse   **25 change of prides** one vanity or extravagance after

another    **26 Nice** lascivious    **mutability** inconstancy    **30 still** constantly
**32 write against** denounce    **33 greater skill** shrewder, more discerning

(3)    CLOTEN    [IV.i.i]

SCENE: Near the cave of Belarius

*{Cloten is planning to wreak some serious havoc. Having learned that Imogen intends to rendezvous with Posthumus here in the Welsh hinterland, Cloten arrives with intentions to murder Posthumus, and then violate Imogen before dragging her back to civilization.}*

I am near to th' place where they should meet, if Pisanio have mapp'd it truly.    1
How fit his garments serve me! Why should his mistress, who was made by
him that made the tailor, not be fit too? The rather—saving reverence of the
word—for 'tis said a woman's fitness comes by fits. Therein I must play the
workman. I dare not speak it to myself, for it is not vainglory for a man and his    5
glass to confer in his own chamber—I mean, the lines of my body are as well
drawn as his; no less young, more strong, not beneath him in fortunes, beyond
him in the advantage of the time, above him in birth, alike conversant in general
services, and more remarkable in single oppositions. Yet this imperceiverant
thing loves him in my despite. What mortality is! Posthumus, thy head, which    10
now is growing upon thy shoulders, shall within this hour be off, thy mistress
enforc'd, thy garments cut to pieces before her face; and all this done, spurn
her home to her father, who may happily be a little angry for my so rough
usage; but my mother, having power of his testiness, shall turn all into my
commendations. My horse is tied up safe. Out, sword, and to a sore purpose!    15
[*Draws his sword.*] Fortune, put them into my hand! This is the very description
of their meeting-place, and the fellow dares not deceive me.

**1 should** intend to    **Pisanio . . . truly** (It was Pisanio who, under duress,
informed Cloten of Imogen's plan to meet up with Posthumus; see
III.v.82–100)    **2 his garments** (Cloten has dressed himself in one of
Posthumus's outfits because, earlier on (see II.iii.133–35), Imogen had
declared that even Posthumus's lowliest garment was dearer to her than
Cloten was. Cloten thus views this ironic touch as the crowning humiliation
of Imogen.)    **3–4 saving . . . word** begging pardon (referring to his indecent
puns on the word "fit")    **4 fitness** sexual inclination    **fits** fits and starts
**5 workman** expert craftsman    **vainglory** a display of vanity    **6 glass**
looking glass    **8 advantage . . . time** cultural and social opportunities
(afforded me)    **8–9 general services** military matters    **9 single**

**oppositions** duels, one-on-one contests  **imperceiverant** undiscerning
**10 in my despite** in defiance of me  **What mortality is** what a thing life is
**12 enforc'd** violated   **13 happily** perchance   **14 mother** i.e., the Queen
(Cloten is son to the Queen by way of her previous husband, not by
Cymbeline.)  **power of** control over   **15 sore** grievous   **16 them**
(referring to Posthumus and Imogen)   **17 the fellow** (referring to Pisanio)

### ALTERNATES

Pisanio       [III.ii.1–22]
Belarius      [III.iii.79–107]
Posthumus   [V.i.1–33]
Posthumus   [V.iv.3–29]

# HAMLET

Only two months after the untimely death of his father, Hamlet's mother Gertrude has already remarried—and to her late husband's brother, at that. Though Hamlet soon discovers that it was this selfsame uncle of his, Claudius, who murdered King Hamlet in the first place, vengeance is inexplicably slow in coming.

Even as he feigns madness and abuses poor Ophelia, Hamlet continuously agonizes over how best to proceed in the matter before him. When Claudius tumbles to the fact that Hamlet is onto him, he devises an elaborate plot designed to do away with his rival. The plan involves goading Hamlet into a friendly little fencing match with Ophelia's brother Laertes, during which the Prince is slated to be mortally wounded by a poison-tipped rapier.

All does not go quite as planned, however. Before the final thrusts and parries are made, Hamlet has indeed met his demise . . . but so too have Gertrude, Laertes, and even Claudius himself.

**CLAUDIUS,** King of Denmark

**HAMLET,** Prince of Denmark, son to the late King Hamlet, nephew to Claudius

**POLONIUS,** counselor to Claudius

**HORATIO,** friend to Hamlet

**LAERTES,** son to Polonius

**REYNALDO,** servant to Polonius

**FORTINBRAS,** Prince of Norway

**GERTRUDE,** Queen of Denmark, mother to Hamlet

**OPHELIA,** daughter to Polonius

(1)                        **HAMLET**                    [I.ii.129]

SCENE: A chamber in Elsinore Castle

*{Less than two months after her husband's untimely death, Hamlet's mother has already remarried—and to her late husband's brother at that. It is a twisted turn of events that Hamlet cannot abide.}*

1    O, that this too too solid flesh would melt,
     Thaw, and resolve itself into a dew!
     Or that the Everlasting had not fix'd
     His cannon 'gainst self-slaughter! O God, God,
5    How weary, stale, flat, and unprofitable
     Seem to me all the uses of this world!
     Fie on 't, ah fie! 'Tis an unweeded garden
     That grows to seed. Things rank and gross in nature
     Possess it merely. That it should come to this!
10   But two months dead—nay, not so much, not two.
     So excellent a king, that was to this
     Hyperion to a satyr; so loving to my mother
     That he might not beteem the winds of heaven
     Visit her face too roughly. Heaven and earth,
15   Must I remember? Why, she would hang on him
     As if increase of appetite had grown
     By what it fed on, and yet, within a month—
     Let me not think on 't. Frailty, thy name is woman!—
     A little month, or ere those shoes were old
20   With which she followed my poor father's body,
     Like Niobe, all tears, why she, even she—
     O God, a beast, that wants discourse of reason,
     Would have mourn'd longer—married with my uncle,
     My father's brother, but no more like my father
25   Than I to Hercules. Within a month,
     Ere yet the salt of most unrighteous tears
     Had left the flushing in her galled eyes,
     She married. O, most wicked speed, to post
     With such dexterity to incestuous sheets!
30   It is not, nor it cannot come to good.
     But break, my heart, for I must hold my tongue.

**2 resolve** dissolve   **4 cannon** law   **6 uses** ways, customs   **7 Fie** (an expression of disgust)   **8 gross** coarse, unrefined   **9 merely** utterly   **11 king** (i.e., Hamlet Sr.)   **to this** i.e., in comparison to Claudius   **12 Hyperion** as Hyperion was (A Titan of Greek mythology, Hyperion was

father to Helios, the sun god.)   **13 beteem** allow   **19 or ere** before
**21 Niobe** Queen of Thebes, whom Greek legend holds was turned into
stone while weeping for her slain children, after which the stone continued to
shed tears   **22 wants . . . reason** lacks the power to reason   **27 flushing**
redness   **galled** irritated (from crying)   **28 post** hasten   **29 dexterity**
deftness, agility   **incestuous** (In Elizabethan England, a marriage like that of
Claudius to his brother's widow was considered to be incestuous in nature.)


(2)                              POLONIUS                              [I.III.55]

SCENE: Polonius's chambers

*{Polonius dispenses a bit of fatherly advice to his son Laertes, who is about to
embark upon a journey to France.}*


Yet here Laertes? Aboard, aboard, for shame!                              1
The wind sits in the shoulder of your sail,
And you are stay'd for. There—my blessing with thee!
And these few precepts in thy memory
Look thou character. Give thy thoughts no tongue,                         5
Nor any unproportion'd thought his act.
Be thou familiar, but by no means vulgar.
Those friends thou hast, and their adoption tried,
Grapple them to thy soul with hoops of steel,
But do not dull thy palm with entertainment                              10
Of each new-hatch'd, unfledg'd courage. Beware
Of entrance to a quarrel, but, being in,
Bear 't that th' opposed may beware of thee.
Give every man thy ear, but few thy voice;
Take each man's censure, but reserve thy judgment.                       15
Costly thy habit as thy purse can buy,
But not express'd in fancy; rich, not gaudy,
For the apparel oft proclaims the man,
And they in France of the best rank and station
Are most select and generous chief in that.                              20
Neither a borrower nor a lender be,
For loan oft loses both itself and friend,
And borrowing dulleth th' edge of husbandry.
This above all: to thine own self be true,
And it must follow, as the night the day,                                25
Thou canst not then be false to any man.
Farewell. My blessing season this in thee!

**3 stay'd** waited  **5 Look thou** be sure to  **character** engrave, inscribe
**6 unproportion'd** unreasonable  **his** its  **7 familiar** friendly  **vulgar**
undiscriminating, common  **8 their adoption tried** their friendship tested
and proven true  **9 Grapple them** bind them closely  **10 dull...**
**entertainment** wear out your hand with greetings  **11 unfledg'd**
immature  **courage** young man of spirit  **13 Bear 't that** conduct yourself
so that  **15 Take** consider  **censure** opinion  **16 habit** attire  **17 fancy**
extravagance  **20 select and generous** distinguished and noble  **chief**
chiefly  **23 husbandry** economy, thrift  **27 season** ripen

(3)                               HAMLET                          [I.iv.39]

SCENE: The guard platform of Elsinore Castle

*{In the dead of night, up amongst the castle's bulwarks, Hamlet encounters for the first time what appears to be the unquiet ghost of his late father.}*

1      Angels and ministers of grace defend us!
       Be thou a spirit of health or goblin damn'd,
       Bring with thee airs from heaven or blasts from hell,
       Be thy intents wicked or charitable,
5      Thou com'st in such a questionable shape
       That I will speak to thee. I'll call thee Hamlet,
       King, father, royal Dane. O, answer me!
       Let me not burst in ignorance; but tell
       Why thy canoniz'd bones, hearsed in death,
10     Have burst their cerements; why the sepulcher
       Wherein we saw thee quietly interr'd
       Hath op'd his ponderous and marble jaws
       To cast thee up again. What may this mean,
       That thou, dead corse, again in complete steel
15     Revisits thus the glimpses of the moon,
       Making night hideous, and we fools of nature
       So horridly to shake our disposition
       With thoughts beyond the reaches of our souls?
       Say, why is this? Wherefore? What should we do?
20     [*The ghost silently beckons Hamlet.*]
       It beckons me to go away with it,
       As if it some impartment did desire
       To me alone. It will not speak.
       Then I will follow it. What should be the fear?
25     I do not set my life at a pin's fee,

And for my soul, what can it do to that,
Being a thing immortal as itself?
It waves me forth again. I'll follow it.

**2 health** well being, good   **3 Bring** bringing   **5 questionable** inviting
question or conversation   **9 canoniz'd** buried in accordance with the
canons of the Church   **hearsed** buried   **10 cerements** burial clothes
**14 corse** corpse   **complete steel** full armor   **15 glimpses…moon**
fleeting moonlight   **16 fools of nature** mere mortals, knowing only of
natural things   **17 disposition** humor, mood   **22 impartment**
communication   **25 set** value   **fee** worth

(4)                       POLONIUS                    [II.1.3]

SCENE: Polonius's chambers

*{With Laertes leading the bachelor's life in Paris, Polonius—concerned parent
and consummate meddler that he is—has decided that a bit of spying on his
son is in order. Before dispatching his manservant Reynaldo to do just that,
Polonius tenders him a primer on the fine art of subterfuge.}*

You shall do marvel's wisely, good Reynaldo,                          1
Before you visit him, to make inquire
Of his behavior. Look you, sir,
Inquire me first what Danskers are in Paris,
And how, and who, what means, and where they keep,                    5
What company, at what expense; and finding
By this encompassment and drift of question
That they do know my son, come you more nearer
Than your particular demands will touch it.
Take you, as 'twere, some distant knowledge of him,                   10
As thus, "I know his father and his friends,
And in part him, but," you may say, "not well.
But, if 't be he I mean, he's very wild,
Addicted so and so," and there put on him
What forgeries you please—marry, none so rank                         15
As may dishonor him, take heed of that—
But, sir, such wanton, wild, and usual slips,
As are companions noted and most known
To youth and liberty; drinking, fencing,
Swearing, quarreling, drabbing—you may go so far.                     20
You must not put another scandal on him

That he is open to incontinency—
That's not my meaning. But breathe his faults so quaintly
That they may seem the taints of liberty,
25    The flash and outbreak of a fiery mind,
A savageness in unreclaimed blood,
Of general assault. Marry, here's my drift;
And, I believe, it is a fetch of wit.
You laying these slight sullies on my son,
30    As 'twere a thing a little soil'd i' th' working,
Mark you,
Your party in converse, him you would sound,
Having ever seen in the prenominate crimes
The youth you breathe of guilty, be assur'd
35    He closes with you in this consequence:
"Good sir," or so, or "friend," or "gentleman,"
According to the phrase or the addition
Of man and country. And then, sir, does 'a this, 'a does—
What was I about to say? By the mass,
40    I was about to say something. Where did I leave?
At "closes in the consequence," ay, marry.
He closes thus: "I know the gentleman;
I saw him yesterday, or th' other day,
Or then or then, with such, or such, and, as you say,
45    There was 'a gaming, there o'ertook in 's rouse,
There falling out at tennis," or perchance,
"I saw him enter such a house of sale,"
Videlicet, a brothel, or so forth. See you now,
Your bait of falsehood takes this carp of truth;
50    And thus do we of wisdom and of reach,
With windlasses and with assays of bias,
By indirections find directions out.
So by my former lecture and advice
Shall you my son. You have me, have you not?

**1 marvel's** marvelously   **4 Danskers** Danes   **5 keep** dwell
**7 encompassment** roundabout approach   **drift of question** guiding of the
conversation   **8–9 come ... it** i.e., you will uncover more than if you were
to make direct inquiries   **10 Take you** pretend as though you have
**14 Addicted** inclined toward   **put on** ascribe to   **15 forgeries** fictions
**rank** foul, offensive   **17 slips** lapses, small offenses   **20 drabbing**
consorting with harlots   **22 incontinency** unrestrained or lewd behavior
**23 quaintly** delicately   **24 of liberty** borne of freedom   **25 outbreak**
outburst   **26 unreclaimed** untamed   **27 Of general assault** i.e., of the
type that afflict youths in general   **Marry** (a mild oath uttered to emphasize a
point)   **28 fetch of wit** clever ruse   **29 sullies** blemishes   **30 a little ...**

**working** i.e., old hat, twice-told   **32 converse** conversation   **sound** sound out   **33 Having ever** as to whether he has ever   **prenominate crimes** aforementioned offenses   **34 breathe** speak   **35 closes...consequence** chimes in with you to this effect   **37 addition** style of address   **38 'a** he **39 By the mass** (a mild oath)   **45 o'ertook in 's rouse** overcome by his liquor   **46 falling out** quarreling   **47 such...sale** a house where a certain commodity was sold   **48 Videlicet** namely   **50 reach** understanding **51 windlasses** circuitous routes   **assays of bias** indirect methods (The image comes from bowls, a popular game of the day.)   **52 find directions out** determine the actual state of things   **53 former lecture** preceding instructions   **54 have me** understand me

(5)                                **POLONIUS**                        [II.ii.86]

SCENE: A chamber in Elsinore Castle

*{Hamlet's recent moodiness and erratic behavior have perplexed one and all around Elsinore. In his typically convoluted manner, Polonius offers Claudius and Gertrude his take on the cause of Hamlet's "madness."}*

My liege, and madam, to expostulate                                                    1
What majesty should be, what duty is,
Why day is day, night night, and time is time,
Were nothing but to waste night, day, and time.
Therefore, since brevity is the soul of wit,                                            5
And tediousness the limbs and outward flourishes,
I will be brief. Your noble son is mad.
Mad call I it, for, to define true madness,
What is 't but to be nothing else but mad?
But let that go.                                                                       10
That he is mad, 'tis true; 'tis true 'tis pity,
And pity 'tis 'tis true—a foolish figure,
But farewell it, for I will use no art.
Mad let us grant him, then, and now remains
That we find out the cause of this effect,                                              15
Or rather say, the cause of this defect,
For this effect defective comes by cause.
Thus it remains, and the remainder thus.
Perpend. [*He produces a letter.*]
I have a daughter—have while she is mine—                                              20
Who in her duty and obedience, mark,
Hath given me this. Now gather, and surmise.

[*He reads from the letter.*]
    "To the celestial and my soul's idol, the most
25       beautified Ophelia"—
That's an ill phrase, a vile phrase; "beautified" is a
vile phrase. But you shall hear. Thus: [*Reads.*]
    "Doubt thou the stars are fire,
    Doubt that the sun doth move,
30      Doubt truth to be a liar,
    But never doubt I love.
    O dear Ophelia, I am ill at these numbers. I have not
    art to reckon my groans. But that I love thee best, O
    most best, believe it. Adieu.
35      Thine evermore, most dear lady, whilst this
    machine is to him, Hamlet."
This in obedience hath my daughter shown me,
And, more above, hath his solicitings,
As they fell out by time, by means, and place,
40   All given to mine ear.
When I had seen this hot love on the wing—
As I perceiv'd it, I must tell you that,
Before my daughter told me—what might you,
Or my dear Majesty your queen here, think
45   If I had play'd the desk or table-book,
Or given my heart a winking, mute and dumb,
Or look'd upon this love with idle sight?
What might you think? No, I went round to work,
And my young mistress thus I did bespeak:
50   "Lord Hamlet is a prince, out of thy star;
This must not be." And then I prescripts gave her,
That she should lock herself from his resort,
Admit no messengers, receive no tokens.
Which done, she took the fruits of my advice;
55   And he, repelled—a short tale to make—
Fell into a sadness, then into a fast,
Thence to a watch, thence into a weakness,
Thence to a lightness, and, by this declension,
Into the madness wherein now he raves,
60   And all we mourn for.

**5 wit** intelligence, understanding   **10 let that go** disregard all that
**12 figure** figure of speech   **13 art** i.e., fanciful oration   **14 remains** it
remains   **17 For . . . cause** for this defective behavior (of Hamlet's) is not
merely accidental, but the effect of some cause   **18 it** i.e., Hamlet's
"madness"   **19 Perpend** consider   **22 gather** deduce   **25 beautified**
beautiful   **30 Doubt** suspect, question   **32 ill . . . numbers** poor at

constructing verse   **33 reckon my groans** convey my deepest feelings
**36 machine...him** body is his own   **38 more above** what's more
**39 fell out** occurred   **41 on the wing** in flight, on the move   **45 play'd...**
**table-book** i.e., remained closed up (thereby withholding information)
**46 winking** closing of the eyes   **47 with idle sight** without concern or
appreciation   **48 round** directly   **49 bespeak** speak to   **50 out...star**
above your lot in life   **51 prescripts** instructions   **52 lock** secure   **resort**
access   **54 took the fruits** reaped the benefits   **57 watch** condition of
sleeplessness   **58 lightness** lightheadedness   **declension** (pattern of)
deterioration

(6)                              HAMLET                        [II.ii.549]

SCENE: A chamber in Elsinore Castle

*{Slowly and unsurely, Hamlet inches toward action. Inspired by the poignant*
*soliloquy of an itinerant actor, the Prince concocts a plan to ferret out Claudius's*
*guilt in the murder of Hamlet, Sr.}* [For a shorter piece, line 40 serves as an
effective end point.]

Now I am alone.                                                              1
O, what a rogue and peasant slave am I!
Is it not monstrous that this player here,
But in a fiction, in a dream of passion,
Could force his soul so to his own conceit                                   5
That from her working all his visage wann'd,
Tears in his eyes, distraction in his aspect,
A broken voice, and his whole function suiting
With forms to his conceit? And all for nothing!
For Hecuba!                                                                 10
What's Hecuba to him, or he to Hecuba,
That he should weep for her? What would he do,
Had he the motive and the cue for passion
That I have? He would drown the stage with tears
And cleave the general ear with horrid speech,                             15
Make mad the guilty and appall the free,
Confound the ignorant, and amaze indeed
The very faculties of eyes and ears. Yet I,
A dull and muddy-mettled rascal, peak
Like John-a-dreams, unpregnant of my cause,                                20
And can say nothing—no, not for a king
Upon whose property and most dear life

A damn'd defeat was made. Am I a coward?
Who calls me villain? Breaks my pate across?
25    Plucks off my beard and blows it in my face?
Tweaks me by the nose? Gives me the lie i' th' throat,
As deep as to the lungs? Who does me this?
Ha, 'swounds, I should take it; for it cannot be
But I am pigeon-liver'd, and lack gall
30    To make oppression bitter, or ere this
I should have fatted all the region kites
With this slave's offal. Bloody, bawdy villain!
Remorseless, treacherous, lecherous, kindless villain!
O, vengeance!
35    Why, what an ass am I! This is most brave,
That I, the son of a dear father murder'd,
Prompted to my revenge by heaven and hell,
Must, like a whore, unpack my heart with words,
And fall a-cursing, like a very drab,
40    A scullion! Fie upon 't, foh!
About, my brains! Hum—I have heard
That guilty creatures sitting at a play
Have by the very cunning of the scene
Been struck so to the soul that presently
45    They have proclaim'd their malefactions;
For murder, though it have no tongue, will speak
With most miraculous organ. I'll have these players
Play something like the murder of my father
Before mine uncle. I'll observe his looks;
50    I'll tent him to the quick. If 'a do blench,
I know my course. The spirit that I have seen
May be the devil, and the devil hath power
T' assume a pleasing shape; yea, and perhaps
Out of my weakness and my melancholy,
55    As he is very potent with such spirits,
Abuses me to damn me. I'll have grounds
More relative than this. The play's the thing
Wherein I'll catch the conscience of the King.

**2 peasant** lowly, base  **5 conceit** imagination  **6 her** i.e., his imagination's
**visage** appearance  **wann'd** grew pale  **7 aspect** gaze  **8–9 his...conceit**
his entire being responding with expressions and actions appropriate to his
thoughts  **10 Hecuba** (a central character in the soliloquy which so moved
Hamlet; see II.ii.501)  **13 cue** prompting  **15 the general** the collective
(i.e., everyone's)  **16 free** guiltless  **19 dull** impassive, inactive
**muddy-mettled** dull-spirited  **peak** mope about  **20 John-a-dreams** a
dreamy do-nothing  **unpregnant of** unmoved by  **23 defeat** annihilation,
ruin  **24 Breaks...across** strikes me alongside the head

**26–27 Gives...lungs** calls me a liar of the very worst sort    **28 'swounds** by God's wounds (a mild oath)    **should** would certainly    **29 pigeon-liver'd** meek (alludes to the popular belief that pigeons and doves had docile natures because their innards produced no gall)    **31 fatted...kites** fattened all of the local kites (hawk-like birds of prey)    **32 offal** innards    **33 kindless** unnatural    **39 drab** harlot    **40 scullion** washerwoman    **Fie, foh** (exclamations of disgust)    **41 About** i.e., move to action, get to work    **44 presently** then and there    **47 most miraculous organ** a most miraculous voice    **50 tent** probe    **'a do** he does    **blench** flinch    **51 The spirit** i.e., the ghost of King Hamlet    **55 spirits** moods, humors    **56 Abuses** deceives    **57 relative** substantial, conclusive

(7)                                    HAMLET                                    [III.1.55]

SCENE: A chamber in Elsinore Castle

*{Completely baffled by his lack of resolve, Hamlet pauses to reflect upon a universal dilemma.}*

To be, or not to be, that is the question:                                    1
Whether 'tis nobler in the mind to suffer
The slings and arrows of outrageous fortune,
Or to take arms against a sea of troubles,
And by opposing, end them. To die, to sleep—                                    5
No more—and by a sleep to say we end
The heartache and the thousand natural shocks
That flesh is heir to. 'Tis a consummation
Devoutly to be wish'd. To die, to sleep;
To sleep, perchance to dream. Ay, there's the rub.                                    10
For in that sleep of death what dreams may come
When we have shuffled off this mortal coil,
Must give us pause. There's the respect
That makes calamity of so long life.
For who would bear the whips and scorns of time,                                    15
Th' oppressor's wrong, the proud man's contumely,
The pangs of despis'd love, the law's delay,
The insolence of office, and the spurns
That patient merit of th' unworthy takes,
When he himself might his quietus make                                    20
With a bare bodkin? Who would fardels bear,
To grunt and sweat under a weary life,
But that the dread of something after death,
The undiscover'd country from whose bourn

25    No traveler returns, puzzles the will,
      And makes us rather bear those ills we have
      Than fly to others that we know not of?
      Thus conscience doth make cowards of us all;
      And thus the native hue of resolution
30    Is sicklied o'er with the pale cast of thought,
      And enterprises of great pitch and moment
      With this regard their currents turn awry,
      And lose the name of action.

**2 suffer** submit to, endure   **3 slings** leather devices used to hurl small
stones   **outrageous** cruel and inconstant   **7 shocks** emotional wounds
**8 consummation** ending   **10 perchance** perhaps   **rub** difficulty
**12 shuffled off** gotten rid of   **mortal coil** turmoil of human existence
**13 respect** reflection, consideration   **14 calamity . . . life** the misery (of
mortal life) so long-lived   **15 time** the world   **16 wrong** wrong-doing
**proud** arrogant   **contumely** contemptuous treatment   **17 despis'd**
disdained, scorned   **delay** procrastination   **18 office** those in positions of
authority   **19 merit** virtue   **th' unworthy takes** those that are undeserving
(of such spurns) must withstand   **20 quietus** release (from life)   **21 bare
bodkin** mere dagger   **fardels** burdens   **24 bourn** boundary   **25 puzzles**
perplexes, paralyzes   **29 native hue** natural complexion   **30 pale cast**
pallor   **31 pitch** height, stature   **moment** importance   **32 regard**
consideration (i.e., of the "something after death")   **currents** courses

(8)                         HAMLET                    [III.1.102]

SCENE: A chamber in Elsinore Castle

*{When Ophelia tries to return some tokens of affection Hamlet gave her in
an earlier, happier time ("Rich gifts wax poor when givers prove unkind," she
explains), the Prince's response is unorthodox to say the least. The question is,
though, whether or not Hamlet realizes that Claudius and Polonius are hovering
nearby, eavesdropping on every word.}*

1     Are you honest? Are you fair? If you be honest and fair, your honesty should
      admit no discourse to your beauty. For the power of beauty will sooner trans-
      form honesty from what it is to a bawd than the force of honesty can translate
      beauty into his likeness. This was sometime a paradox, but now the time gives
5     it proof. I did love you once. Get thee to a nunn'ry. Why wouldst thou be a
      breeder of sinners? I am myself indifferent honest; but yet I could accuse me of
      such things that it were better my mother had not borne me: I am very proud,
      revengeful, ambitious, with more offenses at my beck than I have thoughts to

put them in, imagination to give them shape, or time to act them in. What should such fellows as I do crawling between earth and heaven? We are arrant    10
knaves, all; believe none of us. Go thy ways to a nunn'ry. Where's your father? If at home, let the doors be shut upon him, that he may play the fool nowhere but in 's own house. Farewell. If thou dost marry, I'll give thee this plague for thy dowry: be thou as chaste as ice, as pure as snow, thou shalt not escape calumny. Get thee to a nunn'ry, farewell. Or if thou wilt needs marry, marry a    15
fool; for wise men know well enough what monsters you make of them. To a nunn'ry go, and quickly too. Farewell. I have heard of your paintings too, well enough. God hath given you one face, and you make yourselves another. You jig, you amble, and you lisp, you nickname God's creatures, and make your wantonness your ignorance. Go to, I'll no more on 't; it hath made me mad.    20
I say, we will have no moe marriage. Those that are married already—all but one—shall live. The rest shall keep as they are. To a nunn'ry, go.

**I honest** (1) truthful (2) chaste **fair** (1) beautiful (2) virtuous **honesty**
chastity **2 discourse** intimate dealings **4 sometime** at one time
**a paradox** contrary to popular opinion **the time** the current age
**5 nunn'ry** convent **6 indifferent honest** somewhat decent **7 proud**
vain, haughty **8 beck** command **10 arrant** out and out **13 plague** curse
**15 calumny** malicious slander **wilt needs** must **16 monsters**
i.e., cuckolds **you** you women **17 paintings** use of cosmetics
**18–19 You jig...creatures** i.e., you walk and speak in an affected manner
**19–20 make...ignorance** excuse your affections as being part of your
simpleness **20 on** of **21 moe** more in number

(9)                    HAMLET                    [III.ii.1]

SCENE: A hall in Elsinore Castle

*{The Prince imparts some pre-show advice to a band of traveling players.}*

Speak the speech, I pray you, as I pronounc'd it to you, trippingly on the tongue.    1
But if you mouth it, as many of our players do, I had as lief the town-crier spoke my lines. Nor do not saw the air too much with your hand, thus, but use all gently; for in the very torrent, tempest, and, as I may say, whirlwind of your passion, you must acquire and beget a temperance that may give it smoothness.    5
O, it offends me to the soul to hear a robustious periwig-pated fellow tear a passion to tatters, to very rags, to split the ears of the groundlings, who for the most part are capable of nothing but inexplicable dumb-shows and noise. I would have such a fellow whipp'd for o'erdoing Termagant. It out-herods Herod. Pray you, avoid it. Be not too tame neither, but let your own discretion    10
be your tutor. Suit the action to the word, the word to the action, with this special observance; that you o'erstep not the modesty of nature. For anything

so o'erdone is from the purpose of playing, whose end, both at the first and now, was and is, to hold, as 't were, the mirror up to nature, to show virtue
15    her feature, scorn her own image, and the very age and body of the time his form and pressure. Now this overdone, or come tardy off, though it makes the unskillful laugh, cannot but make the judicious grieve, the censure of which one must in your allowance o'erweigh a whole theatre of others. O, there be players that I have seen play, and heard others praise—and that highly—not to
20    speak it profanely, that, neither having th' accent of Christians nor the gait of Christian, pagan, nor man, have so strutted and bellow'd that I have thought some of nature's journeymen had made men and not made them well, they imitated humanity so abominably. And let those that play your clowns speak no more than is set down for them; for there be of them that will themselves
25    laugh, to set on some quantity of barren spectators to laugh too, though in the mean time some necessary question of the play be then to be consider'd. That's villainous, and shows a most pitiful ambition in the fool that uses it. Go, make you ready.

**2 mouth** enunciate with exaggerated distinctness  **lief** soon, willingly
**6 robustious** noisy, boisterous  **periwig-pated** wig-wearing  **7 passion** passionate speech  **groundlings** common folk who watched a performance from the pit area, i.e., the cheap seats, of the theatre  **8 capable of** able to appreciate  **inexplicable** unintelligible  **dumb-show** a brief pantomime that provides an overview of the play it precedes  **9 Termagant** a notoriously raucous character from early English drama  **10 Herod** i.e., the infamous King of Judea—another role that was typically played with flamboyance and fury  **12 modesty** moderation, self-restraint  **13 from** contrary to
**15 feature** true appearance  **scorn** i.e., show that which is rightfully scorned  **time** i.e., in which we live  **his** its  **16 pressure** character  **come tardy off** inadequately performed  **17 unskillful** i.e., the undiscerning members of the audience  **censure...one** judgment of even one of whom
**20 speak it** mention  **accent** manner of speaking  **Christians** ordinary folk
**22 journeyman** workers who are something less than masters of their trade  **24 of them** some of them  **25 barren** dull, lifeless  **27 fool** (1) foolish person (2) actor playing the role of the fool or clown

(10)                          CLAUDIUS                        [III.iii.36]

SCENE: A chamber in Elsinore Castle

*{Alone and in dire need of something to assuage his guilty conscience, Claudius makes an attempt at repentance.}*

1    O, my offense is rank, it smells to heaven;
     It hath the primal eldest curse upon 't,

A brother's murder. Pray can I not,
Though inclination be as sharp as will.
My stronger guilt defeats my strong intent,                    5
And, like a man to double business bound,
I stand in pause where I shall first begin,
And both neglect. What if this cursed hand
Were thicker than itself with brother's blood;
Is there not rain enough in the sweet heavens                  10
To wash it white as snow? Whereto serves mercy
But to confront the visage of offense?
And what's in prayer but this twofold force,
To be forestalled ere we come to fall,
Or pardon'd being down? Then I'll look up;                     15
My fault is past. But, O, what form of prayer
Can serve my turn? "Forgive me my foul murder?"
That cannot be, since I am still possess'd
Of those effects for which I did the murder;
My crown, mine own ambition, and my queen.                     20
May one be pardon'd and retain th' offense?
In the corrupted currents of this world,
Offense's gilded hand may shove by justice,
And oft 'tis seen the wicked prize itself
Buys out the law. But 'tis not so above.                       25
There is no shuffling, there the action lies
In his true nature, and we ourselves compell'd,
Even to the teeth and forehead of our faults,
To give in evidence. What then? What rests?
Try what repentance can. What can it not?                      30
Yet what can it, when one cannot repent?
O wretched state! O bosom black as death!
O limed soul, that, struggling to be free,
Art more engag'd! Help, angels! Make assay.
Bow, stubborn knees, and heart with strings of steel,          35
Be soft as sinews of the new-born babe!
All may be well.

**2 primal eldest curse** (refers to God's curse on Cain, the very first
murderer, who also slew his brother)   **4 sharp as will** strong as my resolve
(to do so)   **7 pause** hesitation   **9 itself** i.e., its normal size   **11 Whereto**
to what purpose   **12 confront...offense** counteract the effects of sin
**14 forestalled** intercepted   **come to fall** are about to fall (from grace)
**15 look up** take heart   **17 turn** situation   **19 effects** results, fruits
**21 offense** i.e., that which was gained by the offense   **22 currents** courses,
ways   **23 gilded** money-laden (i.e., bribing)   **shove by** push aside
**24 wicked prize** rewards of vice   **25 Buys out** buys off, bribes
**26 shuffling** shady maneuvering   **the action lies** the matter (of our

offense) is judged   **27 his** its   **28 Even...of** even while confronted face to
face with   **29 rests** remains to be done   **33 limed** ensnared (Birdlime is a
sticky substance that was spread about bushes in order to capture birds.)
**34 engag'd** entangled  **assay** (a) supreme effort

(II)                                   HAMLET                              [III.III.73]

SCENE: A chamber in Elsinore Castle

*{On his way to visit Gertrude, Hamlet comes upon Claudius, who is kneeling
in prayer (see preceding entry) and unaware of the Prince's presence. With his
sword drawn and at the ready, Hamlet stays a moment to consider his options.}*

| | |
|---|---|
| 1 | Now might I do it pat, now 'a is a-praying; |
| | And now I'll do 't. And so 'a goes to heaven; |
| | And so am I reveng'd. That would be scann'd: |
| | A villain kills my father, and for that, |
| 5 | I, his sole son, do this same villain send |
| | To heaven. |
| | Why, this is hire and salary, not revenge. |
| | 'A took my father grossly, full of bread, |
| | With all his crimes broad blown, as flush as May; |
| 10 | And how his audit stands who knows save heaven? |
| | But in our circumstance and course of thought, |
| | 'Tis heavy with him. And am I then reveng'd, |
| | To take him in the purging of his soul, |
| | When he is fit and season'd for his passage? |
| 15 | No! |
| | Up, sword, and know thou a more horrid hent. |
| | [*Puts up his sword.*] |
| | When he is drunk asleep, or in his rage, |
| | Or in th' incestuous pleasure of his bed, |
| 20 | At game a-swearing, or about some act |
| | That has no relish of salvation in 't— |
| | Then trip him, that his heels may kick at heaven, |
| | And that his soul may be as damn'd and black |
| | As hell, whereto it goes. My mother stays. |
| 25 | This physic but prolongs thy sickly days. |

**1 pat** opportunely  **'a** he  **3 would be scann'd** requires careful
consideration  **8 grossly** spiritually unprepared  **full of bread** i.e., relishing
the fruits of life  **9 crimes broad blown** sins in full bloom  **flush** full of life,
vigorous  **10 audit** account (with God)  **11 But...thought** i.e., but from

our earthly perspective, as far as we can tell   **12 heavy** grievous   **16 Up**
into the sheath   **know...hent** await my grasp on a more dreadful occasion
**19 incestuous** (In Shakespeare's time, a marriage like the one between
Claudius and his brother's widow was considered to be incestuous in nature.)
**20 game** sport   **21 relish** trace   **24 whereto** to what place  **stays** awaits
(me)   **25 physic** remedy, purging (referring to Claudius's praying)

(12)                    HAMLET                    [III.iv.34]

SCENE: The Queen's private chamber

*{Just moments ago Hamlet unwittingly killed Polonius, stabbing the old man
as he eavesdropped from behind an arras. Disappointed that it wasn't Claudius
instead who was lurking back there, Hamlet now turns his attention toward
an understandably distraught Gertrude.}*

Leave wringing of your hands. Peace, sit you down,                    1
And let me wring your heart, for so I shall,
If it be made of penetrable stuff,
If damned custom have not braz'd it so
That it be proof and bulwark against sense.                    5
[*Showing her two portraits.*]
Look here, upon this picture, and on this,
The counterfeit presentment of two brothers.
See what a grace was seated on this brow:
Hyperion's curls, the front of Jove himself,                    10
An eye like Mars, to threaten and command,
A station like the herald Mercury
New-lighted on a heaven-kissing hill—
A combination and a form indeed,
Where every god did seem to set his seal,                    15
To give the world assurance of a man.
This was your husband. Look you now what follows:
Here is your husband, like a mildew'd ear,
Blasting his wholesome brother. Have you eyes?
Could you on this fair mountain leave to feed,                    20
And batten on this moor? Ha, have you eyes?
You cannot call it love, for at your age
The heyday in the blood is tame, it's humble,
And waits upon the judgment, and what judgment
Would step from this to this? Sense, sure, you have,                    25
Else could you not have motion, but sure that sense

Is apoplex'd, for madness would not err,
Nor sense to ecstasy was ne'er so thrall'd
But it reserv'd some quantity of choice
30   To serve in such a difference. What devil was 't
That thus hath cozen'd you at hoodman-blind?
Eyes without feeling, feeling without sight,
Ears without hands or eyes, smelling sans all,
Or but a sickly part of one true sense
35   Could not so mope.
O shame, where is thy blush? Rebellious hell,
If thou canst mutine in a matron's bones,
To flaming youth let virtue be as wax,
And melt in her own fire. Proclaim no shame
40   When the compulsive ardor gives the charge,
Since frost itself as actively doth burn,
And reason panders will.

**I Leave** stop **Peace** quiet yourself   **4 damned custom** habitual
wickedness **braz'd** hardened   **5 proof** armor   **sense** feeling
**8 counterfeit presentment** painted likenesses   **two brothers** i.e.,
Hamlet Sr. and Claudius, respectively   **10 Hyperion** (A figure from Greek
mythology, Hyperion was a sun god and father of Helios.)   **front** brow,
forehead   **12 station** way of standing or bearing himself   **13 hill** i.e.,
mountain   **18 ear** ear of corn or other grain   **19 blasting** blighting, spoiling
**21 batten** gorge   **23 heyday** state of excitement   **24 waits upon** obeys
**25 Sense** perception through the five senses   **27 apoplex'd** paralyzed
**27–30 madness...difference** madness alone would not account for such
an error in judgment, nor were the five senses ever so overcome with lunacy
that they did not retain the ability to make such an obvious choice (i.e.,
between Hamlet Sr. and Claudius)   **31 cozen'd** cheated   **hoodman-blind**
blindman's bluff   **33 sans** without   **35 so mope** be so bewildered, act so
aimlessly   **37 mutine** rebel, mutiny   **39–42 Proclaim...will** do not
proclaim it as sinful when the heated passions of youth result in wanton
behavior, since even those of more advanced age burn with lust; and reason
acts to abet such desire, instead of restraining it

(13)                       HAMLET                       [IV.IV.32]

SCENE: A field near the coast of Denmark

*{When Hamlet observes Prince Fortinbras and his troops pass by Elsinore on
their way to do battle with the Polish, he cannot help but reflect upon the stark*

*contrast between this army's evident sense of purpose and his own inexplicable
impotence.}*

How all occasions do inform against me,                                              1
And spur my dull revenge! What is a man,
If his chief good and market of his time
Be but to sleep and feed? A beast, no more.
Sure he that made us with such large discourse,                                      5
Looking before and after, gave us not
That capability and god-like reason
To fust in us unus'd. Now whether it be
Bestial oblivion, or some craven scruple
Of thinking too precisely on th' event—                                             10
A thought which, quarter'd, hath but one part wisdom
And ever three parts coward—I do not know
Why yet I live to say "This thing's to do,"
Sith I have cause and will and strength and means
To do 't. Examples gross as earth exhort me:                                        15
Witness this army of such mass and charge
Led by a delicate and tender prince,
Whose spirit with divine ambition puff'd
Makes mouths at the invisible event,
Exposing what is mortal and unsure                                                   20
To all that fortune, death, and danger dare—
Even for an egg-shell. Rightly to be great
Is not to stir without great argument,
But greatly to find quarrel in a straw
When honor's at the stake. How stand I then,                                         25
That have a father kill'd, a mother stain'd,
Excitements of my reason and my blood,
And let all sleep, while, to my shame, I see
The imminent death of twenty thousand men,
That, for a fantasy and trick of fame,                                               30
Go to their graves like beds, fight for a plot
Whereon the numbers cannot try the cause,
Which is not tomb enough and continent
To hide the slain? O, from this time forth,
My thoughts be bloody, or be nothing worth!                                          35

**1 occasions** circumstances, matters  **inform against** accuse, testify against
**2 spur** incite  **dull** impassive, lifeless  **3 market** profit  **5 large discourse**
considerable thought and reflection  **6 before and after** at the future and
the past  **7 That** that same  **8 fust** grow moldy  **9 oblivion** forgetfulness
**craven** cowardly  **10 event** consequence, outcome  **14 Sith** since

**15 gross** plain, evident   **16 mass and charge** massiveness and expense
**17 delicate** noble, refined   **tender** youthful   **18 puff'd** is inflated
**19 mouths** scornful faces   **invisible event** unforseeable outcome (of his
actions)   **22 an egg-shell** i.e., some worthless object   **Rightly** correctly
**23 great argument** a matter of great contention   **26 stain'd** tainted,
corrupted   **30 fantasy** whim   **trick** trifle, trivial amount   **31 plot** i.e., of
ground   **32 Whereon . . . cause** on which there is not room enough for the
opposing armies to engage in combat   **33 continent** container

(14)                          HAMLET                          [V.1.184]

SCENE: A churchyard

*{Hamlet and Horatio were meandering about when they happened upon a pair
of laborers digging up an old grave. Before long it dons on Hamlet that the
grave's previous occupant was the court jester Yorick, a childhood playmate of
his. It's enough to make a prince indulge in a little morbid philosophizing.}*

1   [*He picks up Yorick's skull.*]
    Alas, poor Yorick! I knew him, Horatio; a fellow of infinite jest, of most excellent
    fancy. He hath borne me on his back a thousand times; and now how abhorr'd
    in my imagination it is! My gorge rises at it. Here hung those lips that I have
5   kiss'd I know not how oft. Where be your gibes now? Your gambols, your
    songs, your flashes of merriment that were wont to set the table on a roar?
    Not one now, to mock your own grinning? Quite chap-fall'n? Now get you to
    my lady's chamber, and tell her, let her paint an inch thick, to this favor she
    must come; make her laugh at that. Prithee, Horatio, tell me one thing. Dost
10  thou think Alexander look'd o' this fashion i' th' earth? And smelt so? Pah!
    [*Puts down the skull.*] To what base uses we may return, Horatio! Why may not
    imagination trace the noble dust of Alexander, till 'a find it stopping a bung-
    hole? As thus: Alexander died, Alexander was buried, Alexander returneth to
    dust; the dust is earth; of earth we make loam; and why of that loam, whereto
15  he was converted, might they not stop a beer-barrel?
        Imperious Caesar, dead and turn'd to clay,
        Might stop a hole to keep the wind away.
        O, that the earth which kept the world in awe,
        Should patch a wall t' expel the winter's flaw!
20  But soft, but soft awhile! Here comes the King,
    [*Ophelia's funeral procession enters.*]
    The Queen, the courtiers. Who is this they follow?
    And with such maimed rites? This doth betoken

The corse they follow did with desp'rate hand
Fordo its own life. 'Twas of some estate.                    25
Couch we awhile, and mark.

**3 fancy** imagination   **4 gorge** stomach   **5 gibes** sarcasms   **gambols**
pranks   **6 the table** i.e., those sitting around the table   **7 chap-fall'n**
(1) lacking a lower jaw (2) downcast, dejected   **8 paint** i.e., her face with
cosmetics **favor** countenance   **10 Alexander** Alexander the Great
**11 base** ignoble, low   **12 'a find** one finds   **12–13 bung-hole** hole for
emptying or filling a cask   **14 loam** a mixture composed mainly of clay, used
to make bricks, fill in holes and gaps, etc.   **19 flaw** sudden gust of wind
**20 soft** wait, stop   **23 maimed rites** lack of the customary ceremony
**24 corse** corpse   **25 Fordo** undo, destroy   **estate** high rank in society
**26 Couch** hide   **mark** listen

**ALTERNATES**
Claudius   [I.ii.87-117]
Laertes    [I.iii.1-44]
Ghost      [I.v.2-91]

# HENRY IV, PART 1

Though Hotspur recently spearheaded England's suppression of a Scottish uprising, he now finds himself consorting with the enemy. Enraged over King Henry's treatment of him concerning the status of some war prisoners, Hotspur joined forces with a few other disenchanted noblemen and mounted his own rebellion.

But when push comes to shove at the Battle of Shrewsbury, most of the conspiracy's forces—namely, those of Mortimer, Glendower, and Hotspur's own father, Northumberland—are conspicuously absent. Outmanned if not outfought, Hotspur is eventually slain by King Henry's son, Prince Hal, and his forces are defeated.

Spicing up the above martial adventures are a series of comedic sideshows featuring the high jinks of the fallen knight Falstaff, King Henry's son Prince Hal, and others.

**KING HENRY IV**

**PRINCE HENRY,** also called Prince Hal, son to King Henry IV

**EARL OF NORTHUMBERLAND,** an English noble

**HOTSPUR,** son to the Earl of Northumberland

**EARL OF DOUGLAS,** a Scottish noble, in league with Hotspur

**SIR JOHN FALSTAFF,** a roguish knight, companion to Prince Henry

**EDWARD POINS,** friend to Prince Henry

**LADY PERCY,** wife to Hotspur

(1)                          PRINCE HENRY                          [I.ii.195]

SCENE: An apartment of Prince Henry's

*{Hal has been garnering a considerable amount of notoriety for his shenanigans with Falstaff and company. But now, with a moment to himself, the Prince reveals that there is a method to his merriment.}*

I know you all, and will awhile uphold                                    1
The unyok'd humor of your idleness.
Yet herein will I imitate the sun,
Who doth permit the base contagious clouds
To smother up his beauty from the world,                                  5
That, when he please again to be himself,
Being wanted, he may be more wond'red at
By breaking through the foul and ugly mists
Of vapors that did seem to strangle him.
If all the year were playing holidays,                                   10
To sport would be as tedious as to work;
But when they seldom come, they wish'd for come,
And nothing pleaseth but rare accidents.
So, when this loose behavior I throw off
And pay the debt I never promised,                                       15
By how much better than my word I am,
By so much shall I falsify men's hopes;
And like bright metal on a sullen ground,
My reformation, glitt'ring o'er my fault,
Shall show more goodly and attract more eyes                             20
Than that which hath no foil to set it off.
I'll so offend to make offense a skill,
Redeeming time when men think least I will.

**1 you all** (referring to Falstaff and his cohorts, who've just departed)
**uphold** support, sustain   **2 unyok'd** undisciplined   **idleness** frivolity
**4 base** low-lying   **contagious** noxious   **6 That** so that   **7 wanted** missed
**wond'red** admired   **11 sport** play, make merry   **13 but** as do   **rare**
**accidents** extraordinary events   **14 loose** wanton, dissolute   **17 falsify**
prove to be ill-founded   **hopes** expectations   **18 sullen ground** dull
background   **21 foil** thin sheet of metal laid behind a jewel to increase its
brilliance   **22 to** as to   **skill** clever, skillful policy   **23 Redeeming time**
making up for lost time

(2)                    **HOTSPUR**                    [I.III.29]

SCENE: The royal palace

*{Hotspur has been accused of failing to relinquish a number of important prisoners captured by him during the recent Scottish uprising. Upon his return to London, he appears before King Henry to present his side of the story.}*

1    My liege, I did deny no prisoners.
     But I remember, when the fight was done,
     When I was dry with rage and extreme toil,
     Breathless and faint, leaning upon my sword,
5    Came there a certain lord, neat and trimly dress'd,
     Fresh as a bridegroom, and his chin new reap'd
     Show'd like a stubble-land at harvest-home.
     He was perfumed like a milliner,
     And 'twixt his finger and his thumb he held
10   A pouncet-box, which ever and anon
     He gave his nose and took 't away again,
     Who therewith angry, when it next came there,
     Took it in snuff; and still he smil'd and talk'd,
     And as the soldiers bore dead bodies by
15   He call'd them untaught knaves, unmannerly,
     To bring a slovenly unhandsome corse
     Betwixt the wind and his nobility.
     With many holiday and lady terms
     He questioned me; amongst the rest demanded
20   My prisoners in your Majesty's behalf.
     I then, all smarting with my wounds being cold,
     To be so pest'red with a popinjay,
     Out of my grief and my impatience
     Answer'd neglectingly I know not what—
25   He should, or he should not—for he made me mad
     To see him shine so brisk and smell so sweet
     And talk so like a waiting-gentlewoman
     Of guns and drums and wounds—God save the mark!—
     And telling me the sovereignest thing on earth
30   Was parmaceti for an inward bruise;
     And that it was great pity, so it was,
     This villainous saltpeter should be digg'd
     Out of the bowels of the harmless earth,
     Which many a good tall fellow had destroy'd
35   So cowardly, and but for these vile guns
     He would himself have been a soldier.
     This bald unjointed chat of his, my lord,

I answer'd indirectly, as I said;
And I beseech you, let not his report
Come current for an accusation                                    40
Betwixt my love and your high Majesty.

**5 trimly** prettily, finely   **6 his . . . reap'd** his beard freshly trimmed
**7 Show'd** looked   **harvest-home** the close of the harvest (when the fields
are nearly bare)   **8 milliner** merchant of women's finery   **10 pouncet-box**
small perfume box with a perforated lid   **ever and anon** every now and
then   **12 Who** which   **13 in snuff** in a resentful manner   **still** constantly
**15 untaught** ill-bred, ignorant   **unmannerly** rude   **16 corse** corpse
**18 holiday and lady** dainty and lady-like   **19 questioned** talked to   **the
rest** other things   **22 popinjay** parrot (hence, speaker of worthless drivel)
**23 grief** suffering   **24 neglectingly** without due consideration
**28 God . . . mark** (A common exclamation that is used here to express
disdain and frustration.)   **29 sovereignest thing** most effective remedy
**30 parmaceti** ointment made of whale sperm   **32 saltpeter**
i.e., gunpowder   **34 many . . . destroy'd** has destroyed many a good, brave
fellow   **37 bald** trivial, stupid   **unjointed** disjointed, incoherent   **40 Come
current** become the basis

(3)                              **FALSTAFF**                        [II.ii.10]

SCENE: The highway near Gadshill

*{While Falstaff and his cohorts were en route to one of their favored highway
robbery spots, Poins absconded with the fat knight's horse. Alone and exhausted,
Sir John evidently fails to see the humor of the situation.}*

I am accurs'd to rob in that thief's company. The rascal hath remov'd my horse,    1
and tied him I know not where. If I travel but four foot by the squier further
afoot, I shall break my wind. Well, I doubt not but to die a fair death for all this,
if I scape hanging for killing that rogue. I have forsworn his company hourly
any time this two and twenty years, and yet I am bewitch'd with the rogue's     5
company. If the rascal have not given me medicines to make me love him, I'll
be hang'd. It could not be else, I have drunk medicines. Poins! Hal! A plague
upon you both! Bardolph! Peto! I'll starve ere I'll rob a foot further. An 'twere
not as good a deed as drink to turn true man and to leave these rogues, I am
the veriest varlet that ever chew'd with a tooth. Eight yards of uneven ground    10
is threescore and ten miles afoot with me, and the stony-hearted villains know
it well enough. A plague upon it when thieves cannot be true to one another!
[*A whistle is heard.*] Whew! A plague upon you all! Give me my horse, you
rogues, give me my horse, and be hang'd!

**2 squier** foot-rule (a measuring tool)   **3 break my wind** heave and gasp
for my breath  **for all** despite all   **4 scape** escape   **5 any time** continually
**6 medicines** potions   **8 Bardolph! Peto!** (Falstaff's partners-in-petty-
crime include Bardolph and Peto, along with Poins and Prince Hal.)  **An
'twere** if it were   **9 drink** drinking to one's health  **turn true man** turn into
an honest man   **10 veriest varlet** blackest rogue  **uneven** not level, rough

(4)                    HOTSPUR                    [II.III.I]

SCENE: The Earl of Northumberland's castle

*{Back home for the time being, Hotspur is fuming over a letter that he's just
received. The missive comes from some fair-weather friend who, it would appear,
has opted to sit out the current rebellion.}*

1    [*Reading the letter.*]
"But, for mine own part, my lord, I could be well contented to be there, in
respect of the love I bear your house." He could be contented; why is he not,
then? In respect of the love he bears our house! He shows in this he loves
5    his own barn better than he loves our house. Let me see some more. "The
purpose you undertake is dangerous"—why, that's certain. 'Tis dangerous to
take a cold, to sleep, to drink; but I tell you, my lord fool, out of this nettle,
danger, we pluck this flower, safety. "The purpose you undertake is dangerous,
the friends you have nam'd uncertain, the time itself unsorted, and your whole
10    plot too light for the counterpoise of so great an opposition." Say you so, say
you so? I say unto you again, you are a shallow, cowardly hind, and you lie. What
a lack-brain is this! By the Lord, our plot is a good plot as ever was laid, our
friends true and constant; a good plot, good friends, and full of expectation; an
excellent plot, very good friends. What a frosty-spirited rogue is this! Why,
15    my Lord of York commends the plot and the general course of the action.
'Zounds, an I were now by this rascal, I could brain him with his lady's fan.
Is there not my father, my uncle, and myself? Lord Edmund Mortimer, my
lord of York, and Owen Glendower? Is there not besides the Douglas? Have
I not all their letters to meet me in arms by the ninth of the next month?
20    And are they not some of them set forward already? What a pagan rascal is
this! An infidel! Ha! You shall see now in very sincerity of fear and cold heart,
will he to the King and lay open all our proceedings. O, I could divide myself
and go to buffets, for moving such a dish of skim milk with so honorable an
action! Hang him! Let him tell the King; we are prepar'd. I will set forward
25    tonight.

**3 house** family   **7 take a cold** take a chill, catch cold   **9 unsorted**
ill-chosen   **9–10 your... of** your whole plan is inadequate to compensate
for the threat posed by   **11 hind** yokel, boor   **12 lack-brain** brainless one
**13 expectation** promise   **15 Lord of York** Scroop, the Archbishop of
York (and Hotspur's fellow insurgent)   **16 'Zounds** a contraction of the
popular interjection, "God's Wounds"   **an** if   **18 the Douglas** the Scottish
rebel, Archibald, Earl of Douglas   **19 all... to** letters from all of them, each
vowing to   **20 pagan** unbelieving   **21 very sincerity** the purest form
**22–23 divide... buffets** split in two and commence fighting with myself
(i.e., sort of an Elizabethan version of "I could kick myself")   **23 moving**
appealing to, prevailing upon


(5)                            FALSTAFF                        [II.iv.398]

SCENE: The Boar's Head tavern

*{While carousing at the local pub, Falstaff and Prince Hal decide to indulge in*
*a little scene work. With the Prince slated for an impending appearance before*
*King Henry, the pair figure it couldn't hurt to improvise a dry run of the royal*
*encounter right here and now. The sketch kicks off with Falstaff, as the King,*
*ascending his makeshift throne and addressing "his son."}*


Harry, I do not only marvel where thou spendest thy time, but also how thou       1
art accompanied; for though the camomile, the more it is trodden upon, the
faster it grows, yet youth, the more it is wasted, the sooner it wears. That
thou art my son I have partly thy mother's word, partly my own opinion, but
chiefly a villainous trick of thine eye and a foolish hanging of thy nether lip,      5
that doth warrant me. If then thou be son to me, here lies the point: why,
being son to me, art thou so pointed at? Shall the blessed sun of heaven prove
a micher and eat blackberries? A question not to be ask'd. Shall the son of
England prove a thief and take purses? A question to be ask'd. There is a thing,
Harry, which thou hast often heard of, and it is known to many in our land by      10
the name of pitch. This pitch, as ancient writers do report, doth defile; so doth
the company thou keepest. For, Harry, now I do not speak to thee in drink,
but in tears; not in pleasure, but in passion; not in words only, but in woes also.
And yet there is a virtuous man whom I have often noted in thy company, but I
know not his name. A goodly portly man, i' faith, and a corpulent; of a cheerful    15
look, a pleasing eye, and a most noble carriage; and, as I think, his age some
fifty, or, by 'r lady, inclining to threescore; and now I remember me, his name
is Falstaff. If that man should be lewdly given, he deceiveth me; for, Harry, I see
virtue in his looks. If then the tree may be known by the fruit, as the fruit by

20    the tree, then, peremptorily I speak it, there is virtue in that Falstaff. Him keep
with, the rest banish. And tell me now, thou naughty varlet, tell me, where
hast thou been this month?

> **5 trick** expression, look   **6 warrant** assure   **7 pointed at** i.e., in derision
> and disapproval   **8 micher** truant   **9 England** i.e., England's king
> **11 pitch...defile** (refers to a proverb from Ecclesiasticus 13:1 which deals
> with the defilement of touching pitch)   **13 passion** sorrowful emotion
> **15 portly** dignified, stately   **i' faith** in truth   **corpulent** full-figured (man)
> **17 by 'r lady** by our lady (a common interjection of the day)   **18 lewdly
> given** wickedly inclined   **19–20 If...fruit** (an allusion to Matthew 12:33)
> **20 peremptorily** decisively   **21 naughty varlet** misbehaving boy


(6)                    PRINCE HENRY                    [III.ii.130]

SCENE: The royal palace

*{King Henry and Hal meet face to face at last, and from Hal's point of view,
it's not a pretty sight. The King has been chastising his son for his long-standing
pattern of notorious conduct, asserting that everything which the Prince lacks—
valor, tenacity, prowess on the battlefield—is abundantly evident in his archrival, Hotspur. Having finally heard enough of his father's harangue, Hal responds to the charges levied against him.}*


1       God forgive them that so much have sway'd
        Your Majesty's good thoughts away from me!
        I will redeem all this on Percy's head,
        And in the closing of some glorious day
5       Be bold to tell you that I am your son,
        When I will wear a garment all of blood
        And stain my favors in a bloody mask,
        Which, wash'd away, shall scour my shame with it.
        And that shall be the day, whene'er it lights,
10      That this same child of honor and renown,
        This gallant Hotspur, this all-praised knight,
        And your unthought-of Harry chance to meet.
        For every honor sitting on his helm,
        Would they were multitudes, and on my head
15      My shames redoubled! For the time will come
        That I shall make this northern youth exchange
        His glorious deeds for my indignities.
        Percy is but my factor, good my lord,

To engross up glorious deeds on my behalf;
And I will call him to so strict account                                    20
That he shall render every glory up,
Yea, even the slightest worship of his time,
Or I will tear the reckoning from his heart.
This in the name of God I promise here,
The which if He be pleas'd I shall perform,                                 25
I do beseech your Majesty may salve
The long-grown wounds of my intemperance.
If not, the end of life cancels all bands,
And I will die a hundred thousand deaths
Ere break the smallest parcel of this vow.                                  30

**6 of blood** covered with blood   **7 favors** (facial) features   **9 lights** breaks,
dawns   **13 For** as for   **helm** helmet   **16 northern** (Hotspur hails from
Northumberland, a county of northern England.)   **18 factor** agent,
go-between   **19 engross up** amass, collect   **22 worship** honor   **time**
lifetime   **23 reckoning** amount due   **27 intemperance** excessive
behavior   **28 bands** bonds, solemn obligations   **30 parcel** portion, detail

(7)                           **FALSTAFF**                        [IV.ii.11]

SCENE: A country road near Coventry

*{Falstaff has been placed in command of an infantry company, and it's a sorry
one at that. It seems that Sir John has opted to line his pockets by permitting all
able-bodied men to bribe their way out of service. The motley crew of ragtags
that remains is such a pitiful lot that even Falstaff is embarrassed to be seen in
their company.}*

If I be not asham'd of my soldiers, I am a sous'd gurnet. I have misus'd the King's    1
press damnably. I have got, in exchange of a hundred and fifty soldiers, three
hundred and odd pounds. I press me none but good householders, yeomen's
sons, inquire me out contracted bachelors, such as had been ask'd twice on
the banns—such a commodity of warm slaves as had as lief hear the devil as a    5
drum, such as fear the report of a caliver worse than a struck fowl or a hurt
wild duck. I press'd me none but such toasts-and-butter, with hearts in their
bellies no bigger than pins' heads, and they have bought out their services; and
now my whole charge consists of ancients, corporals, lieutenants, gentlemen
of companies—slaves as ragged as Lazarus in the painted cloth, where the glut-    10
ton's dogs lick'd his sores, and such as indeed were never soldiers, but discarded
unjust servingmen, younger sons to younger brothers, revolted tapsters, and

ostlers trade-fall'n, the cankers of a calm world and a long peace, ten times
more dishonorable ragged than an old feaz'd ancient. And such have I, to fill up
15    the rooms of them as have bought out their services, that you would think that
I had a hundred and fifty totter'd prodigals lately come from swine-keeping,
from eating draff and husks. A mad fellow met me on the way and told me I
had unloaded all the gibbets and press'd the dead bodies. No eye hath seen
such scarecrows. I'll not march through Coventry with them, that's flat. Nay,
20    and the villains march wide betwixt the legs, as if they had gyves on, for indeed
I had the most of them out of prison. There's not a shirt and a half in all my
company, and the half shirt is two napkins tack'd together and thrown over the
shoulders like a herald's coat without sleeves; and the shirt, to say the truth,
stol'n from my host at Saint Albans, or the red-nose innkeeper of Daventry.
25    But that's all one, they'll find linen enough on every hedge.

**1 sous'd** pickled **gurnet** a type of fish **1–2 King's press** royal commission
giving authority to draft military recruits **3 press** draft **householders**
heads of households **yeomen's** small landowner's **4 contracted**
betrothed **4–5 twice . . . banns** (It was customary to proclaim in public on
three consecutive Sundays one's intent to marry.) **5 commodity** quantity,
lot **warm** well-off, pampered **lief** soon **6 drum** (The drum was typically
associated with times of war.) **report** resounding noise **caliver** musket
**than** than do **struck** wounded **7 toasts-and-butter** weaklings,
milquetoasts **8 bought . . . services** bribed their way out of military service
**9 charge** company of soldiers **ancients** ensigns (Falstaff has designated a
disproportionate number of his troops as officers so that he might keep for
himself their higher salaries.) **9–10 gentlemen of companies** gentlemen
volunteers **10 Lazarus** the diseased beggar in the biblical parable of the
rich man and the beggar (Luke 16:19–31) **painted cloth** a type of cheap
wall-hanging **12 unjust** dishonest **servingmen** servants **revolted**
runaway **tapsters** barkeeps **13 ostlers trade-fall'n** employed mule or
horse tenders **cankers** ulcerous sores **14 feaz'd ancient** worn out flag
**16 totter'd** ragged **prodigals** (see Luke 15:11–16) **17 draff and husks**
pig slop and garbage **the way** (Falstaff and his men are bound for the site of
conflict just outside Shrewsbury.) **18 gibbets** gallows **19 flat** final, for
sure **20 gyves** leg irons **24 my host** i.e., the innkeeper **Saint Albans,
Daventry** towns found along the road that runs between London and
Coventry **25 that's all one** never mind, no matter **hedge** (Freshly
washed linen was often laid out on hedges to dry.)

(8)                          FALSTAFF                          [V.iv.iii]

SCENE: The fields near Shrewsbury

{As the battle reaches its climax, hand-to-hand combat abounds. A brief skirmish
between Douglas and Falstaff ended with Sir John "falling down as if he were

*dead," and Douglas sprinting off to fight elsewhere. Just a few paces away, Hal and Hotspur engaged in a duel that saw Hal emerge victorious. Then, with the slain Hotspur and feigning Falstaff lying side by side, Prince Henry remarks that the fat knight must soon be disemboweled, and exits. Alone at last, "Falstaff riseth up."}*

Embowel'd! If thou embowel me today, I'll give you leave to powder me and eat     1
me too tomorrow. 'Sblood, 'twas time to counterfeit, or that hot termagant
Scot had paid me scot and lot too. Counterfeit? I lie, I am no counterfeit. To
die is to be a counterfeit, for he is but the counterfeit of a man who hath not
the life of a man; but to counterfeit dying, when a man thereby liveth, is to     5
be no counterfeit, but the true and perfect image of life indeed. The better
part of valor is discretion, in which better part I have sav'd my life. 'Zounds,
I am afraid of this gunpowder Percy, though he be dead. How if he should
counterfeit too and rise? By my faith, I am afraid he would prove the better
counterfeit. Therefore, I'll make him sure; yea, and I'll swear I kill'd him. Why     10
may not he rise as well as I? Nothing confutes me but eyes, and nobody sees
me. Therefore, sirrah [*He stabs Hotspur's corpse and lifts it onto his back.*], with
a new wound in your thigh, come you along with me.

**1 Embowel'd** disemboweled **powder** salt   **2 'Sblood** God's blood (a mild
oath) **counterfeit** pretend (i.e., that he was dead) **hot** angry **termagant**
violent   **3 paid...too** settled with me in full ("scot and lot" was a type of
municipal tax)   **7 part** quality **'Zounds** God's wounds (a popular
interjection of the day)   **8 gunpowder** i.e., volatile, unpredictable
**10 make him sure** make sure of him (i.e., that he can do no harm)
**11 Nothing...eyes** nothing can disprove my claim except the testimony of
eyewitnesses   **12 sirrah** (a form of address that, in this instance, conveys
disrespect and inappropriate familiarity)

### Alternates

| | |
|---|---|
| Hotspur | [I.iii.158–184] |
| King Henry | [III.ii.4–91] |
| Falstaff | [V.i.127–141] |

# HENRY IV, PART 2

Once again (see *Henry IV, Part 1*), the specter of rebellion appears poised on England's horizon; this time the insurrection is led by the Archbishop of York. Things quickly fall apart, however, when the Archbishop's cause is deserted at the last moment by the Earl of Northumberland. Rather than proceed as planned, the Archbishop instead negotiates a settlement with Prince John. Pursuant to the conditions of said agreement, the Archbishop disbands his army—immediately after which he is arrested and executed. When Northumberland's forces (now back in the game) are subsequently defeated in Yorkshire, the uprising is deemed officially quashed.

But such glad tidings from the battlefield prove to be of little comfort to King Henry; shortly after England's victory, he succumbs to a fatal illness. Assuming Henry's royal responsibilities is his son Prince Hal, who ascends the throne as Henry V.

As in *Henry IV, Part 1*, the amusing misadventures of Falstaff and friends are shuffled in among the narrative's central events. Come story's end, Falstaff gets naught but the bum's rush from the former Prince Hal, his one-time partner in petty crime; the new and improved King Henry orders that the corpulent knight and his cohorts be carted off to prison.

**KING HENRY IV**
**PRINCE HENRY,** also called Prince Hal, son to King Henry IV
**PRINCE JOHN,** son to Henry IV
**EARL OF NORTHUMBERLAND,** adversary to King Henry IV
**ARCHBISHOP OF YORK,** adversary to King Henry IV
**SIR JOHN FALSTAFF,** a roguish knight, companion to Prince Henry

**LADY PERCY,** widow of Hotspur, daughter-in-law to the Earl of Northumberland

(1)                          KING HENRY                          [III.1.4]

SCENE: The royal palace

*{Alone in the dead of night, a restless Henry muses upon the elusive nature of sleep.}*

How many thousand of my poorest subjects                                         1
Are at this hour asleep! O sleep, O gentle sleep,
Nature's soft nurse, how I have frighted thee,
That thou no more wilt weigh my eyelids down
And steep my senses in forgetfulness?                                            5
Why rather, sleep, liest thou in smoky cribs,
Upon uneasy pallets stretching thee
And hush'd with buzzing night-flies to thy slumber,
Than in the perfum'd chambers of the great,
Under the canopies of costly state,                                             10
And lull'd with sound of sweetest melody?
O thou dull god, why liest thou with the vile
In loathsome beds, and leavest the kingly couch
A watch-case or a common 'larum-bell?
Wilt thou upon the high and giddy mast                                          15
Seal up the ship-boy's eyes, and rock his brains
In cradle of the rude imperious surge
And in the visitation of the winds,
Who take the ruffian billows by the top,
Curling their monstrous heads and hanging them                                  20
With deafing clamor in the slippery clouds,
That, with the hurly, death itself awakes?
Canst thou, O partial sleep, give thy repose
To the wet sea-boy in an hour so rude,
And, in the calmest and most stillest night,                                    25
With all appliances and means to boot,
Deny it to a king? Then happy low, lie down!
Uneasy lies the head that wears a crown.

**6 cribs** shacks, hovels   **7 pallets** straw beds   **thee** thyself   **10 costly** lavish
**state** grandeur, magnificence   **12 dull** drowsy   **vile** lowly   **14 watch-case**
sentry box   **'larum-bell** bell wrung to warn of danger   **15 giddy** dizzying,
unstable   **17 In** in the   **rude** harsh, violent   **imperious** domineering
**19 billows** high rolling waves   **21 deafing** deafening   **22 That** so that
**hurly** commotion   **23 partial** showing partiality   **26 appliances and
means** comforts and inducements (to sleep)   **27 low** common folk

(2)                          FALSTAFF                          [IV.III.87]

SCENE: Gaultree Forest

*{After being rudely dismissed by the hard-boiled Prince John, Falstaff can't help but note a marked difference in temperament between John and his older brother, Prince Hal.}*

1    Good faith, this young sober-blooded boy doth not love me, nor a man cannot make him laugh. But that's no marvel—he drinks no wine. There's never none of these demure boys come to any proof, for thin drink doth so over-cool their blood, and making many fish-meals, that they fall into a kind of male green-
5    sickness; and then, when they marry, they get wenches. There are generally fools and cowards, which some of us should be too, but for inflammation. A good sherris-sack hath a twofold operation in it. It ascends me into the brain, dries me there all the foolish and dull and crudy vapors which environ it, makes it apprehensive, quick, forgetive, full of nimble, fiery, and delectable shapes,
10   which, deliver'd o'er to the voice, the tongue, which is the birth, becomes excellent wit. The second property of your excellent sherris is the warming of the blood, which, before cold and settled, left the liver white and pale, which is the badge of pusillanimity and cowardice. But the sherris warms it and makes it course from the inwards to the parts' extremes. It illumineth the face, which
15   as a beacon gives warning to all the rest of this little kingdom, man, to arm; and then the vital commoners and inland petty spirits muster me all to their captain, the heart, who, great and puff'd up with his retinue, doth any deed of courage; and this valor comes of sherris. So that skill in the weapon is nothing without sack, for that sets it a-work; and learning a mere hoard of gold kept by a devil,
20   till sack commences it and sets it in act and use. Hereof comes it that Prince Harry is valiant, for the cold blood he did naturally inherit of his father, he hath, like lean, sterile, and bare land, manur'd, husbanded, and till'd with excellent en-deavor of drinking good and good store of fertile sherris, that he is become very hot and valiant. If I had a thousand sons, the first humane principle I would teach
25   them should be to forswear thin potations and to addict themselves to sack.

**3 demure** solemn  **come . . . proof** amount to anything  **thin drink** lighter spirits such as beer or ale  **4–5 green-sickness** an anemic condition which usually afflicted young women and gave them a greenish tint to their complexion  **5 get** beget  **6 inflammation** arousal through drinking
**7 sherris-sack** (Both sherris and sack, terms that are often used individually, belong to a general class of strong, dry white wines, usually imported from the south of Europe.)  **ascends me** ascends  **8 crudy** thick
**9 apprehensive** perceptive  **forgetive** creative  **shapes** imaginations, ideas
**11 wit** intellect, mental capacity  **12 liver** (The liver was at one time thought to be the seat of a person's courage.)  **14 inwards** inner parts, innards  **parts' extremes** body's limbs  **15 man** i.e., man's body

**16 vital . . . spirits** (It was once thought that vital, highly-refined substances and fluids permeated the body's blood system and internal regions.) **muster me all** all gather   **18 in the** with a   **20 commences it** enables it to realize its potential **act** operation **Hereof** of this   **22 lean** meager **husbanded** farmed   **24 humane** human, civilized

(3)               PRINCE HENRY             [IV.v.21]

SCENE: The royal palace

*{Although King Henry's demise appears imminent, for the moment he merely lies fast asleep in his sickbed. When Prince Hal enters the chamber, his attention is quickly torn between the gravely ill King and the royal crown that rests nearby.}*

| | |
|---|---:|
| Why doth the crown lie there upon his pillow, | 1 |
| Being so troublesome a bedfellow? | |
| O polish'd perturbation! Golden care! | |
| That keep'st the ports of slumber open wide | |
| To many a watchful night! Sleep with it now! | 5 |
| Yet not so sound and half so deeply sweet | |
| As he whose brow with homely biggen bound | |
| Snores out the watch of night. O majesty! | |
| When thou dost pinch thy bearer, thou dost sit | |
| Like a rich armor worn in heat of day, | 10 |
| That scald'st with safety. By his gates of breath | |
| There lies a downy feather which stirs not. | |
| Did he suspire, that light and weightless down | |
| Perforce must move. My gracious lord! My father! | |
| This sleep is sound indeed. This is a sleep | 15 |
| That from this golden rigol hath divorc'd | |
| So many English kings. Thy due from me | |
| Is tears and heavy sorrows of the blood, | |
| Which nature, love, and filial tenderness | |
| Shall, O dear father, pay thee plenteously. | 20 |
| My due from thee is this imperial crown, | |
| Which, as immediate from thy place and blood, | |
| Derives itself to me. Lo, where it sits, | |
| [*He puts on the crown.*] | |
| Which God shall guard. And put the world's whole strength | 25 |
| Into one giant arm, it shall not force | |
| This lineal honor from me. This from thee | |
| Will I to mine leave, as 'tis left to me. | |

**3 perturbation** cause of agitation  **care** apprehension, disquiet  **4 ports**
gates  **5 watchful** sleepless  **Sleep** may you (King Henry) sleep  **6 Yet not**
i.e., yet even so your sleep will still not be  **7 homely biggen** plain nightcap
**9 thou** (referring to the crown)  **pinch** afflict, torment  **11 scald'st with**
**safety** burns the wearer even while safeguarding him  **his...breath**
i.e., King Henry's lips  **13 suspire** breathe  **16 rigol** ring (referring to the
crown)  **17 due** rightful claim  **18 blood** (The blood was considered to be
the seat of one's emotions.)  **22 immediate from** the one who is nearest
to  **23 Derives itself** descends  **25 Which** (referring to King Henry's
head)  **27 lineal** inherited

(4)                     KING HENRY                     [IV.v.93]

SCENE: The royal palace

*{After prematurely presuming his father's demise and donning the royal crown
(see preceding entry), Prince Hal is suddenly confronted by a down-but-not-
yet-out King Henry who unexpectedly regains consciousness.}*

1     I stay too long by thee, I weary thee.
      Dost thou so hunger for mine empty chair
      That thou wilt needs invest thee with my honors
      Before thy hour be ripe? O foolish youth,
5     Thou seek'st the greatness that will overwhelm thee.
      Stay but a little, for my cloud of dignity
      Is held from falling with so weak a wind
      That it will quickly drop. My day is dim.
      Thou hast stol'n that which after some few hours
10    Were thine without offense, and at my death
      Thou hast seal'd up my expectation.
      Thy life did manifest thou lov'dst me not,
      And thou wilt have me die assur'd of it.
      Thou hid'st a thousand daggers in thy thoughts,
15    Which thou hast whetted on thy stony heart,
      To stab at half an hour of my life.
      What, canst thou not forbear me half an hour?
      Then get thee gone and dig my grave thyself,
      And bid the merry bells ring to thine ear
20    That thou art crowned, not that I am dead.
      Let all the tears that should bedew my hearse
      Be drops of balm to sanctify thy head.
      Only compound me with forgotten dust;

Give that which gave thee life unto the worms.
Pluck down my officers, break my decrees,                                    25
For now a time is come to mock at form.
Harry the Fifth is crown'd! Up, vanity!
Down, royal state! All you sage counselors, hence!
And to the English court assemble now,
From every region, apes of idleness!                                          30
Now, neighbor confines, purge you of your scum.
Have you a ruffin that will swear, drink, dance,
Revel the night, rob, murder, and commit
The oldest sins the newest kinds of ways?
Be happy, he will trouble you no more.                                        35
England shall double gild his treble guilt,
England shall give him office, honor, might;
For the fifth Harry from curb'd license plucks
The muzzle of restraint, and the wild dog
Shall flesh his tooth on every innocent.                                      40
O my poor kingdom, sick with civil blows!
When that my care could not withhold thy riots,
What wilt thou do when riot is thy care?
O, thou wilt be a wilderness again,
Peopled with wolves, thy old inhabitants!                                     45

**2 chair** i.e., throne   **3 wilt needs** find it necessary to   **honors** titles
**6 Stay** wait   **11 seal'd up** confirmed   **expectation** fears   **17 forbear**
endure, bear with   **22 balm** oil used to anoint the King at his coronation
**23 compound** mix   **26 form** ceremony   **27 vanity** folly   **28 hence** away
**30 apes of idleness** frivolous fools   **31 confines** territories, regions
**32 ruffin** ruffian   **38 license** licentiousness, vice   **40 flesh ... on** plunge his
teeth into the flesh of   **41 civil blows** civil strife and upheaval   **42 care**
i.e., careful maintenance of discipline   **withhold** keep in check   **riots**
debauchery, profligate living   **43 care** concern

**ALTERNATES**
Archbishop of York   [I.iii.85–108]
Prince Henry         [IV.v.138–176]
King Henry           [IV.v.177–219]

# HENRY V

Henry readies England for war after his claims on certain lands possessed by the French are ungraciously dismissed by France's royal heir apparent, the Dauphin. Tarrying just long enough to thwart a budding insurgency among a few of his noblemen, Henry and his armies finally cross the channel and embark upon their campaign in France.

After easily capturing the French town of Harfleur, England's forces meet much stiffer opposition when confronted by France's armies near Agincourt. But despite being greatly outnumbered by the French contingent, Henry's armies emerge victorious, and France is forced to sue for peace. Under the terms of surrender, it is agreed that Henry shall marry the French king's daughter, Katharine, and be acknowledged as heir to France's throne.

KING HENRY V, formerly Prince Henry
EARL OF WESTMORLAND, an English noble
NYM, a rogue
BARDOLPH, a rogue
PISTOL, a rogue
BOY, servant to King Henry V
LEWIS, THE DAUPHIN, son to the King of France

PRINCESS KATHARINE, daughter to the King of France
HOSTESS, formerly Mistress Quickly, wife to Pistol

(1)                    **KING HENRY**                    [I.ii.259]

SCENE: The royal palace

*{Though Hal now maintains an appropriately regal existence as King Henry the Fifth, the dissolute lifestyle of his past has not been entirely forgotten. A while back Henry laid claim to certain French dukedoms as rightfully belonging to England. By way of reply, Lewis the Dauphin has sent Henry a chest full of tennis balls—the implication being that frivolous games are more suited to Henry's nature than are the rigors of ruling a kingdom.}*

We are glad the Dauphin is so pleasant with us.                    1
His present and your pains we thank you for.
When we have match'd our rackets to these balls,
We will in France, by God's grace, play a set
Shall strike his father's crown into the hazard.                    5
Tell him he hath made a match with such a wrangler
That all the courts of France will be disturb'd
With chases. And we understand him well,
How he comes o'er us with our wilder days,
Not measuring what use we made of them.                    10
We never valu'd this poor seat of England,
And therefore, living hence, did give ourself
To barbarous license; as 'tis ever common
That men are merriest when they are from home.
But tell the Dauphin I will keep my state,                    15
Be like a king, and show my sail of greatness
When I do rouse me in my throne of France.
For that I have laid by my majesty
And plodded like a man for working-days,
But I will rise there with so full a glory                    20
That I will dazzle all the eyes of France,
Yea, strike the Dauphin blind to look on us.
And tell the pleasant Prince this mock of his
Hath turn'd his balls to gun-stones, and his soul
Shall stand sore charged for the wasteful vengeance                    25
That shall fly with them; for many a thousand widows
Shall this his mock mock out of their dear husbands;
Mock mothers from their sons, mock castles down;
And some are yet ungotten and unborn
That shall have cause to curse the Dauphin's scorn.                    30
But this lies all within the will of God,
To whom I do appeal, and in whose name
Tell you the Dauphin I am coming on

To venge me as I may, and to put forth
35    My rightful hand in a well-hallow'd cause.
So get you hence in peace, and tell the Dauphin
His jest will savor but of shallow wit,
When thousands weep more than did laugh at it.

**I We are** I am (Henry is employing the royal plural.)   **Dauphin** (Generically, the term "dauphin" applies to the eldest son of the King of France, who is by definition next in line to the throne.)   **2 your** (Henry is addressing the French ambassadors who delivered the Dauphin's message.)   **5 Shall** that shall   **hazard** an opening in the wall around an Elizabethan-era tennis court (Henry also infers the common "danger" sense of the word.)   **6 wrangler** opponent   **7 courts** (1) tennis courts (2) royal courts   **8 chases** (1) failed return in tennis (2) pursuits   **9 comes o'er us** taunts me   **10 measuring** appreciating   **11 seat** throne   **15 keep my state** maintain a dignity befitting my royal status   **16 sail of greatness** powers under full sail   **17 rouse me** raise myself up   **18 that** i.e., the French kingdom (to which Henry lays claim)   **laid by** put aside   **24 balls to gun-stones** tennis balls into cannon balls   **25 sore charged** sorely burdened with responsibility   **wasteful** ruinous   **34 may** can   **37 savor** smack, reek

(2)                            KING HENRY                            [III.1.1]

SCENE: Before the city of Harfleur

*{Henry and his troops have landed in France, and currently surround the city of Harfleur. Even as his soldiers storm the city's walls, Henry exhorts them on to the sort of heroics that befit their English heritage.}*

I    Once more into the breach, dear friends, once more;
Or close the wall up with our English dead!
In peace there's nothing so becomes a man
As modest stillness and humility.
5    But when the blast of war blows in our ears,
Then imitate the action of the tiger:
Stiffen the sinews, summon up the blood,
Disguise fair nature with hard-favor'd rage.
Then lend the eye a terrible aspect;
10    Let it pry through the portage of the head
Like the brass cannon; let the brow o'erwhelm it
As fearfully as doth a galled rock
O'erhang and jutty his confounded base,
Swill'd with the wild and wasteful ocean.
15    Now set the teeth and stretch the nostril wide,

Hold hard the breath, and bend up every spirit
To his full height. On, on, you noblest English,
Whose blood is fet from fathers of war-proof!
Fathers that, like so many Alexanders,
Have in these parts from morn till even fought,                    20
And sheath'd their swords for lack of argument.
Dishonor not your mothers; now attest
That those whom you call'd fathers did beget you.
Be copy now to men of grosser blood,
And teach them how to war. And you, good yeomen,                   25
Whose limbs were made in England, show us here
The mettle of your pasture. Let us swear
That you are worth your breeding, which I doubt not,
For there is none of you so mean and base
That hath not noble luster in your eyes.                           30
I see you stand like greyhounds in the slips,
Straining upon the start. The game's afoot!
Follow your spirit, and upon this charge
Cry "God for Harry, England, and Saint George!"

**1 breach** (i.e., in the city's walls of defense)   **4 stillness** quietness of
behavior   **7 blood** zeal, anger   **10 portage** portholes (i.e., eyes)
**11 o'erwhelm** overhang   **12 fearfully** menacingly   **galled** worn away
**13 jutty** project beyond   **confounded** ruined, wasted   **14 Swill'd** awash
**wasteful** destructive   **16 bend up** strain, raise up   **17 his** its   **18 fet**
derived   **of war-proof** whose valor was proved in battle   **19 Alexanders**
(Alexander the Great is credited with bemoaning the fact that there were no
more worlds for him to conquer.)   **21 argument** something to fight over
**24 copy** example   **grosser** less refined   **25 yeomen** owners of small landed
estates (who usually made up the bulk of England's infantry)   **27 mettle . . .**
**pasture** quality of your rearing   **29 mean** undignified, low-born   **31 slips**
leashes   **32 upon the start** to get started, to set off   **34 Saint George**
patron saint of England

(3)                            Boy                    [III.ii.28]

SCENE: Before the city of Harfleur

*{An English lad, young in years but evidently well versed in the ways of the world,
takes time out from the battle to reflect upon his three rascally comrades-in-arms,
Nym, Bardolph, and Pistol.}*

As young as I am, I have observ'd these three swashers. I am boy to them all      1
three, but all they three, though they would serve me, could not be man to

me; for indeed three such antics do not amount to a man. For Bardolph, he is white-liver'd and red-fac'd, by the means whereof 'a faces it out, but fights not.

5    For Pistol, he hath a killing tongue and a quiet sword, by the means whereof 'a breaks words, and keeps whole weapons. For Nym, he hath heard that men of few words are the best men, and therefore he scorns to say his prayers, lest 'a should be thought a coward; but his few bad words are match'd with as few good deeds, for 'a never broke any man's head but his own, and that was

10    against a post when he was drunk. They will steal anything, and call it purchase. Bardolph stole a lute-case, bore it twelve leagues, and sold it for three half-pence. Nym and Bardolph are sworn brothers in filching, and in Calais they stole a fire-shovel. I knew by that piece of service the men would carry coals. They would have me as familiar with men's pockets as their gloves or their

15    handkerchers; which makes much against my manhood, if I should take from another's pocket to put into mine, for it is plain pocketing up of wrongs. I must leave them, and seek some better service. Their villainy goes against my weak stomach, and therefore I must cast it up.

**1 swashers** braggarts, swaggerers   **2 man** manservant   **3 antics** buffoons
**4 white-liver'd** cowardly   **red-fac'd** ruddy complexioned (much like one
who has consumed too much strong drink)   **'a...out** he puts forth a bold
front   **6 breaks words** (1) corrupts the meaning of words (2) goes back on
his word   **10 purchase** booty   **11 leagues** (One league equals about
three miles.)   **11–12 three half-pence** (i.e., a ridiculously inconsequential
compensation for his labors)   **13 carry coals** i.e., willingly suffer insults and
degradation   **15 makes** offends   **16 pocketing...wrongs** (1) submitting
to insults (2) receiving stolen goods   **17–18 goes...stomach** makes me ill
**18 cast** vomit

(4)                     KING HENRY                     [IV.III.18]

SCENE: The English camp at Agincourt

*{Prior to the big showdown with France—a battle in which the French will
outnumber England's forces by a margin of five to one—Henry overhears one
of his noblemen, Westmorland, grousing about the poor odds and wishing that
there were a few more Englishmen set to take the field.}*

1    What's he that wishes so?
     My cousin Westmorland? No, my fair cousin.
     If we are mark'd to die, we are enow
     To do our country loss; and if to live,
5    The fewer men, the greater share of honor.
     God's will, I pray thee, wish not one man more.
     By Jove, I am not covetous for gold,

Nor care I who doth feed upon my cost;
It yearns me not if men my garments wear;
Such outward things dwell not in my desires.　　　　　10
But if it be a sin to covet honor,
I am the most offending soul alive.
No, faith, my coz, wish not a man from England.
God's peace, I would not lose so great an honor
As one man more, methinks, would share from me　　　15
For the best hope I have. O, do not wish one more!
Rather proclaim it, Westmorland, through my host,
That he which hath no stomach to this fight,
Let him depart; his passport shall be made
And crowns for convoy put into his purse.　　　　　20
We would not die in that man's company
That fears his fellowship to die with us.
This day is call'd the feast of Crispian.
He that outlives this day, and comes safe home,
Will stand a' tiptoe when this day is nam'd,　　　　25
And rouse him at the name of Crispian.
He that shall see this day, and live old age,
Will yearly on the vigil feast his neighbors,
And say, "Tomorrow is Saint Crispian."
Then will he strip his sleeve and show his scars,　　30
And say, "These wounds I had on Crispin's day."
Old men forget; yet all shall be forgot,
But he'll remember with advantages
What feats he did that day. Then shall our names,
Familiar in his mouth as household words,　　　　　35
Harry the King, Bedford and Exeter,
Warwick and Talbot, Salisbury and Gloucester,
Be in their flowing cups freshly rememb'red.
This story shall the good man teach his son;
And Crispin Crispian shall ne'er go by,　　　　　　40
From this day to the ending of the world,
But we in it shall be remembered—
We few, we happy few, we band of brothers.
For he today that sheds his blood with me
Shall be my brother; be he ne'er so vile,　　　　　45
This day shall gentle his condition.
And gentlemen in England now a-bed
Shall think themselves accurs'd they were not here,
And hold their manhoods cheap whiles any speaks
That fought with us upon Saint Crispin's day.　　　50

**1 What's** who's　**3 enow** enough　**8 upon my cost** at my expense
**9 yearns** grieves　**13 faith** by my faith (a mild oath)　**coz** cousin　**15 share**

**from me** deprive me of   **18 to** for   **20 crowns for convoy** money for
traveling   **21 We** (Henry is employing the royal plural)   **22 fears** is
apprehensive about   **23 feast of Crispian** Saint Crispian's day   **25 a' tiptoe**
i.e., at attention   **26 rouse him** stir himself   **27 live** live to see   **28 the
vigil** i.e., the eve of St. Crispin's day   **33 advantages** embellishments (that
he's added)   **45 vile** low in rank, common   **46 gentle his condition** raise
him to the rank of gentleman

(5)                              KING HENRY                         [V.II.122]

SCENE: The King of France's palace

*{England has emerged victorious in its war against France, with one of Henry's
conditions for peace being his marriage to France's Princess Katharine. Since
time is of the essence, England's king wastes none: Henry immediately begins
courting Kate's favor, lacing his straightforward suit with a generous helping of
humility.}*

1    Kate, my wooing is fit for thy understanding. I am glad thou  canst speak no
     better English, for if thou couldst, thou wouldst find me such a plain king that
     thou wouldst think I had sold my farm to buy my crown. I know no ways to
     mince it in love, but directly to say, "I love you." Then if you urge me farther
5    than to say, "do you in faith?" I wear out my suit. Marry, if you would put me to
     verses or to dance for your sake, Kate, why you undid me. For the one, I have
     neither words nor measure; and for the other, I have no strength in measure,
     yet a reasonable measure in strength. If I could win a lady at leap-frog, or by
     vaulting into my saddle with my armor on my back, under the correction of
10   bragging be it spoken, I should quickly leap into a wife. Or if I might buffet for
     my love, or bound my horse for her favors, I could lay on like a butcher and sit
     like a jackanapes, never off. But, before God, Kate, I cannot look greenly, nor
     gasp out my eloquence, nor I have no cunning in protestation; only downright
     oaths, which I never use till urg'd, nor never break for urging. If thou canst
15   love a fellow of this temper, Kate, whose face is not worth sunburning, that
     never looks in his glass for love of anything he sees there, let thine eye be thy
     cook. I speak to thee plain soldier. If thou canst love me for this, take me. If
     not, to say to thee that I shall die, is true; but for thy love, by the Lord, no—
     yet, I love thee too. And while thou liv'st, dear Kate, take a fellow of plain and
20   uncoin'd constancy, for he perforce must do thee right, because he hath not
     the gift to woo in other places. For these fellows of infinite tongue, that can
     rhyme themselves into ladies' favors, they do always reason themselves out
     again. What? A speaker is but a prater, a rhyme is but a ballad. A good leg will
     fall, a straight back will stoop, a black beard will turn white, a curl'd pate will

grow bald, a fair face will wither, a full eye will wax hollow; but a good heart,    25
Kate, is the sun and the moon—or rather the sun and not the moon, for it
shines bright and never changes, but keeps his course truly. If thou would have
such a one, take me. And take me, take a soldier; take a soldier, take a king.
And what say'st thou then to my love? Speak, my fair, and fairly, I pray thee.
Put off your maiden blushes, avouch the thoughts of your heart with the looks    30
of an empress, take me by the hand and say, "Harry of England, I am thine."
Which word thou shalt no sooner bless mine ear withal, but I will tell thee
aloud, "England is thine, Ireland is thine, France is thine, and Henry Plantagenet
is thine"—who, though I speak it before his face, if he be not fellow with the
best king, thou shalt find the best king of good fellows. Come, your answer in    35
broken music! For thy voice is music and thy English broken. Therefore, queen
of all, Katharine, break thy mind to me in broken English. Wilt thou have me?

**1 fit . . . understanding** (Henry is referring to the fact that Katharine speaks
and comprehends very little English.)    **5 in faith** in truth, truly  **wear . . .
suit** exhaust my courtship skills  **Marry** indeed, to be sure
**5–6 put . . . verses** urge me to recite verse    **6 For** as for    **7 measure**
meter  **in measure** in dance    **8 measure in** amount of    **9 correction**
reproof, admonition    **10 buffet** fight    **11 bound** cause to leap and prance
**lay on** inflict blows, strike hard    **11–12 sit . . . off** maintain my seat on a
horse as deftly as a monkey ("jackanapes") could, never falling off
**12 greenly** bashful (like a "green" boy smitten with love)    **13 downright**
direct, straightforward    **15 temper** temperament    **16 glass** looking glass
**16–17 let . . . cook** (Henry is urging Kate to embellish what few qualities he
might already possess—to dress up his appearance, as it were, in the way a
cook might garnish a meal in order to increase its appeal.)    **17 plain soldier**
openly, honestly    **20 uncoin'd** not fabricated, genuine    **21 tongue** speech
**22 reason** talk    **24 fall** wither and lose its shape    **28 take me, take** if you
take me, you take    **29 fair** beloved, beautiful woman    **30 Put off** dispense
with  **avouch** declare, affirm    **32 withal** with    **34 fellow with** equal to
**36 broken music** music arranged for an ensemble of different instruments,
"broken" down into individual parts    **37 break** reveal, disclose

## Alternates

# HENRY VI, PART 1

Mother England's present situation is not a pretty one: Good King Henry V has recently died, his young son is not yet of sufficient age to assume his royal duties as Henry VI, and England's war with France has reached full speed. To make matters worse, a young Frenchwoman by the name of Joan La Pucelle (also known as Joan of Arc) takes the battlefield by storm, inspiring France's forces to one victory after another.

As if that weren't enough, young Henry's game attempt to smooth over a smoldering feud between the Duke of Somerset and the Duke of York has but a transient effect. A tenuous truce between the two houses soon disintegrates into a barrage of mutual recriminations on the French battlefield. Yet, just when England appears on the brink of defeat, Joan of Arc's spiritual mentors suddenly desert her, and France's troops are routed. La Pucelle is subsequently taken prisoner by the Duke of York and burned at the stake.

Meanwhile, the Earl of Suffolk has taken a prisoner of his own: Margaret, daughter to the King of Naples. Suffolk sees Margaret as his personal spoil of war, and by engineering a marriage between her and King Henry, he intends to control both the next queen and the crown.

**KING HENRY VI**
**SOMERSET,** an English earl, adversary to York
**YORK,** an English earl, adversary to Somerset
**SUFFOLK,** also called William De La Pole, an English earl
**LORD TALBOT,** an English noble
**SIR JOHN FALSTAFF**
**CHARLES,** Dauphin of France
**DUKE OF BURGUNDY,** a French lord

**MARGARET,** daughter to the King of Naples, afterward wife to King Henry VI
**JOAN LA PUCELLE,** a young Frenchwoman, commonly called Joan of Arc

(1)                    LORD TALBOT                    [IV.i.13]

SCENE: The royal palace in Paris

*{When Sir John Falstaff arrives to inform King Henry of Burgundy's defection to the French, Lord Talbot is quick to lash out at the unsuspecting messenger. Talbot not only strips Falstaff of his garter (which serves as the badge of Sir John's order, the Knights of the Garter), but launches an impressive verbal assault as well.}* [Note that this is not the same Falstaff character found in both parts of *Henry IV* and *The Merry Wives of Windsor*. This Sir John is a historical figure whose real name was "Fastolfe." That being said, there does seem to be a striking resemblance between the two.]

Shame to the Duke of Burgundy and thee!                              1
I vow'd, base knight, when I did meet thee next,
To tear the garter from thy craven's leg,
Which I have done, because unworthily
Thou wast installed in that high degree.                             5
Pardon me, princely Henry, and the rest.
This dastard, at the battle of Patay,
When but in all I was six thousand strong
And that the French were almost ten to one,
Before we met or that a stroke was given,                            10
Like to a trusty squire did run away;
In which assault we lost twelve hundred men.
Myself and divers gentlemen beside
Were there surpris'd and taken prisoners.
Then judge, great lords, if I have done amiss;                       15
Or whether that such cowards ought to wear
This ornament of knighthood, yea or no?
When first this order was ordain'd, my lords,
Knights of the garter were of noble birth,
Valiant and virtuous, full of haughty courage,                      20
Such as were grown to credit by the wars;
Not fearing death, nor shrinking for distress,
But always resolute in most extremes.
He then that is not furnish'd in this sort
Doth but usurp the sacred name of knight,                            25
Profaning this most honorable order,
And should, if I were worthy to be judge,
Be quite degraded, like a hedge-born swain
That doth presume to boast of gentle blood.

**5 installed . . . degree** i.e., inducted into knighthood   **6 rest** (referring to
Gloucester, Winchester and other noblemen also in attendance)   **7 dastard**
coward   **8 but . . . strong** I had but six thousand men under my command
**9 were** i.e., outnumbered us   **11 Like . . . squire** (Talbot speaks sarcastically
here)   **13 divers** several   **gentlemen** soldiers ranking between sergeants
and officers   **20 haughty** noble, high-minded   **21 were . . . credit** did rise
to fame   **by** i.e., by their performance in   **23 most extremes** the most
trying of circumstances   **28 degraded** dropped in rank   **hedge-born
swain** low-born peasant   **29 gentle blood** noble lineage

<br>

(2)                               KING HENRY                          [IV.i.134]

SCENE: The royal palace in Paris

*{With hard feelings between Somerset and York continuing to fester and detract
from England's effort to defeat the French, young Henry takes his best shot at
patching up things between the two lords.}*

<br>

| | |
|---|---|
| 1 | Come hither, you that would be combatants; |
| | Henceforth I charge you, as you love our favor, |
| | Quite to forget this quarrel and the cause. |
| | And you, my lords: remember where we are, |
| 5 | In France, amongst a fickle wavering nation. |
| | If they perceive dissension in our looks |
| | And that within ourselves we disagree, |
| | How will their grudging stomachs be provok'd |
| | To willful disobedience, and rebel! |
| 10 | Beside, what infamy will there arise |
| | When foreign princes shall be certified |
| | That for a toy, a thing of no regard, |
| | King Henry's peers and chief nobility |
| | Destroy'd themselves, and lost the realm of France? |
| 15 | O, think upon the conquest of my father, |
| | My tender years, and let us not forgo |
| | That for a trifle that was bought with blood! |
| | Let me be umpire in this doubtful strife. |
| | I see no reason, if I wear this rose, |
| 20 | [*He puts on a red rose.*] |
| | That anyone should therefore be suspicious |
| | I more incline to Somerset than York. |
| | Both are my kinsmen, and I love them both. |
| | As well they may upbraid me with my crown, |

Because, forsooth, the King of Scots is crown'd.                    25
But your discretions better can persuade
Than I am able to instruct or teach;
And therefore, as we hither came in peace,
So let us still continue peace and love.

**2 our** my (Henry is employing the royal plural)   **8 grudging stomachs**
resentful dispositions, unruly tempers   **11 certified** informed   **12 toy**
trifling matter   **16 My tender years** (Henry succeeded to the English
throne when he was just nine months old, and is underage even at this
point.)   **17 That...that** for a trifle that which   **19 rose** (In the "Wars of
the Roses," as it came to be known, wearing a white rose indicated allegiance
to the house of York, while red roses were sported by supporters of
Somerset.)   **24 As...crown** they might just as well reproach me for
wearing my crown   **26 discretions** sound judgments

(3)                     EARL OF SUFFOLK                [V.III.46]

SCENE: The fields near Angiers

*{Suffolk has taken as prisoner the fair Margaret, daughter to a French nobleman.*
*Smitten by the maid's beauty, Suffolk seeks, in this moment alone with her, some*
*means by which he might enjoy the full compliment of her company—and at*
*the same time keep his marriage intact.}*

O fairest beauty, do not fear nor fly!                              1
For I will touch thee but with reverent hands.
An earl I am, and Suffolk am I call'd.
Be not offended, nature's miracle,
Thou art allotted to be ta'en by me.                               5
So doth the swan her downy cygnets save,
Keeping them prisoner underneath her wings.
Yet if this servile usage once offend,
Go and be free again as Suffolk's friend.
[*She starts to leave.*]                                           10
O, stay! [*Aside.*] I have no power to let her pass;
My hand would free her, but my heart says no.
As plays the sun upon the glassy streams,
Twinkling another counterfeited beam,
So seems this gorgeous beauty to mine eyes.                        15
Fain would I woo her, yet I dare not speak.
I'll call for pen and ink, and write my mind.

Fie, de la Pole, disable not thyself.
Hast not a tongue? Is she not here?
20   Wilt thou be daunted at a woman's sight?
Ay, beauty's princely majesty is such,
Confounds the tongue and makes the senses rough.
How canst thou tell she will deny thy suit,
Before thou make a trial of her love?
25   She's beautiful, and therefore to be woo'd;
She is a woman, therefore to be won.
Fond man, remember that thou hast a wife.
Then how can Margaret be thy paramour?
There all is marr'd; there lies a cooling card.
30   And yet a dispensation may be had.
I'll win this Lady Margaret. For whom?
Why, for my king. Tush, that's a wooden thing!
Yet so my fancy may be satisfied,
And peace established between these realms.
35   But there remains a scruple in that too;
For though her father be the King of Naples,
Duke of Anjou and Maine, yet is he poor,
And our nobility will scorn the match.
It shall be so, disdain they ne'er so much.
40   Henry is youthful and will quickly yield.
[To Margaret.]
Madam, I have a secret to reveal.

**5 Thou** that thou **allotted** destined   **6 cygnets** baby swans   **8 once offend** at all offends you   **14 Twinkling** causing to twinkle   **16 Fain** gladly
**18 Fie** (an expression of disgust)   **disable** belittle   **22 Confounds** that it confounds **rough** dull   **27 Fond** foolish   **29 marr'd** ruined, spoiled
**cooling card** card played by an opponent that spoils one's chance to win
**30 dispensation** permission from the Pope to do that which would normally be forbidden by the Church's edicts   **32 Tush** (an exclamation of contempt)   **wooden** stupid   **35 scruple** problem, objection


**ALTERNATES**
Lord Talbot      [IV.vii.1–31]
Earl of Suffolk   [V.v.48–78]

# HENRY VI, PART 2

When the Duke of Gloucester dares to criticize certain provisions of England's recent treaty with France—a peace that resulted in, among other things, the marriage of Margaret to King Henry—the new (and seditious) Queen does not take it well. Ably assisted by her fellow conspirators, the Earl of Suffolk and Cardinal Beaufort, Margaret immediately sets about eliminating Gloucester and his influence on the King. Before long Margaret has seen to it that the Duchess of Gloucester is banished, and that Gloucester himself is accused of treason, and ultimately murdered.

Direct from Ireland enters rabble-rouser nonpareil, Jack Cade. Somehow, this oddest of ducks manages to lead a motley crew of insurgents all the way to the streets of London. But the ad hoc rebellion quickly fizzles out when Cade's men accept King Henry's offer of amnesty, and an embittered Jack Cade takes to his heels.

Elsewhere, the Wars of the Roses have begun in earnest. Claiming that he is the rightful King of England, the Duke of York leads his armies to an initial victory over the King's forces at the Battle of St. Alban's, at which point the action moves on to London and *Henry IV, Part 3.*

**KING HENRY VI**
**HUMPHREY, DUKE OF GLOUCESTER,** uncle to King Henry VI
**RICHARD, DUKE OF YORK**
**LORD SAY,** an English noble
**JACK CADE,** a rebel


**MARGARET,** Queen to King Henry VI
**ELEANOR, DUCHESS OF GLOUCESTER,** wife to Humphrey

## (1)    DUKE OF GLOUCESTER    [III.1.142]

SCENE: The Abbey at Bury St. Edmunds

*{In an attempt to eliminate both the Duke of Gloucester and his influence over young Henry, Margaret and the other conspirators have falsely accused Gloucester of various crimes against England. In the face of such slander, the honorable Humphrey has come before King and court to warn Henry of the treachery that surrounds him.}*

| | |
|---|---|
| 1 | Ah, gracious lord, these days are dangerous! |
| | Virtue is chok'd with foul ambition |
| | And charity chas'd hence by rancor's hand. |
| | Foul subornation is predominant |
| 5 | And equity exil'd your Highness' land. |
| | I know their complot is to have my life; |
| | And, if my death might make this island happy |
| | And prove the period of their tyranny, |
| | I would expend it with all willingness. |
| 10 | But mine is made the prologue to their play; |
| | For thousands more, that yet suspect no peril, |
| | Will not conclude their plotted tragedy. |
| | Beaufort's red sparkling eyes blab his heart's malice, |
| | And Suffolk's cloudy brow his stormy hate; |
| 15 | Sharp Buckingham unburdens with his tongue |
| | The envious load that lies upon his heart; |
| | And dogged York, that reaches at the moon, |
| | Whose overweening arm I have pluck'd back, |
| | By false accuse doth level at my life. |
| 20 | And you, my sovereign lady, with the rest, |
| | Causeless have laid disgraces on my head |
| | And with your best endeavor have stirr'd up |
| | My liefest liege to be mine enemy. |
| | Ay, all of you have laid your heads together— |
| 25 | Myself had notice of your conventicles— |
| | And all to make away my guiltless life. |
| | I shall not want false witness to condemn me, |
| | Nor store of treasons to augment my guilt. |
| | The ancient proverb will be well effected: |
| 30 | "A staff is quickly found to beat a dog." |

**4 subornation** inducing others to do evil or illegal acts (including perjury) through the use of bribes and other nefarious means   **5 exil'd** exiled from   **6 complot** plot, conspiracy   **8 prove the period** mark the end

**14 cloudy** troubled, menacing   **15 Sharp** harsh, disagreeable   **16 envious** hateful, malicious   **18 overweening** presumptuous, arrogant   **19 accuse** accusation   **level at** draw aim upon   **20 you** (he refers to Queen Margaret) **23 liefest liege** dearest sovereign lord (i.e., Henry)   **24 all of you** (referring to Beaufort, York, and the other conspirators, all of whom are present)   **25 conventicles** secret meetings   **26 make away** do away with, end   **27 want** lack   **28 store** an abundance   **29 effected** realized

(2)                         KING HENRY                         [III.1.198]

SCENE: The Abbey at Bury St. Edmunds

*{Gloucester's eloquent appeal to Henry (see preceding entry) was all for naught. But as the Duke is led away to prison, Henry laments both his dear uncle's fate and his own inability to do what he knows is right.}*

My heart is drown'd with grief,                                          1
Whose flood begins to flow within mine eyes;
My body round engirt with misery—
For what's more miserable than discontent?
Ah, uncle Humphrey, in thy face I see                                     5
The map of honor, truth, and loyalty;
And yet, good Humphrey, is the hour to come
That e'er I prov'd thee false or fear'd thy faith.
What louring star now envies thy estate,
That these great lords and Margaret our queen                            10
Do seek subversion of thy harmless life?
Thou never didst them wrong nor no man wrong.
And as the butcher takes away the calf
And binds the wretch and beats it when it strays,
Bearing it to the bloody slaughter-house,                                15
Even so remorseless have they borne him hence;
And as the dam runs lowing up and down,
Looking the way her harmless young one went,
And can do naught but wail her darling's loss;
Even so myself bewails good Gloucester's case                            20
With sad unhelpful tears, and with dimm'd eyes
Look after him and cannot do him good,
So mighty are his vowed enemies.
His fortunes I will weep, and 'twixt each groan
Say, "Who's a traitor, Gloucester he is none."                           25

**3 round engirt** surrounded    **7 yet … come** never yet, Humphrey, has there been a time    **8 fear'd thy faith** doubted your loyalty    **9 louring** gloomy, threatening    **envies thy estate** shows malice toward your state of affairs    **11 subversion** destruction    **16 they** (referring to the guards) **17 dam** mother    **lowing** calling out    **21 dimm'd** dull, saddened **25 Who's** whoever is

(3)                          DUKE OF YORK                          [III.1.331]

SCENE: The Abbey at Bury St. Edmunds

*{Bound for Ireland to quell a rebellion, York takes a moment alone to assess the progress made in his quest for the English crown.}* [Line 24 serves as an effective alternate end point.]

1    Now, York, or never, steel thy fearful thoughts,
     And change misdoubt to resolution.
     Be that thou hop'st to be, or what thou art
     Resign to death; it is not worth th' enjoying.
5    Let pale-fac'd fear keep with the mean-born man,
     And find no harbor in a royal heart.
     Faster than springtime show'rs comes thought on thought,
     And not a thought but thinks on dignity.
     My brain more busy than the laboring spider
10   Weaves tedious snares to trap mine enemies.
     Well, nobles, well, 'tis politicly done,
     To send me packing with an host of men.
     I fear me you but warm the starved snake,
     Who, cherish'd in your breasts, will sting your hearts.
15   'Twas men I lack'd, and you will give them me;
     I take it kindly. Yet be well assur'd
     You put sharp weapons in a madman's hands.
     Whiles I in Ireland nourish a mighty band,
     I will stir up in England some black storm
20   Shall blow ten thousand souls to heaven or hell;
     And this fell tempest shall not cease to rage
     Until the golden circuit on my head,
     Like to the glorious sun's transparent beams,
     Do calm the fury of this mad-bred flaw.
25   And, for a minister of my intent,
     I have seduc'd a headstrong Kentishman,

John Cade of Ashford,
To make commotion, as full well he can,
Under the title of John Mortimer.
In Ireland have I seen this stubborn Cade                                   30
Oppose himself against a troop of kerns,
And fought so long, till that his thighs with darts
Were almost like a sharp-quill'd porpentine;
And, in the end being rescued, I have seen
Him caper upright like a wild Morisco,                                      35
Shaking the bloody darts as he his bells.
Full often, like a shag-hair'd crafty kern,
Hath he conversed with the enemy,
And undiscover'd come to me again
And given me notice of their villainies.                                    40
This devil here shall be my substitute;
For that John Mortimer, which now is dead,
In face, in gait, in speech, he doth resemble.
By this I shall perceive the commons' mind,
How they affect the house and claim of York.                               45
Say he be taken, rack'd, and tortured,
I know no pain they can inflict upon him
Will make him say I mov'd him to those arms.
Say that he thrive, as 'tis great like he will,
Why then from Ireland come I with my strength                              50
And reap the harvest which that rascal sow'd.
For, Humphrey being dead, as he shall be,
And Henry put apart, the next for me.

**1 steel** harden, strengthen  **fearful** timid  **2 misdoubt** suspicion
**5 mean-born** low-born, common  **8 dignity** i.e., the dignity inherent in
being king  **10 tedious** intricate  **11 politicly** prudently (used here
sarcastically)  **12 send...men** (York was placed in command of a sizable
army when he was selected to deal with the Irish uprising.)  **13 starved** stiff
and numb with cold  **14 cherish'd** nurtured  **20 Shall** that shall  **21 fell**
fierce, deadly  **22 circuit** circlet (i.e., the crown)  **24 mad-bred flaw**
commotion created by madness (referring to the mismanagement and strife
running rampant in the royal court)  **29 Mortimer** (Mortimer was the
surname of a powerful family with certain claims to the English throne. Cade
usurped the name, and thereby a debatable claim to royalty, in order to
justify his "commotion.")  **31 kerns** light-armed foot soldiers of Ireland or
Scotland  **32 darts** light spears  **33 porpentine** porcupine  **35 Morisco**
one who dances the morris, a particularly colorful dance  **36 he** i.e., the
Morisco  **37 Full** quite  **like** disguised like  **42 For that** because  **John
Mortimer** i.e., the legitimate John Mortimer  **44 commons'** common

peoples' **45 affect** regard, react to   **46 rack'd** tormented on the rack
**47 know** know of   **48 Will** that will   **mov'd** incited, provoked   **49 great
like** very likely   **53 put apart** gotten rid of   **next for me** next in line for
the throne is me

(4)                          JACK CADE                          [IV.vii.25]

SCENE: A street in London

*{Jack Cade is a colorful fellow: terrorist, rabble-rouser, egomaniac, warrior
supreme . . . and apparently an ardent foe of literacy in any form. Cade's progress
in his attempt to capture London has led him to proclaim himself "lord of the
city." As such, he now sits in judgment before his luckless prisoner, Lord Say.}*

1    Ah, thou say, thou serge, nay, thou buckram lord!  Now art thou within point-
     blank of our jurisdiction regal. What canst thou answer to my Majesty for
     giving up of Normandy unto Monsieur Basimecu, the Dauphin of France? Be
     it known unto thee by these presence, even the presence of Lord Mortimer,
5    that I am the besom that must sweep the court clean of such filth as thou art.
     Thou hast most traitorously corrupted the youth of the realm in erecting a
     grammar school; and whereas before, our forefathers had no other books but
     the score and the tally, thou hast caus'd printing to be us'd, and contrary to
     the King his crown and dignity, thou hast built a paper-mill. It will be prov'd to
10   thy face that thou hast men about thee that usually talk of a noun and a verb,
     and such abominable words as no Christian ear can endure to hear. Thou hast
     appointed justices of the peace, to call poor men before them about matters
     they were not able to answer. Moreover, thou hast put them in prison, and
     because they could not read, thou hast hang'd them, when, indeed, only for
15   that cause they have been most worthy to live. Away with him! Go, take him
     away, I say, and strike off his head presently; and then break into his son-in-law's
     house, Sir James Cromer, and strike off his head, and bring them both upon
     two poles hither. The proudest peer in the realm shall not wear a head on his
     shoulders, unless he pay me tribute. There shall not a maid be married, but
20   she shall pay to me her maidenhead ere they have it. Men shall hold of me in
     capite; and we charge and command that their wives be as free as heart can
     wish or tongue can tell.

     **I say, serge, buckram** cloths made of silk, wool and coarse linen,
     respectively (Cade begins his progression from fine to common material with
     a play on Say's surname.)   **3 Basimecu** Cade's corruption of
     "Baise-mon-cul," which is French for "kiss my ass"   **4 these presence** these
     present documents (a legal phrase)   **Lord Mortimer** (referring to himself)

**5 besom** broom   **8 score…tally** a crude means of keeping accounts, utilizing a notched stick in lieu of a ledger   **10 usually** habitually, are accustomed to   **14 could not read** i.e., could not demonstrate their literacy in Latin and thereby claim exemption from civil prosecution
**20 maidenhead** virginity   **they** i.e., the maids' new husbands   **20–21 in capite** as tenant in chief, i.e., by direct grant from the crown   **21 free** (1) legally unencumbered (2) promiscuous

ALTERNATES
Duke of York   [I.i.214–259]
John Hume      [I.ii.87–107]

# HENRY VI, PART 3

When his forces suffer defeat at the first Battle of St. Alban's (see *Henry VI, Part 2*) King Henry has little choice but to strike a bargain with his adversary, the Duke of York. Their agreement calls for Henry to continue ruling England as long as he lives, with York winning official recognition as the royal heir. But since this also amounts to the disinheritance of her son, Queen Margaret declares the arrangement unacceptable.

Joining forces with Lord Clifford, Margaret resolves to wage war against York and his followers. Round one of the ensuing struggle goes to the Queen's faction as York's army is routed at Wakefield, and York himself is stabbed to death by Margaret and Clifford.

York's sons, Edward and Richard, mount an impressive comeback, however. Clifford is slain and the royal forces are defeated at Towton, after which Edward assumes the title of King Edward IV and ascends England's throne.

As for Margaret, her alliance with King Lewis of France proves insufficient to avert a resounding defeat at Tewkesbury. Margaret is taken captive and eventually returned to France in exchange for a healthy ransom. Meanwhile, Margaret's husband suffers a somewhat more dreadful fate: while a prisoner in the Tower of London, Henry is mercilessly butchered by the Duke of Gloucester—a slaying designed to shove Gloucester one step closer to his reign as King Richard III.

KING HENRY VI

LEWIS XI, King of France

LORD CLIFFORD, an English noble in league with Margaret

RICHARD, DUKE OF YORK, adversary to King Henry VI

RICHARD, DUKE OF GLOUCESTER, son to the Duke of York

QUEEN MARGARET, wife to King Henry VI

(1)                    **DUKE OF YORK**              [I.iv.iii]

SCENE: A field of battle in the English countryside

*{The Duke of York has been taken prisoner, and his fate now rests upon the mercy of Queen Margaret. Unfortunately for York, mercy is not one of the Queen's strong suits. A display of viciousness by Margaret (see I.iv.66 for the particulars) elicits from York a reply in kind.}*

| | |
|---|---:|
| She-wolf of France, but worse than wolves of France, | 1 |
| Whose tongue more poisons than the adder's tooth! | |
| How ill-beseeming is it in thy sex | |
| To triumph, like an Amazonian trull, | |
| Upon their woes whom fortune captivates! | 5 |
| But that thy face is, vizard-like, unchanging, | |
| Made impudent with use of evil deeds, | |
| I would assay, proud queen, to make thee blush. | |
| To tell thee whence thou cam'st, of whom deriv'd, | |
| Were shame enough to shame thee, wert thou not shameless. | 10 |
| Thy father bears the type of King of Naples, | |
| Of both the Sicils and Jerusalem, | |
| Yet not so wealthy as an English yeoman. | |
| Hath that poor monarch taught thee to insult? | |
| It needs not, nor it boots thee not, proud Queen, | 15 |
| Unless the adage must be verified, | |
| That beggars mounted run their horse to death. | |
| 'Tis beauty that does oft make women proud; | |
| But, God he knows, thy share thereof is small. | |
| 'Tis virtue that doth make them most admir'd; | 20 |
| The contrary doth make thee wond'red at. | |
| 'Tis government that makes them seem divine; | |
| The want thereof makes thee abominable. | |
| Thou art as opposite to every good | |
| As the Antipodes are unto us, | 25 |
| Or as the south to the septentrion. | |
| O tiger's heart wrapt in a woman's hide! | |
| How couldst thou drain the life-blood of the child, | |
| To bid the father wipe his eyes withal, | |
| And yet be seen to bear a woman's face? | 30 |
| Women are soft, mild, pitiful, and flexible; | |
| Thou stern, obdurate, flinty, rough, remorseless. | |
| Bid'st thou me rage? Why, now thou hast thy wish. | |
| Wouldst have me weep? Why, now thou hast thy will. | |
| For raging wind blows up incessant showers, | 35 |

And, when the rage allays, the rain begins.
These tears are my sweet Rutland's obsequies,
And every drop cries vengeance for his death.
That face of his the hungry cannibals
40    Would not have touch'd, would not have stain'd with blood.
But you are more inhuman, more inexorable,
O, ten times more, than tigers of Hyrcania.
See, ruthless queen, a hapless father's tears!
This cloth thou dip'dst in blood of my sweet boy,
45    And I with tears do wash the blood away.
Keep thou the napkin, and go boast of this;
[*Gives back the bloodstained cloth.*]
And if thou tell'st the heavy story right,
Upon my soul, the hearers will shed tears.
50    Yea even my foes will shed fast-falling tears
And say, "Alas, it was a piteous deed!"
There, take the crown, and, with the crown, my curse;
[*Removes his paper crown*]
And in thy need such comfort come to thee
55    As I now reap at thy too cruel hand!
Hard-hearted Clifford, take me from the world.
My soul to heaven, my blood upon your heads!

**4 Amazonian** (The Amazons were a legendary race of female warriors, known for their strength, height, and masculine traits.) **trull** whore
**5 captivates** subdues, conquers  **6 But** were it not  **vizard-like** mask-like
**8 assay** attempt  **11 type** title  **12 both the Sicils** Sicily and Naples
(known as the "Kingdom of the Two Sicilies")  **13 yeoman** landowner
beneath the rank of gentleman  **15 It needs not** it's not necessary  **boots**
profits  **22 government** self-discipline  **25 Antipodes** people dwelling on
the opposite side of the earth  **26 septentrion** the Big Dipper
(representative of the north)  **28–29 How...withal** (see I.iv.79–83)
**31 pitiful** capable of feeling pity  **32 flinty** unyielding, stern  **36 allays**
calms  **37 obsequies** funeral rites  **42 Hyrcania** a region of ancient Persia
noted for its abundance of wild beasts  **48 heavy** sorrowful, unhappy

(2)                    LORD CLIFFORD                    [II.ii.9]

SCENE: Before the city gates of York

*{Clifford attempts to convince King Henry that violence recently perpetrated against the Duke of York—this in spite of a bargain struck between Henry and the Duke—was completely justified.}*

My gracious liege, this too much lenity                                    1
And harmful pity must be laid aside.
To whom do lions cast their gentle looks?
Not to the beast that would usurp their den.
Whose hand is that the forest bear doth lick?                             5
Not his that spoils her young before her face.
Who scapes the lurking serpent's mortal sting?
Not he that sets his foot upon her back.
The smallest worm will turn, being trodden on;
And doves will peck in safeguard of their brood.                        10
Ambitious York did level at thy crown,
Thou smiling while he knit his angry brows.
He, but a duke, would have his son a king,
And raise his issue, like a loving sire;
Thou, being a king, bless'd with a goodly son,                          15
Didst yield consent to disinherit him,
Which argued thee a most unloving father.
Unreasonable creatures feed their young;
And though man's face be fearful to their eyes,
Yet, in protection of their tender ones,                                20
Who hath not seen them, even with those wings,
Which sometime they have us'd with fearful flight,
Make war with him that climb'd unto their nest,
Offering their own lives in their young's defense?
For shame, my liege; make them your precedent!                          25
Were it not pity that this goodly boy
Should lose his birthright by his father's fault,
And long hereafter say unto his child,
"What my great-grandfather and grandsire got,
My careless father fondly gave away?"                                   30
Ah, what a shame were this! Look on the boy,
And let his manly face, which promiseth
Successful fortune, steel thy melting heart
To hold thine own and leave thine own with him.

**1 liege** sovereign lord  **lenity** leniency   **6 spoils** carries off as prey
**7 scapes** escapes   **11 level** aim   **14 raise** elevate the dignity   **17 argued**
showed, proved   **18 Unreasonable creatures** beasts incapable of reason
**20 tender** young   **21 Who** who among us   **25 precedent** example, role
model   **29 great-grandfather and grandsire** Henry IV and Henry V,
respectively   **30 fondly** foolishly   **33 steel** strengthen

(3)                          KING HENRY                        [II.v.i]

SCENE: A field of battle in the English countryside

*{Wandering alone on the outskirts of the battlefield, a solemn Henry wonders*
*if perhaps the simple life might not also be the richest.}*

1     This battle fares like to the morning's war,
      When dying clouds contend with growing light;
      What time the shepherd, blowing of his nails,
      Can neither call it perfect day nor night.
5     Now sways it this way, like a mighty sea
      Forc'd by the tide to combat with the wind;
      Now sways it that way, like the selfsame sea
      Forc'd to retire by fury of the wind.
      Sometime the flood prevails, and then the wind;
10    Now one the better, then another best;
      Both tugging to be victors, breast to breast,
      Yet neither conqueror nor conquered;
      So is the equal poise of this fell war.
      Here on this molehill will I sit me down. [*Sits.*]
15    To whom God will, there be the victory!
      For Margaret my queen, and Clifford too,
      Have chid me from the battle, swearing both
      They prosper best of all when I am thence.
      Would I were dead, if God's good will were so!
20    For what is in this world but grief and woe?
      O God, methinks it were a happy life
      To be no better than a homely swain;
      To sit upon a hill, as I do now,
      To carve out dials quaintly, point by point,
25    Thereby to see the minutes how they run:
      How many makes the hour full complete,
      How many hours brings about the day,
      How many days will finish up the year,
      How many years a mortal man may live.
30    When this is known, then to divide the times:
      So many hours must I tend my flock,
      So many hours must I take my rest,
      So many hours must I contemplate,
      So many hours must I sport myself,
35    So many days my ewes have been with young,
      So many weeks ere the poor fools will ean,
      So many years ere I shall shear the fleece,
      So minutes, hours, days, months, and years,

Pass'd over to the end they were created,
Would bring white hairs unto a quiet grave.                                          40
Ah, what a life were this; how sweet, how lovely!
Gives not the hawthorn bush a sweeter shade
To shepherds looking on their silly sheep
Than doth a rich embroider'd canopy
To kings that fear their subjects' treachery?                                        45
O, yes, it doth; a thousandfold it doth.
And to conclude, the shepherd's homely curds,
His cold thin drink out of his leather bottle,
His wonted sleep under a fresh tree's shade,
All which secure and sweetly he enjoys,                                              50
Is far beyond a prince's delicates—
His viands sparkling in a golden cup,
His body couched in a curious bed—
When care, mistrust, and treason waits on him.

**3 What time** when  **of his nails** on his hands   **13 poise** weight, balance
**fell** deadly   **17 chid** chided, scolded   **18 thence** absent   **22 homely** plain,
simple **swain** shepherd   **24 dials** sundials   **quaintly** painstakingly
**34 sport** amuse   **36 fools** (used here as a term of endearment)   **ean** bring
forth (lambs)   **39 end they** end result for which they were created
**43 silly** helpless   **47 curds** clotted milk   **49 wonted sleep** accustomed
nap   **fresh** cool, refreshing   **51 delicates** luxuries   **53 curious** elaborate,
exquisite   **54 care** worry

(4)          RICHARD, DUKE OF GLOUCESTER          [III.ii.124]

SCENE: The royal palace in London

*{Despite the logjam of royal heirs ahead of him, Gloucester (later to become Richard III) resolves that no obstacle—human or otherwise—shall deter him from ascending to the English throne.}* [This lengthy soliloquy can be abridged in a number of ways. Effective alternate endings include lines 29, 41, and 49.]

Ay, Edward will use women honorably.                                                 1
Would he were wasted, marrow, bones, and all,
That from his loins no hopeful branch may spring,
To cross me from the golden time I look for!
And yet, between my soul's desire and me—                                            5
The lustful Edward's title buried—

Is Clarence, Henry, and his young son Edward,
And all the unlook'd-for issue of their bodies,
To take their rooms, ere I can place myself.
10   A cold premeditation for my purpose!
Why, then, I do but dream on sovereignty,
Like one that stands upon a promontory
And spies a far-off shore where he would tread,
Wishing his foot were equal with his eye,
15   And chides the sea that sunders him from thence,
Saying, he'll lade it dry to have this way.
So do I wish the crown, being so far off;
And so I chide the means that keeps me from it;
And so, I say, I'll cut the causes off,
20   Flattering me with impossibilities.
My eye's too quick, my heart o'erweens too much,
Unless my hand and strength could equal them.
Well, say there is no kingdom then for Richard;
What other pleasure can the world afford?
25   I'll make my heaven in a lady's lap,
And deck my body in gay ornaments,
And witch sweet ladies with my words and looks.
O miserable thought; and more unlikely
Than to accomplish twenty golden crowns!
30   Why, love forswore me in my mother's womb;
And for I should not deal in her soft laws,
She did corrupt frail nature with some bribe,
To shrink mine arm up like a wither'd shrub;
To make an envious mountain on my back,
35   Where sits deformity to mock my body;
To shape my legs of an unequal size;
To disproportion me in every part,
Like to a chaos, or an unlick'd bear-whelp
That carries no impression like the dam.
40   And am I then a man to be belov'd?
O monstrous fault, to harbor such a thought!
Then since this earth affords no joy to me
But to command, to check, to o'erbear such
As are of better person than myself,
45   I'll make my heaven to dream upon the crown,
And, whiles I live, t' account this world but hell,
Until my misshap'd trunk that bears this head
Be round impaled with a glorious crown.
And yet I know not how to get the crown,
50   For many lives stand between me and home;
And I—like one lost in a thorny wood,

That rends the thorns and is rent with the thorns,
Seeking a way and straying from the way,
Not knowing how to find the open air,
But toiling desperately to find it out—                                          55
Torment myself to catch the English crown;
And from that torment I will free myself,
Or hew my way out with a bloody axe.
Why, I can smile, and murder whiles I smile,
And cry "Content" to that which grieves my heart,                    60
And wet my cheeks with artificial tears,
And frame my face to all occasions.
I'll drown more sailors than the mermaid shall;
I'll slay more gazers than the basilisk;
I'll play the orator as well as Nestor,                                          65
Deceive more slyly than Ulysses could,
And, like a Sinon, take another Troy.
I can add colors to the chameleon,
Change shapes with Proteus for advantages,
And set the murderous Machiavel to school.                            70
Can I do this, and cannot get a crown?
Tut! Were it farther off, I'll pluck it down.

**1 Ay . . . honorably** (Richard is mocking his brother's parting words, that everyone "use her honorably"—i.e., treat Lady Grey, Edward's future queen, with all due respect and consideration.) **2 wasted** physically spent, decayed **3 hopeful branch** i.e., potential heir to the throne **4 cross** impede, thwart **golden time** i.e., when Richard will wear the golden crown **6 The . . . buried** even with the hard-living Edward and his reign eliminated **8 unlook'd-for** unforseeable **9 rooms** places **10 cold premeditation** chilling consideration **15 sunders** separates **16 lade it dry** empty it by using a ladle **18 means** obstacles **19 causes** (of my frustration) **20 Flattering me** deluding myself **21 quick** hasty **o'erweens** presumes **26 ornaments** attire **27 witch** charm, bewitch **29 accomplish** gain **31 for** so that **deal in** have anything to do with **soft laws** gentle rules of love **32 frail** easily led to evil **34 envious** malicious, spiteful **38 chaos** shapeless lump **unlick'd bear-whelp** (It was at one time believed that mother bears licked their new-borns from formless lumps into the appropriate cub-like shapes.) **39 impression** embodiment, shape **dam** mother **41 fault** error **43 check** control **o'erbear** subdue, dominate **46 account** regard, consider **48 impaled** encircled, enclosed **50 home** my goal **60 "Content"** agreed, I am content **62 frame . . . to** manipulate my appearance to suit **63 mermaid** (Legend had it that, with their singing or weeping, mermaids were able to lure sailors into drowning.) **64 basilisk** a mythic reptile that could kill with its gaze **65 Nestor** aged Greek leader known for his wisdom **66 Ulysses** Greek warrior noted for his cunning

**67 Sinon** key figure in the famous "Trojan Horse" episode that eventually brought about the fall of Troy   **68 add colors to** present myself in more variations than   **69 with** as well as   **Proteus** Greek sea god able to assume different forms   **for advantages** as it serves my purpose   **70 set...school** teach even Machiavelli himself something about being cunning and deadly (Machiavelli being notorious for his unscrupulous political maneuvers)   **72 Were it** even if it were   **off** out of reach

---

(5)                RICHARD, DUKE OF GLOUCESTER                [V.VI.61]

SCENE: The Tower of London

*{Moments ago the Duke of Gloucester found his way to Henry's prison cell and summarily murdered the deposed king. Now, as he stands over his victim with bloody sword in hand, Richard pauses to consider that which still lies before him in his pursuit of the crown.}*

1    What, will the aspiring blood of Lancaster
     Sink in the ground? I thought it would have mounted.
     See how my sword weeps for the poor king's death!
     O, may such purple tears be alway shed
5    From those that wish the downfall of our house!
     If any spark of life be yet remaining,
     Down, down to hell, and say I sent thee thither!
     [He *stabs the body again.*]
     I, that have neither pity, love, nor fear.
10   Indeed, 'tis true that Henry told me of;
     For I have often heard my mother say
     I came into the world with my legs forward.
     Had I not reason, think ye, to make haste,
     And seek their ruin that usurp'd our right?
15   The midwife wonder'd and the women cried,
     "O, Jesus bless us, he is born with teeth!"
     And so I was, which plainly signified
     That I should snarl and bite and play the dog.
     Then, since the heavens have shap'd my body so,
20   Let hell make crook'd my mind to answer it.
     I have no brother, I am like no brother;
     And this word "love," which greybeards call divine,
     Be resident in men like one another,
     And not in me. I am myself alone.
25   Clarence, beware; thou keep'st me from the light.

But I will sort a pitchy day for thee;
For I will buzz abroad such prophecies
That Edward shall be fearful of his life;
And then, to purge his fear, I'll be thy death.
King Henry and the Prince his son are gone;                    30
Clarence, thy turn is next, and then the rest—
Counting myself but bad till I be best.
I'll throw thy body in another room
And triumph, Henry, in thy day of doom.

**1 aspiring** ambitious  **Lancaster** (Henry was of the House of Lancaster.)
**2 mounted** ascended  **4 purple tears** drops of blood  **alway** always
**10 told me of** (Just prior to his being murdered, Henry was recounting
what he'd heard of Richard's unusual birth.)  **26 sort** pick  **pitchy**
pitch-black  **27 buzz** whisper  **28 fearful of** afraid for  **32 bad** inadequate

**ALTERNATES**

Duke of York    [I.iv.1–29]
Lord Clifford   [II.vi.1–30]
King Henry      [III.i.13–54]

# HENRY VIII

Less a cohesive story than a series of historically related episodes, *Henry VIII* deals with—in order of appearance—Cardinal Wolsey's successful attempt to destroy the Duke of Buckingham; the scandal of Henry's divorce from Queen Katharine and his subsequent marriage to young Anne Bullen; the fall from grace of Cardinal Wolsey; Henry's defense of the Archbishop of Canterbury against charges of heresy; and finally, the christening of Mother England's savior-in-waiting, Princess Elizabeth.

**KING HENRY VIII**
**CARDINAL WOLSEY,** counselor to King Henry VIII
**CARDINAL CAMPEIUS,** counselor to King Henry VIII
**PORTER'S MAN,** a servant at the royal palace

**QUEEN KATHARINE,** wife to King Henry VIII

| (1) | **CARDINAL WOLSEY** | [III.ii.203] |
|---|---|---|

SCENE: An antechamber to the King's apartments

*{Although he doesn't know it yet, the devious Wolsey has been brought down by his own hand. First, a series of letters he wrote to the Pope opposing Henry's divorce came to the King's attention. Then the Cardinal himself unwittingly turned over to Henry an inventory of all the Cardinal's misbegotten wealth. When some time later Henry concludes an innocuous chat with Wolsey by handing him the damning documents ("Read o'er this," Henry orders before leaving), a perplexed Wolsey wonders aloud.}*

1    What should this mean?
     What sudden anger 's this? How have I reap'd it?
     He parted frowning from me, as if ruin
     Leap'd from his eyes. So looks the chafed lion
5    Upon the daring huntsman that has gall'd him,
     Then makes him nothing. I must read this paper;
     I fear, the story of his anger. [*He reads.*] 'Tis so!

This paper has undone me. 'Tis th' account
Of all that world of wealth I have drawn together
For mine own ends—indeed, to gain the popedom                    10
And fee my friends in Rome. O negligence!
Fit for a fool to fall by. What cross devil
Made me put this main secret in the packet
I sent the King? Is there no way to cure this?
No new device to beat this from his brains?                      15
I know 'twill stir him strongly; yet I know
A way, if it take right, in spite of fortune
Will bring me off again. What's this? "To th' Pope?"
The letter, as I live, with all the business
I writ to 's Holiness. Nay then, farewell!                       20
I have touch'd the highest point of all my greatness,
And, from that full meridian of my glory,
I haste now to my setting. I shall fall
Like a bright exhalation in the evening,
And no man see me more.                                          25
This is the state of man: today he pus forth
The tender leaves of hopes; tomorrow blossoms,
And bears his blushing honors thick upon him;
The third day comes a frost, a killing frost,
And when he thinks, good easy man, full surely                   30
His greatness is a-ripening, nips his root,
And then he falls as I do. I have ventur'd
Like little wanton boys that swim on bladders,
This many summers in a sea of glory,
But far beyond my depth. My high-blown pride                     35
At length broke under me and now has left me,
Weary and old with service, to the mercy
Of a rude stream that must forever hide me.
Vain pomp and glory of this world, I hate ye!
I feel my heart new open'd. O, how wretched                      40
Is that poor man that hangs on princes' favors!
There is, betwixt that smile we would aspire to,
That sweet aspect of princes, and their ruin,
More pangs and fears than wars or women have;
And when he falls, he falls like Lucifer,                        45
Never to hope again.

**4 chafed** enraged   **5 gall'd** wounded   **6 makes him nothing** destroys
(the hunter)   **11 fee** bribe   **12 cross** perverse   **13 main** critically
important **packet** (The inventory of Wolsey's wealth was inadvertently
included among a packet of other papers he'd sent to the King.)   **15 device**
scheme **beat** drive   **17 take right** succeed   **18 bring me off** rescue me

**22 meridian** the highest point in the sky reached by the sun
**24 exhalation** meteor   **28 blushing** glowing   **30 easy** easygoing, easily
persuaded **full surely** completely assured that   **33 wanton** playful
**bladders** buoyant devices   **35 high-blown** inflated   **38 rude** turbulent,
rough   **43 their ruin** the ruin they cause

(2)                        PORTER'S MAN                        [V.III.12]

SCENE: The palace yard

*{The royal grounds are being overrun with boisterous well-wishers, all of them
straining to get a decent view of the procession for Princess Elizabeth's christening.
Caught in the middle of this madness is the poor, beleaguered Porter's Man. His
instructions were to disperse the clamoring mob. But that, he quickly points out
to his boss, is a task easier assigned than done.}*

|   |   |
|---|---|
| 1 | Pray sir, be patient. 'Tis as much impossible— |
|   | Unless we sweep 'em from the door with cannons— |
|   | To scatter 'em, as 'tis to make 'em sleep |
|   | On May-day morning, which will never be. |
| 5 | We may as well push against Paul's as stir 'em. |
|   | I am not Samson, nor Sir Guy, nor Colbrand, |
|   | To mow 'em down before me; but if I spar'd any |
|   | That had a head to hit, either young or old, |
|   | He or she, cuckold or cuckold-maker, |
| 10 | Let me ne'er hope to see a chine again— |
|   | And that I would not for a cow, God save her! |

There is a fellow somewhat near the door, he should be a brazier by his face,
for, o' my conscience, twenty of the dog-days now reign in 's nose; all that stand
about him are under the line, they need no other penance. That fire-drake did I
hit three times on the head, and three times was his nose discharg'd against me.
He stands there, like a mortar-piece, to blow us. There was a haberdasher's
wife of small wit near him, that rail'd upon me till her pink'd porringer fell off
her head, for kindling such a combustion in the state. I miss'd the meteor once,
and hit that woman, who cried out "Clubs!" when I might see from far some
forty truncheoners draw to her succor, which were the hope o' th' Strand,
where she was quarter'd. They fell on; I made good my place. At length, they
came to th' broom-staff to me. I defied 'em still, when suddenly a file of boys
behind 'em, loose shot, deliver'd such a show'r of pebbles that I was fain to
draw mine honor in, and let 'em win the work. The devil was amongst 'em, I
think, surely.

Line numbers 15, 20, 25 appear in the left margin alongside the prose passage above.

**4 May-day morning** (It was the custom to arise before dawn on May-day, early morning festivities being a favorite part of the day's celebration.)
**5 Paul's** St. Paul's cathedral   **6 Sir Guy, Colbrand** (In the popular English romance "Guy of Warwick," Sir Guy defeats a Danish giant by the name of Colbrand.)   **10 see** i.e., eat   **chine** cut of meat that includes the backbone (likely a playful reference to the many backsides he has clobbered)
**11 would…cow** would not want to see happen for anything ("cow" is perhaps suggested by "chine")   **12 brazier** one who works with brass (and thus with a forge)   **13 dog-days** hot days of midsummer (likened here to the radiant glow of the man's nose)   **14 under the line** living on the equator   **fire-drake** fiery dragon   **16 mortar-piece** small cannon   **blow us** explode upon us   **17 of small wit** stupid, foolish   **pink'd porringer** small cap ornamented with small holes   **combustion** commotion   **18 meteor** i.e., the radiating brazier   **19 "Clubs!"** (A rallying cry often heard on the streets of London, meant to draw help to the scene of a brawl.)
**20 truncheoners** men armed with clubs   **draw…succor** come to her aid   **hope** young up-and-comers   **Strand** a particularly upscale street located in the heart of London   **21 fell on** attacked   **made…place** held my ground
**22 came…me** cornered me into a tight spot   **23 loose shot** throwers not formally aligned with any particular company   **fain** forced   **24 work** fort

ALTERNATE
Cardinal Wolsey   [III.ii.407–457]

# JULIUS CAESAR

Fearing that Caesar's immense popularity will one day translate into the end of Roman democracy, Cassius and a few other prominent Roman citizens have decided the time has come for action. The budding conspiracy's final piece falls into place when Brutus's devotion to the republic outweighs even his love for Caesar, and he reluctantly agrees to sign on to the plan.

Shortly after entering the Capitol building, Caesar is surrounded by the group of conspirators, and stabbed to death. Though Brutus manages to tranquilize an irate Roman citizenry with his considerable oratory prowess, the pacifying effect proves short-lived. Mark Antony soon arrives on the scene and, with an impassioned elocutionary display of his own, moves the masses so profoundly that Brutus and the other conspirators are forced to flee.

A triumvirate of Antony, Octavius, and Lepidus is formed to lead Rome and its armies in battle against the forces of Brutus and Cassius. After a series of confrontations, the rebel forces are finally defeated on the plains of Philippi. Rather than face being captured, both Cassius and Brutus elect to die by their own swords.

**JULIUS CAESAR**
**MARK ANTONY,** advisor to Caesar, afterward a triumvir
**CICERO,** a Roman senator
**CASCA,** conspirator against Julius Caesar
**BRUTUS,** conspirator against Julius Caesar

**CALPURNIA,** wife to Julius Caesar
**PORTIA,** wife to Brutus

(1)                    **CASSIUS**                    [I.ii.92]

SCENE: A street in Rome

*{The feeling exists among some of Rome's leading citizens that Caesar has grown too powerful, too revered. Cassius is one of those citizens. Convinced that the Republic's very existence is in jeopardy, he attempts to goad Brutus into joining him in a budding insurgency.}*

Well, honor is the subject of my story.                          1
I cannot tell what you and other men
Think of this life, but as for my single self,
I had as lief not be as live to be
In awe of such a thing as I myself.                              5
I was born free as Caesar; so were you.
We both have fed as well, and we can both
Endure the winter's cold as well as he.
For once, upon a raw and gusty day,
The troubled Tiber chafing with her shores,                     10
Caesar said to me, "Dar'st thou, Cassius, now
Leap in with me into this angry flood,
And swim to yonder point?" Upon the word,
Accoutred as I was, I plunged in
And bade him follow; so indeed he did.                          15
The torrent roar'd, and we did buffet it,
With lusty sinews throwing it aside
And stemming it with hearts of controversy.
But ere we could arrive the point propos'd,
Caesar cried, "Help me, Cassius, or I sink!"                    20
Ay, as Aeneas, our great ancestor,
Did from the flames of Troy upon his shoulder
The old Anchises bear, so from the waves of Tiber
Did I the tired Caesar. And this man
Is now become a god, and Cassius is                             25
A wretched creature, and must bend his body
If Caesar carelessly but nod on him.
He had a fever when he was in Spain,
And when the fit was on him, I did mark
How he did shake. 'Tis true, this god did shake.               30
His coward lips did from their color fly,
And that same eye whose bend doth awe the world
Did lose his luster. I did hear him groan.
Ay, and that tongue of his that bade the Romans
Mark him and write his speeches in their books,                35

"Alas," it cried, "Give me some drink, Titinius,"
As a sick girl. Ye gods, it doth amaze me
A man of such a feeble temper should
So get the start of the majestic world
40      And bear the palm alone.
Why, man, he doth bestride the narrow world
Like a Colossus, and we petty men
Walk under his huge legs and peep about
To find ourselves dishonorable graves.
45      Men at some time are masters of their fates.
The fault, dear Brutus, is not in our stars,
But in ourselves, that we are underlings.
Brutus and Caesar: what should be in that "Caesar?"
Why should that name be sounded more than yours?
50      Write them together, yours is as fair a name;
Sound them, it doth become the mouth as well;
Weigh them, it is as heavy; conjure with 'em,
"Brutus" will start a spirit as soon as "Caesar."
Now, in the names of all the gods at once,
55      Upon what meat doth this our Caesar feed
That he is grown so great? Age, thou art sham'd!
Rome, thou hast lost the breed of noble bloods!
When went there by an age, since the great flood,
But it was fam'd with more than with one man?
60      When could they say, till now, that talk'd of Rome,
That her wide walks encompass'd but one man?
Now is it Rome indeed and room enough,
When there is in it but one only man.
O, you and I have heard our fathers say
65      There was a Brutus once that would have brook'd
Th' eternal devil to keep his state in Rome
As easily as a king.

**4 lief not be** soon not exist   **5 as I myself** a mere mortal like myself
**10 Tiber** river flowing through Rome   **14 Accoutred** outfitted, dressed
**16 buffet** battle   **17 lusty sinews** vigorous strength   **18 stemming**
making headway against   **hearts of controversy** hearts fueled by rivalry and
competition   **21 Aeneas** legendary founder of Rome who carried his aged
father Anchises from the burning ruins of Troy   **26 bend his body** bow
**29 fit** symptoms of a fever   **31 color** normal complexion   **32 bend** glance
**33 his** its   **38 temper** constitution   **39 the start of** an advantage on (as
with one who leads in a race)   **40 palm** i.e., victor's trophy   **41 bestride**
stand over   **42 Colossus** a gigantic statue that supposedly stood astride the
entrance to the harbor of the Greek island of Rhodes   **52 conjure** summon
a spirit by incantation   **53 start** raise   **58 great flood** the flood of Noah's

time  **59 it** (referring to Rome)  **fam'd** made famous  **65 Brutus** Lucius
Brutus, who founded the Roman republic  **brook'd** tolerated  **66 to...**
**state** in order to maintain his position of dignity  **67 As...king** as soon as
he would have tolerated the presence of a king

(2)  CASCA  [I.III.3]

SCENE: A street in Rome

*{With fantastic spectacles unfolding throughout the streets of Rome, a shaken*
*Casca betrays to Cicero his fear that these harrowing events may be portents of*
*things to come.}*

Are you not mov'd when all the sway of earth  1
Shakes like a thing unfirm? O Cicero,
I have seen tempests when the scolding winds
Have riv'd the knotty oaks, and I have seen
Th' ambitious ocean swell and rage and foam  5
To be exalted with threat'ning clouds;
But never till tonight, never till now,
Did I go through a tempest dropping fire.
Either there is a civil strife in heaven,
Or else the world, too saucy with the gods,  10
Incenses them to send destruction.
A common slave—you know him well by sight—
Held up his left hand, which did flame and burn
Like twenty torches join'd, and yet his hand,
Not sensible of fire, remain'd unscorch'd.  15
Besides—I ha' not since put up my sword—
Against the Capitol I met a lion,
Who glaz'd upon me, and went surly by
Without annoying me. And there were drawn
Upon a heap a hundred ghastly women,  20
Transformed with their fear, who swore they saw
Men, all in fire, walk up and down the streets.
And yesterday the bird of night did sit
Even at noon-day upon the market-place,
Hooting and shrieking. When these prodigies  25
Do so conjointly meet, let not men say
"These are their reasons, they are natural,"
For I believe they are portentous things
Unto the climate that they point upon.

**1 sway** realm   **4 riv'd** split   **6 exalted with** raised up to the level of
**9 strife** war   **10 saucy** insolent   **15 Not sensible of** insensitive to
**16 put up** sheathed   **17 Against** near   **18 glaz'd upon** glared at
**19 annoying** harming   **20 Upon a heap** into a huddled mass   **ghastly** pale
with terror   **23 bird of night** owl   **25 prodigies** unnatural events
**26 conjointly** at the same time   **27 These** this and that, such and such
**29 climate** region, country

(3)                          BRUTUS                          [II.1.162]

SCENE: The garden of Brutus's house

*{The conspirators have at last resolved to assassinate Caesar. When Cassius
suggests that, just to be on the safe side, it might be prudent to dispatch Antony
as well, Brutus quickly voices an objection.}*

1    Our course will seem too bloody, Caius Cassius,
     To cut the head off and then hack the limbs,
     Like wrath in death and envy afterwards;
     For Antony is but a limb of Caesar.
5    Let's be sacrificers, but not butchers, Caius.
     We all stand up against the spirit of Caesar,
     And in the spirit of men there is no blood.
     O, that we then could come by Caesar's spirit,
     And not dismember Caesar! But, alas,
10   Caesar must bleed for it. And, gentle friends,
     Let's kill him boldly, but not wrathfully;
     Let's carve him as a dish fit for the gods,
     Not hew him as a carcass fit for hounds.
     And let our hearts, as subtle masters do,
15   Stir up their servants to an act of rage,
     And after seem to chide 'em. This shall make
     Our purpose necessary, and not envious—
     Which so appearing to the common eyes,
     We shall be call'd purgers, not murderers.
20   And for Mark Antony, think not of him;
     For he can do no more than Caesar's arm
     When Caesar's head is off. If he love Caesar,
     All that he can do is to himself—
     Take thought and die for Caesar.

3 **envy** malice   10 **gentle** noble   14 **subtle** cunning   15 **their servants**
i.e., our passions   17 **envious** spiteful, malicious   24 **Take thought**
despair, grieve

(4)                     MARK ANTONY                     [III.1.254]

SCENE: Inside the Capitol

*{Alone with Caesar's corpse, Antony rethinks his conciliatory attitude toward
Brutus and the other conspirators.}*

| | |
|---|---:|
| O pardon me, thou bleeding piece of earth, | 1 |
| That I am meek and gentle with these butchers! | |
| Thou art the ruins of the noblest man | |
| That ever lived in the tide of times. | |
| That I did love thee, Caesar, O, 'tis true! | 5 |
| If then thy spirit look upon me now, | |
| Shall it not grieve thee dearer than thy death | |
| To see thy Antony making his peace, | |
| Shaking the bloody fingers of thy foes— | |
| Most noble!—in the presence of thy corse? | 10 |
| Had I as many eyes as thou hast wounds, | |
| Weeping as fast as they stream forth thy blood, | |
| It would become me better than to close | |
| In terms of friendship with thine enemies. | |
| Woe to the hand that shed this costly blood! | 15 |
| Over thy wounds now do I prophesy— | |
| Which, like dumb mouths, do ope their ruby lips | |
| To beg the voice and utterance of my tongue— | |
| A curse shall light upon the limbs of men; | |
| Domestic fury and fierce civil strife | 20 |
| Shall cumber all the parts of Italy; | |
| Blood and destruction shall be so in use | |
| And dreadful objects so familiar | |
| That mothers shall but smile when they behold | |
| Their infants quartered with the hands of war— | 25 |
| All pity chok'd with custom of fell deeds; | |
| And Caesar's spirit, ranging for revenge, | |
| With Ate by his side come hot from hell, | |
| Shall in these confines with a monarch's voice | |

30      Cry "Havoc!" and let slip the dogs of war,
        That this foul deed shall smell above the earth
        With carrion men, groaning for burial.

**4 tide of times** course of history   **10 corse** corpse   **13 close** join, agree
**15 costly** (1) precious (2) expensive (i.e., in terms of the consequences that
will come from the shedding of it)   **17 dumb** speechless   **21 cumber**
disturb, trouble   **22 in use** commonplace   **23 objects** spectacles
**25 quartered** slaughtered  **with** by   **26 with...deeds** by familiarity with
cruel deeds   **27 ranging** roving in search   **28 Ate** goddess of discord and
moral chaos   **29 confines** regions   **30 "Havoc!"** the command given an
army as a signal to commence pillaging  **slip** loose   **31 That** so that
**32 carrion** dead, rotting

(5)                        BRUTUS                        [III.ii.13]

SCENE: The Forum in Rome

*{Standing before a Roman mob that's growing uglier by the minute, Brutus
attempts to explain (and justify) the whys and wherefores of Caesar's assassination.}* [For a piece that's shorter—and arguably stronger—consider line 15
as an end point.]

1       Romans, countrymen, and lovers, hear me for my cause, and be silent, that you
        may hear. Believe me for mine honor, and have respect to mine honor, that
        you may believe. Censure me in your wisdom, and awaken your senses, that
        you may the better judge. If there be any in this assembly, any dear friend of
5       Caesar's, to him I say that Brutus' love to Caesar was no less than his. If then
        that friend demand why Brutus rose against Caesar, this is my answer: Not
        that I lov'd Caesar less, but that I lov'd Rome more. Had you rather Caesar
        were living and die all slaves, than that Caesar were dead, to live all free men?
        As Caesar lov'd me, I weep for him; as he was fortunate, I rejoice at it; as he
10      was valiant, I honor him; but as he was ambitious, I slew him. There is tears
        for his love, joy for his fortune, honor for his valor, and death for his ambition.
        Who is here so base that would be a bondman? If any, speak, for him have I
        offended. Who is here so rude that would not be a Roman? If any, speak, for
        him have I offended. Who is here so vile that will not love his country? If any,
15      speak, for him have I offended. I pause for a reply. [*No one speaks.*] Then none
        have I offended. I have done no more to Caesar than you shall do to Brutus.
        The question of his death is enroll'd in the Capitol; his glory not extenuated,
        wherein he was worthy, nor his offenses enforc'd, for which he suffer'd death.
        [*Enter Mark Antony with Caesar's body.*] Here comes his body, mourn'd by Mark
20      Antony, who, though he had no hand in his death, shall receive the benefit of

his dying, a place in the commonwealth, as which of you shall not? With this I depart, that, as I slew my best lover for the good of Rome, I have the same dagger for myself, when it shall please my countrymen to need my death.

**1 lovers** friends   **that** so that   **2 have respect to** bear in mind
**3 Censure** judge   **senses** mental faculties   **8 die all** all of you die   **9 As** inasmuch as   **fortunate** blessed by good fortune   **12 bondman** slave, serf
**13 rude** uncivilized   **16 shall do** should do   **17 question** matter, circumstances   **enroll'd** set down in writing   **extenuated** understated
**18 enforc'd** exaggerated

(6)                      **MARK ANTONY**                      [III.ii.73]

SCENE: The Forum in Rome

*{Having bucked the odds in pacifying the Roman citizenry (see preceding entry), Brutus exited the stage in triumph. Now, however, it's Antony's turn to take a shot at winning over the same crowd's sympathies.}*

Friends, Romans, countrymen; lend me your ears.                    1
I come to bury Caesar, not to praise him.
The evil that men do lives after them;
The good is oft interred with their bones.
So let it be with Caesar. The noble Brutus                    5
Hath told you Caesar was ambitious.
If it were so, it was a grievous fault,
And grievously hath Caesar answer'd it.
Here, under leave of Brutus and the rest—
For Brutus is an honorable man;                    10
So are they all, all honorable men—
Come I to speak in Caesar's funeral.
He was my friend, faithful and just to me;
But Brutus says he was ambitious,
And Brutus is an honorable man.                    15
He hath brought many captives home to Rome,
Whose ransoms did the general coffers fill.
Did this in Caesar seem ambitious?
When that the poor have cried, Caesar hath wept;
Ambition should be made of sterner stuff.                    20
Yet Brutus says he was ambitious,
And Brutus is an honorable man.
You all did see that on the Lupercal
I thrice presented him a kingly crown,

25    Which he did thrice refuse. Was this ambition?
      Yet Brutus says he was ambitious,
      And, sure, he is an honorable man.
      I speak not to disprove what Brutus spoke,
      But here I am to speak what I do know.
30    You all did love him once, not without cause.
      What cause withholds you then to mourn for him?
      O judgment, thou art fled to brutish beasts,
      And men have lost their reason.
      But yesterday the word of Caesar might
35    Have stood against the world. Now lies he there,
      And none so poor to do him reverence.
      O masters, if I were dispos'd to stir
      Your hearts and minds to mutiny and rage,
      I should do Brutus wrong, and Cassius wrong,
40    Who, you all know, are honorable men.
      I will not do them wrong; I rather choose
      To wrong the dead, to wrong myself and you,
      Than I will wrong such honorable men.
      But here's a parchment with the seal of Caesar.
45    I found it in his closet; 'tis his will.
      [*He shows the will.*]
      Let but the commons hear this testament—
      Which, pardon me, I do not mean to read—
      And they would go and kiss dead Caesar's wounds
50    And dip their napkins in his sacred blood;
      Yea, beg a hair of him for memory,
      And, dying, mention it within their wills,
      Bequeathing it as a rich legacy
      Unto their issue. But I must not read it.
55    It is not meet you know how Caesar lov'd you.
      You are not wood, you are not stones, but men;
      And, being men, hearing the will of Caesar,
      It will inflame you, it will make you mad.
      'Tis good you know not that you are his heirs;
60    For if you should, O, what would come of it!
      I have o'ershot myself to tell you of it.
      I fear I wrong the honorable men
      Whose daggers have stabb'd Caesar. I do fear it.

**1 lend** give  **ears** attention  **8 answer'd** paid for  **9 leave** permission
**12 in** at  **17 ransoms** (Important persons taken captive were often
released in exchange for the payment of a sizable ransom.)  **23 Lupercal**
Lupercalia, the Roman festival celebrated on February 15  **27 sure** certainly
**31 withholds** prevents  **34 But** just  **36 none . . . reverence** no one, not

even the lowliest person, will show him his due reverence **38 mutiny** riot,
disorder **45 closet** private chamber **47 commons** common people
**50 napkins** handkerchiefs **54 issue** children, heirs **55 meet** fitting,
appropriate **61 o'ershot myself** gone too far, said too much


(7)          **MARK ANTONY**          [III.II.169]

SCENE: The Forum in Rome

*{As everyone gathers around Caesar's lifeless body, Antony continues (see preceding entry) with his address to the Roman citizenry.}* [Though it's possible to combine this entry with the preceding one, doing so will result in a very long piece rife with staging problems.]


| | |
|---|--:|
| If you have tears, prepare to shed them now. | 1 |
| You all do know this mantle. I remember | |
| The first time ever Caesar put it on; | |
| 'Twas on a summer's evening, in his tent, | |
| That day he overcame the Nervii. | 5 |
| Look, in this place ran Cassius' dagger through; | |
| See what a rent the envious Casca made; | |
| Through this the well-beloved Brutus stabb'd, | |
| And, as he pluck'd his cursed steel away, | |
| Mark how the blood of Caesar followed it, | 10 |
| As rushing out of doors to be resolv'd | |
| If Brutus so unkindly knock'd or no; | |
| For Brutus, as you know, was Caesar's angel. | |
| Judge, O you gods, how dearly Caesar lov'd him! | |
| This was the most unkindest cut of all; | 15 |
| For when the noble Caesar saw him stab, | |
| Ingratitude, more strong than traitors's arms, | |
| Quite vanquish'd him. Then burst his mighty heart, | |
| And, in his mantle muffling up his face, | |
| Even at the base of Pompey's statue, | 20 |
| Which all the while ran blood, great Caesar fell. | |
| O, what a fall was there, my countrymen! | |
| Then I, and you, and all of us fell down, | |
| Whilst bloody treason flourish'd over us. | |
| O now you weep, and I perceive you feel | 25 |
| The dint of pity. These are gracious drops. | |
| Kind souls, what weep you when you but behold | |
| Our Caesar's vesture wounded? Look you here, | |

Here is himself, marr'd, as you see, with traitors.
30    [*He lifts Caesar's mantle, exposing the corpse.*]
Good friends, sweet friends, let me not stir you up
To a sudden flood of mutiny.
They that have done this deed are honorable.
What private griefs they have, alas, I know not,
35    That made them do it. They are wise and honorable,
And will no doubt with reasons answer you.
I come not, friends, to steal away your hearts.
I am no orator, as Brutus is,
But, as you know me all, a plain blunt man
40    That love my friend; and that they know full well
That gave me public leave to speak of him.
For I have neither wit, nor words, nor worth,
Action, nor utterance, nor the power of speech
To stir men's blood. I only speak right on.
45    I tell you that which you yourselves do know,
Show you sweet Caesar's wounds—poor, poor dumb mouths—
And bid them speak for me. But were I Brutus,
And Brutus Antony, there were an Antony
Would ruffle up your spirits, and put a tongue
50    In every wound of Caesar that should move
The stones of Rome to rise and mutiny.

**2 mantle** loose, sleeveless garment usually worn over other clothes
**5 Nervii** Belgian tribe defeated by Caesar's forces in 57 B.C.    **7 envious**
malicious    **11 As** as if    **be resolv'd** know for certain    **12 unkindly** cruelly
**13 angel** trusted companion, guiding spirit (i.e., one considered incapable of
evil)    **17 arms** daggers    **26 dint** force, impression    **gracious** kind,
righteous    **27 what** why    **28 vesture** clothing    **29 with** by    **34 griefs**
grievances    **40 they** (Brutus and the other assassins granted Antony
permission to speak to the masses.)    **42 wit** intellect    **worth** stature
authority    **43 Action** gesticulation, gestures    **utterance** delivery    **44 right
on** straightforwardly    **46 dumb** speechless    **48 were** would be
**49 Would** that would    **ruffle up** incite (to anger)

### Alternates
Marullus    [I.i.32–55]
Casca    [I.ii.235–275]
Brutus    [II.i.10–34]
Brutus    [II.i.114–140]

# KING JOHN

Full-scale war between their two countries is apparently averted when England's King John and France's King Philip agree to a royal marriage between John's niece and Philip's son. The truce soon falls by the wayside, however. Under threat of excommunication by the Catholic church, Philip reneges on his agreement with John (whom the Church has declared a heretic), and the war is back on.

England's armies emerge victorious on the battlefield near Angiers, where young Arthur—living in France with his mother, Constance, and arguably the rightful heir to the English throne—is taken captive and returned to England.

Viewing Arthur as a threat to his grip on the crown, John intimates to Hubert de Burgh that it would be better if the boy were dead. Though good Hubert proves unable to commit the foul deed, Arthur dies while attempting to escape.

When word spreads of Arthur's death, a number of English noblemen defect to France, which in turn renews its fight with England. The French invasion founders, though, when Philip the Bastard assumes England's helm and the renegade nobles return to the fold.

King John, meanwhile, has retired to Swinstead Abbey. His death there by poison clears the way for the reign of his son, Henry III.

KING JOHN
ARTHUR, nephew to King John
EARL OF SALISBURY, an English noble
HUBERT DE BURGH, confidant and aide to King John
PHILIP THE BASTARD, illegitimate son to the late Richard I, nephew to King John
PHILIP, King of France
LEWIS, Dauphin of France, son to King Philip
LYMOGES, DUKE OF AUSTRIA, a member of King Philip's court
CARDINAL PANDULPH, the Pope's legate

CONSTANCE, mother to Arthur, widow to King John's brother Geffrey
BLANCHE, a Spanish gentlewoman, niece to King John

(1)                 PHILIP THE BASTARD                [II.1.561]

SCENE: Before the city gates of Angiers

*{A just-concluded truce between France and England does not sit well with the Bastard. Alone on the outskirts of the city, he ruminates upon the ability of power and money to corrupt.}*

| | |
|---|---|
| 1 | Mad world, mad kings, mad composition! |
| | John, to stop Arthur's title in the whole, |
| | Hath willingly departed with a part, |
| | And France, whose armor conscience buckled on, |
| 5 | Whom zeal and charity brought to the field |
| | As God's own soldier, rounded in the ear |
| | With that same purpose-changer, that sly devil, |
| | That broker, that still breaks the pate of faith, |
| | That daily break-vow, he that wins of all, |
| 10 | Of kings, of beggars, old men, young men, maids, |
| | Who, having no external thing to lose |
| | But the word "maid," cheats the poor maid of that, |
| | That smooth-fac'd gentleman, tickling commodity, |
| | Commodity, the bias of the world— |
| 15 | The world, who of itself is peised well, |
| | Made to run even upon even ground, |
| | Till this advantage, this vile-drawing bias, |
| | This sway of motion, this commodity, |
| | Makes it take head from all indifferency, |
| 20 | From all direction, purpose, course, intent. |
| | And this same bias, this commodity, |
| | This bawd, this broker, this all-changing word, |
| | Clapp'd on the outward eye of fickle France, |
| | Hath drawn him from his own determin'd aid, |
| 25 | From a resolv'd and honorable war, |
| | To a most base and vile-concluded peace. |
| | And why rail I on this commodity? |
| | But for because he hath not woo'd me yet. |
| | Not that I have the power to clutch my hand |
| 30 | When his fair angels would salute my palm, |
| | But for my hand, as unattempted yet, |
| | Like a poor beggar, raileth on the rich. |
| | Well, whiles I am a beggar, I will rail |
| | And say there is no sin but to be rich; |
| 35 | And being rich, my virtue then shall be |
| | To say there is no vice but beggary. |
| | Since kings break faith upon commodity, |
| | Gain, be my lord, for I worship thee. |

1 **composition** agreement, alliance   2 **Arthur's title** Arthur's claim to the
English throne   3 **departed** parted   6 **rounded** spoke privately, whispered
7 **With** by   8 **broker** intermediary, go-between   **still** ever   **pate** head
9 **break-vow** breaker of vows   11 **Who** i.e., the maids   11–12 **having...**
**"maid"** having nothing of value to lose but her reputation as a virtuous
woman   13 **smooth-fac'd** deceptively alluring   **tickling** flattering
**commodity** self-interest, expediency   14 **bias** overriding influence
15 **peised** poised, balanced   16 **run even** run equably   17 **vile-drawing**
evil-attracting   18 **sway** control   19 **take head** rush away   **indifferency**
sense of balance, impartiality   23 **Clapp'd on** presented to   **France**
(referring to Philip, King of France)   24 **drawn** lured   28 **But for** merely
29 **clutch** close up   30 **angels** gold coins bearing the figure of an angel
**salute** come into contact with   31 **as unattempted yet** as yet untempted
37 **upon** because of

(2)                          ARTHUR                        [IV.i.39]

SCENE: A room in a castle

*{In thinly veiled terms, King John has instructed Hubert to do away with young
Arthur. Though Hubert would like nothing better than to spare the lad, it
would appear his sense of duty is about to prevail. As Arthur awaits the searing
irons that are being readied to blind him, all he can do is beg good Hubert for
mercy.}*

Must you with hot irons burn out both mine eyes?                    1
Have you the heart? When your head did but ache,
I knit my handkercher about your brows—
The best I had, a princess wrought it me—
And I did never ask it you again;                                   5
And with my hand at midnight held your head;
And like the watchful minutes to the hour
Still and anon cheer'd up the heavy time,
Saying "What lack you?" and "Where lies your grief?"
Or "What good love may I perform for you?"                          10
Many a poor man's son would have lien still
And ne'er have spoke a loving word to you,
But you at your sick service had a prince.
Nay, you may think my love was crafty love
And call it cunning. Do, an if you will.                            15
If heaven be pleas'd that you must use me ill,
Why then you must. Will you put out mine eyes?
These eyes that never did nor never shall

So much as frown on you?
20    Ah, none but in this iron age would do it!
The iron of itself, though heat red-hot,
Approaching near these eyes, would drink my tears
And quench his fiery indignation
Even in the matter of mine innocence—
25    Nay, after that, consume away in rust,
But for containing fire to harm mine eye.
Are you more stubborn-hard than hammer'd iron?
An if an angel should have come to me
And told me Hubert should put out mine eyes,
30    I would not have believ'd him—no tongue but Hubert's.
O save me, Hubert, save me!

**3 knit** tied    **4 wrought it** embroidered it for    **5 you** from you
**7 watchful . . . hour** minutes that mark the passing of the hour    **8 Still and
anon** continually    **9 grief** pain    **10 love** loving service    **11 lien** lain
**13 at . . . service** to wait on you when you were sick    **15 an if** if    **20 iron
age** hard, merciless time (with a play on the image of "hot irons")    **21 heat**
heated    **23 his** its    **24 the . . . innocence** that which is evidence of my
innocence (i.e., his tears)    **26 But** merely

(3)                          KING JOHN                          [IV.ii.216]

SCENE: King John's palace

*{When Hubert arrived at the palace to report that Arthur was dead, a number
of King John's noblemen immediately smelled a rat. Suspecting their monarch
of complicity in the matter (and justifiably so; see preceding entry), the nobles
stormed off threatening retribution. Shaken by this unseemly turn of events,
John lambastes both Hubert and himself for their reckless actions.}*

1    O, when the last account 'twixt heaven and earth
Is to be made, then shall this hand and seal
Witness against us to damnation!
How oft the sight of means to do ill deeds
5    Make deeds ill done! Hadst not thou been by,
A fellow by the hand of nature mark'd
Quoted, and sign'd to do a deed of shame,
This murder had not come into my mind.
But, taking note of thy abhorr'd aspect,
10    Finding thee fit for bloody villainy,
Apt, liable to be employ'd in danger,

I faintly broke with thee of Arthur's death;
And thou, to be endeared to a king,
Made it no conscience to destroy a prince.
Hadst thou but shook thy head or made a pause                    15
When I spake darkly what I purposed,
Or turn'd an eye of doubt upon my face,
As bid me tell my tale in express words,
Deep shame had struck me dumb, made me break off,
And those thy fears might have wrought fears in me.               20
But thou didst understand me by my signs
And didst in signs again parley with sin;
Yea, without stop didst let thy heart consent,
And consequently thy rude hand to act
The deed which both our tongues held vile to name.               25
Out of my sight, and never see me more!
My nobles leave me, and my state is brav'd,
Even at my gates, with ranks of foreign pow'rs.
Nay, in the body of this fleshly land,
This kingdom, this confine of blood and breath,                  30
Hostility and civil tumult reigns
Between my conscience and my cousin's death.

**2 hand and seal** i.e., Arthur's death warrant, bearing John's signature and
the royal seal, which Hubert has just now produced  **7 Quoted, and sign'd**
designated and assigned  **9 abhorr'd aspect** hateful countenance
**11 liable** fit  **12 faintly broke** indirectly broached the subject
**14 conscience** matter of conscience  **16 darkly** obscurely of, indirectly of
**purposed** proposed  **18 As** as if to  **express** exact, explicit  **19 had** would
have  **21 signs** subtle indications  **24 rude** violent, brutal  **act** perform
**27 state is brav'd** kingdom is challenged, authority is defied  **29 body...**
**land** (referring here to his own body)  **30 confine** prison

(4)                  PHILIP THE BASTARD                  [V.i.44]

SCENE: King John's palace

*{Even as the French invade his country's shore, a despondent King John finds he
is incapable of dealing with the crisis at hand. So it is that the Bastard steps
forward, gamely attempting to rejuvenate his King's flagging spirits with a spot
of last-minute encouragement.}*

Wherefore do you droop? Why look you sad?                         1
Be great in act, as you have been in thought.

Let not the world see fear and sad distrust
Govern the motion of a kingly eye.
5      Be stirring as the time; be fire with fire;
Threaten the threat'ner, and outface the brow
Of bragging horror. So shall inferior eyes,
That borrow their behaviors from the great,
Grow great by your example, and put on
10     The dauntless spirit of resolution.
Away, and glister like the god of war
When he intendeth to become the field!
Show boldness and aspiring confidence.
What, shall they seek the lion in his den,
15     And fright him there, and make him tremble there?
O, let it not be said! Forage, and run
To meet displeasure farther from the doors,
And grapple with him ere he come so nigh.
Shall we, upon the footing of our land,
20     Send fair-play orders and make compromise,
Insinuation, parley, and base truce
To arms invasive? Shall a beardless boy,
A cock'red silken wanton, brave our fields,
And flesh his spirit in a warlike soil,
25     Mocking the air with colors idly spread,
And find no check? Let us, my liege, to arms!

**6 outface** defy, stare down   **7 bragging** blustering, menacing   **11 glister**
glisten, radiate   **12 become** grace   **16 Forage** seek out (the enemy)
**19 upon...land** standing on our own land   **20 fair-play orders**
conditions of honorable conduct   **21 Insinuation** self-ingratiation   **base**
contemptible, cowardly   **22 arms invasive** invading forces   **23 cock'red**
pampered   **silken wanton** effeminate child   **brave** make an arrogant show
of force in   **24 flesh** initiate in bloodshed   **25 idly** carelessly

# KING LEAR

Lear's plan to divide his kingdom among his three daughters hits a snag when his youngest child, Cordelia, refuses to join her two older sisters in showering their father with disingenuous praise. Goneril and Regan thus split the spoils in half, while Cordelia rebounds from her disinheritance by marrying the King of France.

The madness of Lear's method soon becomes evident, however, when both Goneril and Regan humiliate the King by refusing to accommodate his retinue of boisterous knights. Enraged by his daughters' ingratitude, Lear storms off into the tempestuous night.

Elsewhere, the Earl of Gloucester has his own problems. Through a series of sinister machinations, the Earl has been convinced by his bastard son Edmund that his other (and legitimate) son, Edgar, covets his wealth and wishes him dead. Edgar, fearing for his life, takes on the guise of a madman and escapes into the countryside. It is there that, some time later, Edgar encounters his father, who has been blinded by Regan's husband Cornwall for providing assistance to Lear. Both the blind Gloucester, led by his son Edgar, and the mad Lear, aided by his true friend Kent, end up near Dover, where Cordelia has landed with French troops in order to rescue her father. Cordelia is reunited with her father, but her soldiers suffer defeat at the hands of Edmund and his forces, and both Cordelia and Lear are taken captive.

Before all the shouting is over, Cordelia is hanged by order of Edmund, Goneril poisons Regan before dying by her own hand, Edmund is slain by Edgar, and poor old Lear dies of grief.

**LEAR,** King of Britain
**DUKE OF ALBANY,** husband to Goneril
**EARL OF KENT,** an English noble, friend to Lear
**EARL OF GLOUCESTER,** an English noble
**EDGAR,** son to Gloucester
**EDMUND,** illegitimate son to Gloucester
**OSWALD,** steward to Goneril

**GONERIL,** daughter to Lear
**REGAN,** daughter to Lear
**CORDELIA,** daughter to Lear

(1)                          EDMUND                          [I.ii.1]

SCENE: The Earl of Gloucester's castle

*{Edmund can hardly wait to see his vile plan underway, a plot designed to discredit his brother Edgar and gain for himself sole claim on the family fortune. Having contrived a letter in which Edgar advocates the death of their father (a letter that Edmund now holds in his hand), he takes a moment alone to ponder his lot in life.}*

| | |
|---|---|
| 1 | Thou, Nature, art my goddess; to thy law |
| | My services are bound. Wherefore should I |
| | Stand in the plague of custom, and permit |
| | The curiosity of nations to deprive me, |
| 5 | For that I am some twelve or fourteen moonshines |
| | Lag of a brother? Why bastard? Wherefore base? |
| | When my dimensions are as well compact, |
| | My mind as generous, and my shape as true, |
| | As honest madam's issue? Why brand they us |
| 10 | With base? With baseness? Bastardy? Base, base? |
| | Who, in the lusty stealth of nature, take |
| | More composition and fierce quality |
| | Than doth within a dull, stale, tired bed |
| | Go to th' creating a whole tribe of fops |
| 15 | Got 'tween asleep and wake? Well then, |
| | Legitimate Edgar, I must have your land. |
| | Our father's love is to the bastard Edmund |
| | As to th' legitimate. Fine word, "legitimate!" |
| | Well, my legitimate, if this letter speed |
| 20 | And my invention thrive, Edmund the base |
| | Shall top th' legitimate. I grow, I prosper. |
| | Now, gods, stand up for bastards! |

**1 Nature** the natural order, law of the jungle   **3 Stand in** submit to, be bound by   **custom** i.e., the convention regarding bastards ("custom" being the opposite of "Nature")   **4 curiosity of nations** nitpicking distinctions of society   **5 For that** because   **moonshines** months   **6 Lag of** behind   **7 dimensions** bodily proportions   **compact** composed, knit together   **8 generous** noble   **true** well-proportioned   **9 As honest** as a virtuous   **11 lusty...nature** furtive satisfaction of sexual appetite   **12 More... quality** greater character and robust energy   **14 fops** fools   **15 Got** begotten   **19 speed** succeed   **20 invention** scheme

(2)                          **LEAR**                    [I.IV.252]

SCENE: The Duke of Albany's palace

*{Deeming Lear's retinue as nothing more than a "disorder'd rabble," Goneril has informed her father that he must drastically reduce the number of his followers. Unaccustomed as he is to taking orders, an enraged and humiliated Lear strikes back.}*

Darkness and devils!                                              1
Saddle my horses; call my train together.
Degenerate bastard! I'll not trouble thee.
Yet have I left a daughter.
Ingratitude, thou marble-hearted fiend,                          5
More hideous when thou show'st thee in a child
Than the sea-monster!
My train are men of choice and rarest parts,
That all particulars of duty know,
And in the most exact regard support                            10
The worships of their name. O most small fault,
How ugly didst thou in Cordelia show!
Which, like an engine, wrench'd my frame of nature
From the fix'd place; drew from my heart all love,
And added to the gall. O Lear, Lear, Lear!                      15
[*Striking his head.*]
Beat at this gate, that let thy folly in
And thy dear judgment out! Hear, Nature, hear!
Suspend thy purpose, if thou didst intend
To make this creature fruitful!                                 20
Into her womb convey sterility;
Dry up in her the organs of increase,
And from her derogate body never spring
A babe to honor her! If she must teem,
Create her child of spleen, that it may live                    25
And be a thwart disnatur'd torment to her!
Let it stamp wrinkles in her brow of youth,
With cadent tears fret channels in her cheeks,
Turn all her mother's pains and benefits
To laughter and contempt, that she may feel                     30
How sharper than a serpent's tooth it is
to have a thankless child! I am asham'd
That thou hast power to shake my manhood thus,

That these hot tears, which break from me perforce,
35    Should make thee worth them. Blasts and fogs upon thee!
Th' untented woundings of a father's curse
Pierce every sense about thee! Old fond eyes,
Beweep this cause again, I'll pluck ye out,
And cast you, with the waters that you loose,
40    To temper clay. Yea, is 't come to this?
Ha! Let it be so. I have another daughter,
Who, I am sure, is kind and comfortable.
When she shall hear this of thee, with her nails
She'll flay thy wolvish visage. Thou shalt find
45    That I'll resume the shape which thou dost think
I have cast off for ever.

**2 train** retinue  **8 rarest parts** most exceptional qualities  **11 The...
name** their honorable reputations  **12 Cordelia** (For an account of Lear's
estrangement from Cordelia, see I.i.82.)  **13 engine** evil mechanical device,
instrument of torture  **13–14 frame...place** natural self from its very
foundation (Lear is comparing his own fall to that of a building's.)  **18 dear**
worthy  **20 this creature** (referring to Goneril)  **22 increase**
reproduction  **23 derogate** debased  **24 teem** bear a child  **25 spleen**
malice, ill will  **26 thwart** perverse  **disnatur'd** unnatural  **28 cadent**
falling  **fret** create by wearing away  **29 mother's** motherly  **benefits**
kindnesses  **30 laughter** mockery  **34 perforce** by force  **35 Blasts**
blights  **fogs** (It was thought at the time that fog harbored diseases.)
**36 untented** uncleansed (and therefore likely to fester)  **37 fond** foolish
**38 Beweep** (if you) weep for  **39 loose** let loose  **40 temper** moisten
**42 comfortable** comforting, consoling  **44 visage** face

(3)                           EARL OF KENT                    [II.ii.13]

SCENE: Before the Earl of Gloucester's castle

*{Kent and Oswald square off for a second time, and it's clear once more that
Oswald is not among those who the Earl counts as his friends.}*

1    Fellow, I know thee—[for] a knave, a rascal, an eater of broken meats; a base,
proud, shallow, beggarly, three-suited, hundred-pound, filthy, worsted-stocking
knave; a lily-liver'd, action-taking, whoreson, glass-gazing, superservicable, finical rogue; one-trunk-inheriting slave; one that wouldst be a bawd in way of
5    good service, and art nothing but the composition of a knave, beggar, coward,

pander, and the son and heir of a mongrel bitch; one whom I will beat into clamorous whining, if thou deny'st the least syllable of thy addition. What a brazen-fac'd varlet art thou, to deny thou knowest me! Is it two days since I tripp'd up thy heels and beat thee before the King? Draw, you rogue, for thou it be night, yet the moon shines. I'll make a sop o' th' moonshine of you. You   10 whoreson cullionly barber-monger, draw! [*Draws his sword.*] Draw, you rascal! You come with letters against the King, and take Vanity the puppet's part against the royalty of her father. Draw, you rogue, or I'll so carbonado your shanks. Draw, you rascal! Come your ways. Strike, you slave! Stand, rogue, stand, you neat slave! Strike!   15

**1 broken meats** food scraps   **2 proud** insolent   **three-suited** having three suits of apparel (which was then the typical clothing allotment for a servant) **hundred-pound** (possibly a reference to the bare minimum of property required of anyone aspiring to the status of gentleman)   **worsted-stocking** wearing wool stockings (implying he is too lowly to afford silk stockings) **3 lily-liver'd** cowardly   **action-taking** prone to initiating lawsuits in order to settle disputes (rather than by fisticuffs or duel)   **whoreson** son of a whore, detestable   **glass-glazing** fond of looking in the mirror, vain **superservicable** officious   **3–4 finical** foppish   **4 one-trunk-inheriting** possessing only one trunk's worth of personal effects   **bawd** pimp **5 composition** combination   **7 thy addition** i.e., these titles I have given you   **8 varlet** rogue, knave   **deny . . . me** (Kent is in disguise, which prompted Oswald to claim, "I know thee not." Kent's direct reply to Oswald begins this piece.)   **9 beat thee** (see I.v.84–92)   **10 I'll . . . you** I'll so riddle your body with holes that it will soak up the moonlight like a sop (a piece of bread floating in a drink) soaks up liquor   **11 cullionly** rascally **barber-monger** frequent patron of barber shops (hence, foppish and conceited)   **12 letters** (see I.iii.25–26)   **Vanity the puppet's** (referring to Goneril, who Kent is equating to a stock character in the old morality puppet-shows)   **13 carbonado** hack, slash (To carbonado was to carve a piece of meat in a crosswise fashion prior to cooking it.)   **14 Come your ways** come on   **15 neat** foppish

(4)                              LEAR                              [II.IV.264]

SCENE: Before the Earl of Gloucester's castle

*{Lear and his followers have abandoned Goneril's inhospitality (see entry [2]) in hopes of finding more sympathetic treatment at the home of his other daughter, Regan. Once there, however, Lear's hopes are quickly dashed; rather than a warm*

*welcome, he receives a rude awakening. For it seems that the two sisters have banded together, and are now denying their father any entourage whatsoever. After all, Regan impertinently inquires, "What need one?"}*

| | |
|---|---|
| 1 | O, reason not the need! Our basest beggars |
| | Are in the poorest thing superfluous. |
| | Allow not nature more than nature needs, |
| | Man's life is cheap as beast's. Thou art a lady; |
| 5 | If only to go warm were gorgeous, |
| | Why, nature needs not what thou gorgeous wear'st, |
| | Which scarcely keeps thee warm. But, for true need— |
| | You heavens, give me that patience, patience I need! |
| | You see me here, you gods, a poor old man, |
| 10 | As full of grief as age, wretched in both. |
| | If it be you that stirs these daughters' hearts |
| | Against their father, fool me not so much |
| | To bear it tamely; touch me with noble anger, |
| | And let not women's weapons, water-drops, |
| 15 | Stain my man's cheeks! No, you unnatural hags, |
| | I will have such revenges on you both |
| | That all the world shall—I will do such things— |
| | What they are, yet I know not; but they shall be |
| | The terrors of the earth! You think I'll weep: |
| 20 | No, I'll not weep. |
| | I have full cause of weeping, but this heart |
| | Shall break into a hundred thousand flaws |
| | Or ere I'll weep. O fool, I shall go mad! |

**1 reason not** do not coldly calculate  **2 Are...superfluous** have some humble possession they can get along without  **3 Allow not** if you do not allow  **5 go** keep  **6 needs...wear'st** doesn't require that which you wear in order to be attractive  **10 as** as I am of  **12–13 fool...To** do not make me so foolish as to  **15 unnatural** devoid of normal human feelings, cruel  **22 flaws** fragments  **23 Or ere** before

| | | |
|---|---|---|
| (5) | **LEAR** | [III.ii.1] |

SCENE: An open field in Gloucestershire

*{Lear's descent into madness has begun. Moments ago, he rashly bolted out of doors into the night's fierce storm, and now stands alone, raging with the elements against the cruelty of his fate.}*

Blow, winds, and crack your cheeks! Rage, blow!                              1
You cataracts and hurricanoes, spout
Till you have drench'd our steeples, drown'd the cocks!
You sulph'rous and thought-executing fires,
Vaunt-couriers of oak-cleaving thunderbolts,                                 5
Singe my white head! And thou, all-shaking thunder,
Strike flat the thick rotundity o' th' world!
Crack nature's molds, all germains spill at once,
That makes ingrateful man!
Rumble thy bellyful! Spit, fire! Spout, rain!                                10
Nor rain, wind, thunder, fire are my daughters.
I tax not you, you elements, with unkindness;
I never gave you kingdom, call'd you children;
You owe me no subscription. Then let fall
Your horrible pleasure. Here I stand, your slave,                           15
A poor, infirm, weak, and despis'd old man.
But yet I call you servile ministers,
That will with two pernicious daughters join
Your high-engender'd battles 'gainst a head
So old and white as this. Let the great gods,                               20
That keep this dreadful pudder o'er our heads,
Find out their enemies now. Tremble, thou wretch,
That hast within thee undivulged crimes,
Unwhipp'd of justice! Hide thee, thou bloody hand,
Thou perjur'd, and thou simular of virtue                                   25
That art incestuous! Caitiff, to pieces shake,
That under covert and convenient seeming
Has practic'd on man's life! Close pent-up guilts,
Rive your concealing continents, and cry
These dreadful summoners grace! I am a man                                  30
More sinn'd against than sinning!

2 **cataracts** floodgates of heaven **hurricanoes** waterspouts   3 **cocks**
weathercocks   4 **sulph'rous** of lightning (It was thought that lightning was
burning sulpher.) **thought-executing** acting with the speed of thought
5 **Vaunt-couriers** harbingers   8 **molds** i.e., the molds used to produce
men **germains** seeds **spill** destroy   11 **Nor** neither   12 **tax** charge,
accuse   14 **subscription** allegiance   17 **ministers** agents   18 **daughters**
i.e., Regan and Goneril   19 **high-engender'd battles** forces created in the
heavens   21 **keep** carry on **pudder** commotion   22 **Find...enemies**
expose criminals and other transgressors (by their obvious displays of fear)
25 **simular** counterfeiter, pretender   26 **Caitiff** despicable wretch
27 **covert...seeming** a false pretense of virtue   28 **practic'd on** plotted
against **Close** secret   29 **Rive** split apart, burst **continents** enclosures,
covers   29–30 **cry...grace** beg mercy of these mighty and revered officers
of justice

(6)                          LEAR                      [IV.vi.83]

SCENE: The fields near Dover

*{Wandering about in the open countryside, a deranged Lear bursts upon the blind Gloucester and his son Edgar.}*

1    No, they cannot touch me for coining; I am the King himself. Nature's above
     art in that respect. There's your press-money. That fellow handles his bow
     like a crow-keeper; draw me a clothier's yard. Look, look, a mouse! Peace,
     peace; this piece of toasted cheese will do 't. There's my gauntlet; I'll prove
5    it on a giant. Bring up the brown bills. O, well flown, bird! I' th' clout, i' th'
     clout—hewgh! Give the word. Pass. [*Seeing Gloucester.*] Ha! Goneril with a
     white beard? They flatter'd me like a dog, and told me I had white hairs in my
     beard ere the black ones were there. To say "ay" and "no" to everything that I
     said! "Ay," and "no" too, was no good divinity. When the rain came to wet me
10   once, and the wind to make me chatter, when the thunder would not peace
     at my bidding, there I found 'em, there I smelt 'em out. Go to, they are not
     men o' their words. They told me I was everything.
     'Tis a lie, I am not ague-proof; [though] every inch a king.
     When I do stare, see how the subject quakes.
15   I pardon that man's life. What was thy cause?
     Adultery?
     Thou shalt not die. Die for adultery? No.
     The wren goes to 't, and the small gilded fly
     Does lecher in my sight.
20   Let copulation thrive; for Gloucester's bastard son
     Was kinder to his father than my daughters
     Got 'tween the lawful sheets.
     To 't, luxury, pell-mell, for I lack soldiers.
     Behold yond simp'ring dame,
25   Whose face between her forks presages snow,
     That minces virtue, and does shake the head
     To hear of pleasure's name;
     The fitchew, nor the soil'd horse, goes to 't
     With a more riotous appetite.
30   Down from the waist they are Centaurs,
     Though women all above.
     But to the girdle do the gods inherit;
     Beneath is all the fiend's.
     There's hell, there's darkness, there is the sulphurous pit, Burning, scalding,
35   stench, consumption. Fie, fie, fie! Pah, pah! Give me an ounce of civet; good
     apothecary, sweeten my imagination. There's money for thee. Dost thou squiny
     at me? No, do thy worst, blind Cupid; I'll not love. Read thou this challenge;
     mark but the penning of it. Read. O ho, are you there with me? No eyes in
     your head, nor no money in your purse? Your eyes are in a heavy case, your

purse in a light; yet  you see how this world goes. A man may see how this   40
world goes with no eyes. Look with thine ears. See how yond justice rails upon
yond simple thief. Hark in thine ear: change places, and, handy-dandy, which is
the justice, which is the thief? Thou hast seen a farmer's dog bark at a beggar?
And the creature run from the cur? There thou mightst behold the great image
of authority; a dog's obey'd in office.                                        45
Thou rascal beadle, hold thy bloody hand!
Why dost thou lash that whore? Strip thy own back;
Thou hotly lusts to use her in that kind
For which thou whipp'st her. The usurer hangs the cozener.
Through tatter'd clothes small vices do appear;                                50
Robes and furr'd gowns hide all. Plate sin with gold,
And the strong lance of justice hurtless breaks;
Arm it in rags, a pigmy's straw does pierce it.
None does offend, none, I say, none! I'll able 'em.
Take that of me, my friend, who have the power                                 55
To seal th' accuser's lips. Get thee glass eyes,
And, like a scurvy politician, seem
To see the things thou dost not. Now, now, now, now!
Pull off my boots. Harder, harder! So.
If thou wilt weep my fortunes, take my eyes.                                   60
I know thee well enough; thy name is Gloucester.
Thou must be patient. We came crying hither.
Thou know'st, the first time that we smell the air
We wawl and cry. I will preach to thee. Mark.
When we are born, we cry that we are come                                      65
To this great stage of fools.—This' a good block.
It were a delicate stratagem to shoe
A troop of horse with felt. I'll put 't in proof,
And when I have stol'n upon these son-in-laws,
Then, kill, kill, kill, kill, kill, kill!                                       70
[*A gentleman and attendants enter, and approach him.*]
No rescue? What, a prisoner? I am even
The natural fool of fortune. Use me well;
You shall have ransom. Let me have surgeons;
I am cut to th' brains.                                                         75
No seconds? All myself?
Why, this would make a man a man of salt
To use his eyes for garden water-pots,
Ay, and laying autumn's dust.
I will die bravely, like a smug bridegroom. What?                              80
I will be jovial. Come, come, I am a king,
Masters, know you that? There's life in 't.
Come; an you get it, you shall get it by running.
Sa, sa, sa, sa.
[*He exits running, with attendants in pursuit.*]                              85

**1 coining** minting coins   **1–2 Nature's . . . respect** i.e., the natural or given right of kings to mint currency supersedes that of the counterfeiter, who can do so only with his learned "art"   **2 press-money** money paid to a soldier upon being drafted into military service ("pressed")   **3 crow-keeper** one who is hired to keep crows away from cornfields   **clothier's yard** an arrow the length of a cloth yard, shot with a long bow   **4 do 't** i.e., entrap Lear's imagined mouse   **gauntlet** challenge to combat   **4–5 prove it on** try my cause against   **5 brown bills** any of a variety of pike-type weapons, in this case painted brown to help prevent corrosion   **well flown, bird** (Lear invokes a little falconing lingo to describe the flight of his imaginary arrow.) **I' th' clout** on the mark, bull's eye   **6 hewgh** (an approximation of the whooshing sound made by an arrow in flight)   **word** password
**7 They . . . dog** they fawned all over me like dogs   **7–8 white . . . beard** i.e., wisdom   **8 To . . . "no"** to mindlessly agree   **9 no good divinity** not in keeping with biblical teaching (see James 5:12)   **11 found 'em** discovered their true natures   **Go to** (a common interjection used to convey disapproval or incredulity)   **13 ague** fever   **14 the subject** my subjects, my people   **15 cause** offense   **18 goes to 't** copulates   **19 Does lecher** acts lewdly   **22 Got** who were begotten   **23 luxury** lust   **25 Whose . . . snow** whose cold and detached appearance warns of similar frigidity to be found between her legs ("forks")   **26 minces** pretends, feigns   **27 of pleasure's name** talk of sexual pleasure   **28 The fitchew** (neither) the polecat   **soil'd** high-spirited from feeding on fresh-cut grass   **29 riotous** unrestrained
**32 But to** only down to   **girdle** waist   **inherit** possess, control   **33 fiend's** devil's   **35 Fie** (an expression of disgust)   **civet** perfume derived from the civet cat   **36 squiny** (1) squint (2) look sideways in the manner of a harlot
**37 blind Cupid** (Traditionally portrayed as blind, Cupid often graced the sign over a brothel.)   **38 are . . . me** is that the way things are (Lear has at last comprehended that Gloucester cannot see.)   **39 heavy case** grievous state   **40 light** empty state   **42 simple** humble, poor   **handy-dandy** choose whichever one you will (the phrase comes from a popular child's game)   **45 a dog's . . . office** even one with a bestial nature is obeyed if in a position of authority   **46 beadle** parish officer (who is empowered to administer whippings)   **48 that kind** the same way   **49 cozener** cheater (Lear is pointing out the hypocrisy of one transgressor punishing another.) **52 hurtless** harmlessly   **54 able 'em** authorize them, vouch for them   **55 that** i.e., assurance of immunity   **56 glass eyes** eyeglasses   **57 politician** schemer   **64 wawl** wail   **66 This'** this is   **block** style of hat (Lear refers to the weeds entangled in his hair, which he proceeds to remove, as one would a hat, before beginning his sermon.)   **67 delicate** ingenious   **68 with felt** (thereby enabling them to pass unheard)   **in proof** to the test   **72 even** quite, simply   **73 natural** born   **fool** dupe, plaything   **74 ransom** (A sizable sum of money was often paid as ransom to secure the release of important persons taken prisoner.)   **76 seconds** supporters   **All** just, merely   **77 salt** salty tears   **79 laying** allaying, i.e., wetting down   **80 smug** smartly dressed

("Die bravely" is a punning reference to a "bridegroom's" successful completion of the sexual act.)  **82 Masters** (a polite form of address, equivalent to "sirs")  **life in 't** still hope   **83 an** if   **84 Sa** (a hunting cry)


(7)                          **LEAR**                    [IV.VII.44]

SCENE: A tent in the French camp near Dover

*{Cordelia has at last rescued her father. Both she and the Earl of Kent are close by Lear's side as, emerging from a deep sleep, he utters a pitiful reply to Cordelia's query, "How fares your Majesty?"}*


You do me wrong to take me out o' th' grave.                    1
Thou art a soul in bliss; but I am bound
Upon a wheel of fire, that mine own tears
Do scald like molten lead.
You are a spirit, I know. When did you die?                    5
Where have I been? Where am I? Fair daylight?
I am mightily abus'd. I should e'en die with pity
To see another thus. I know not what to say.
I will not swear these are my hands. Let's see;
I feel this pin prick. Would I were assur'd                    10
Of my condition!
I am a very foolish fond old man,
Fourscore and upward, not an hour more nor less;
And, to deal plainly,
I fear I am not in my perfect mind.                    15
Methinks I should know you, and know this man,
Yet I am doubtful; for I am mainly ignorant
What place this is, and all the skill I have
Remembers not these garments, nor I know not
Where I did lodge last night. Do not laugh at me;                    20
For, as I am a man, I think this lady
To be my child Cordelia.
Be your tears wet? Yes, faith. I pray weep not.
If you have poison for me, I will drink it.
I know you do not love me, for your sisters                    25
Have, as I do remember, done me wrong.
You have some cause, they have not.
Do not abuse me. You must bear with me.
Pray you now, forget and forgive.
I am old and foolish.                    30

**1 You** (Lear is responding to Cordelia's inquiries, "How does my royal lord? How fares your majesty?")   **3 wheel of fire** (a form of torment found in hell)   **7 abus'd** confused   **12 fond** silly   **14 deal plainly** be honest   **17 mainly** entirely   **18 skill** power of reason   **23 faith** truly   **28 abuse** take advantage of, deceive

**ALTERNATES**

Edgar        [II.iii.1–21]
Edgar        [III.iv.46–147]
Gentleman    [IV.iii.11–32]

# LOVE'S LABOR'S LOST

No sooner do the King of Navarre and three of his lords forswear the company of women for the next three years than up pops the Princess of France for a diplomatic visit. Naturally, the King proceeds to fall head over heels for the Princess, even as each of his lords is in turn smitten by one of the Princess's ladies. Before long the "No Women" rule is a rule in name only.

Elsewhere, the Spaniard Don Armado has managed to quell his own passion for a country lass named Jaquenetta long enough to prepare an evening's entertainment for the King and his guests. The merry presentation is going just swell until news from France arrives that the Princess's father has died.

Though the Princess is compelled to return home at once, she and her ladies indicate that wedding bells within a year's time is a distinct possibility—if their would-be husbands behave themselves in the interim.

**FERDINAND,** King of Navarre
**BEROWNE,** lord attending on the King
**LONGAVILLE,** lord attending on the King
**DUMAINE,** lord attending on the King
**DON ARMADO,** an eccentric Spaniard

**PRINCESS OF FRANCE**
**ROSALINE,** lady attending on the Princess of France
**JAQUENETTA,** a country girl

(1)                          ARMADO                          [I.II.167]

SCENE: The King of Navarre's park

*{Despite a recent ban on consorting with women, Armado is forced to admit that he has nonetheless fallen into love. Complicating matters even further is the fact that the object of his lust—a common country girl named Jaquenetta—is an inappropriate match for a gentleman like himself.}*

1   I do affect the very ground, which is base, where her shoe, which is baser, guided by her foot, which is basest, doth tread. I shall be forsworn, which is a great argument of falsehood, if I love. And how can that be true love which is falsely attempted? Love is a familiar, Love is a devil; there is no evil angel but
5   Love. Yet was Samson so tempted, and he had an excellent strength; yet was Solomon so seduced, and he had a very good wit. Cupid's butt-shaft is too hard for Hercules' club, and therefore too much odds for a Spaniard's rapier. The first and second cause will not serve my turn; the passado he respects not, the duello he regards not. His disgrace is to be called boy, but his glory
10   is to subdue men. Adieu, valor! Rust, rapier! Be still, drum! For your manager is in love; yea, he loveth. Assist me, some extemporal god of rhyme, for I am sure I shall turn sonnet. Devise, wit; write, pen; for I am for whole volumes in folio.

**1 affect** love   **2 be forsworn** renounce my oath (to avoid women)
**3 argument** proof   **4 falsely** improperly   **familiar** attendant evil spirit,
demon   **6 wit** intellect, judgment   **butt-shaft** unbarbed arrow (the sort
used for target practice)   **7 odds for** competition for, of an advantage
against   **8 first . . . turn** (Armado is alluding to circumstances that, according
to the accepted code of honor, necessitated a duel. His complaint is that
Cupid refuses to abide by these rules.)   **passado** thrusting a sword forward
in fencing   **9 duello** dueling code   **disgrace** misfortune, humiliation
**10 drum** (The drum was commonly associated with combat.)   **manager**
expert wielder (of the rapier)   **12 turn sonnet** i.e., become a poet   **am for**
am ready (to compose)   **13 folio** a book of the largest size

(2)                          BEROWNE                          [III.I.174]

SCENE: The King of Navarre's park

*{While lamenting the fact that his status as a confirmed bachelor appears to be in jeopardy, Berowne concedes that he can no longer resist the considerable charms of Rosaline.}*

I, forsooth, in love! I, that have been love's whip,                              1
A very beadle to a humorous sigh,
A critic, nay, a night-watch constable,
A domineering pedant o'er the boy,
Than whom no mortal so magnificent!                                               5
This wimpled, whining, purblind, wayward boy,
This senior-junior, giant-dwarf, Dan Cupid,
Regent of love-rhymes, lord of folded arms,
Th' anointed sovereign of sighs and groans,
Liege of all loiterers and malcontents,                                          10
Dread prince of plackets, king of codpieces,
Sole imperator and great general
Of trotting paritors—O my little heart!—
And I to be a corporal of his field,
And wear his colors like a tumbler's hoop!                                       15
What? I love, I sue, I seek a wife?
A woman, that is like a German clock,
Still a-repairing, ever out of frame,
And never going aright, being a watch,
But being watch'd that it may still go right?                                    20
Nay, to be perjur'd, which is worst of all;
And, among three, to love the worst of all,
A whitely wanton with a velvet brow,
With two pitch-balls stuck in her face for eyes;
Ay, and, by heaven, one that will do the deed                                    25
Though Argus were her eunuch and her guard.
And I to sigh for her, to watch for her,
To pray for her! Go to! It is a plague
That Cupid will impose for my neglect
Of his almighty dreadful little might.                                           30
Well, I will love, write, sigh, pray, sue, groan;
Some men must love my lady, and some Joan.

**1 forsooth** indeed   **2 beadle** local officer responsible for punishing minor offenders with a whipping   **4 pedant** schoolmaster   **boy** Cupid   **5 Than . . . magnificent** as was no other mortal with such skill and assurance   **6 wimpled** blindfolded   **purblind** completely blind   **7 Dan** Sir   **8 folded arms** (considered a mannerism typical of the lovesick)   **10 loiterers** slackers, mopers   **11 plackets** slits in petticoats (with a bawdy reference to that which lies beneath them)   **codpieces** flaps or pouches covering the crotches of men's trousers (with a bawdy reference to that which lies beneath them)   **12 imperator** absolute ruler   **13 paritor** an officer of the court who frequently realized a profit by ferreting out sexual offenders   **14 corporal . . . field** field officer   **15 tumbler's hoop** (which typically were brightly decorated, and thus very obvious)   **16 sue** court, woo

**18 Still a-repairing** always in need of repair  **frame** order  **20 But being watch'd** unless it's carefully monitored (as one would a wayward wife)  **still go** forever behave  **21 perjur'd** (By doting on Rosaline, Berowne is forswearing his oath to avoid women; see I.i.153–157)  **23 whitely** pale, sallow  **wanton** willful or contrary woman  **24 pitch-balls** i.e., deep black orbs  **25 do the deed** engage in sexual intercourse (including adulterously)  **26 Argus** a monster of mythology who had a hundred eyes  **27 watch for** loose sleep over  **28 Go to!** (a common interjection of the day, used to express amazement and/or disapproval)  **29 neglect** disregard  **32 my lady** milady, a lady of breeding and quality  **Joan** stock name for a common peasant woman

(3)                          BEROWNE                          [IV.III.I]

SCENE: The King of Navarre's park

*{Wandering alone in the park, Berowne continues (see preceding entry) to fret over his acute case of love-sickness.}*

1    The King he is hunting the deer; I am coursing myself. They have pitch'd a toil; I am toiling in a pitch—pitch that defiles. Defile! A foul word. Well, set thee down, sorrow! For so they say the fool said, and so say I, and I the fool. Well prov'd, wit! By the Lord, this love is as mad as Ajax. It kills sheep; it kills me, I
5    a sheep. Well prov'd again o' my side! I will not love; if I do, hang me. I' faith, I will not. O, but her eye! By this light, but for her eye, I would not love her; yes, for her two eyes. Well, I do nothing in the world but lie, and lie in my throat. By heaven, I do love, and it hath taught me to rhyme and to be mallicholy; and here is part of my rhyme, and here my mallicholy. Well, she hath one o' my
10   sonnets already. The clown bore it, the fool sent it, and the lady hath it: sweet clown, sweeter fool, sweetest lady! By the world, I would not care a pin, if the other three were in. Here comes one with a paper. God give him grace to groan!

**1 coursing** pursuing  **pitch'd a toil** set a trap  **2 pitch** (alludes to his earlier description of Rosaline's eyes as being like two "pitch-balls"; see preceding entry, line 24)  **2–3 set thee down** (in modern vernacular, akin to "pull up a chair")  **4 prov'd** argued, put  **wit** intellect  **Ajax** (According to legend, Ajax was so incensed over being deprived of the slain Achilles's armor that he attacked a flock of sheep, imagining them to be the enemy.)  **5 o' my side** on my part  **I' faith** truly  **7 in my throat** profoundly  **8 rhyme** write poems  **mallicholy** melancholy  **9 here** (referring to the sonnet he's written, which he holds in his hand)  **10 clown** country-dweller (referring in this case to Costard, who Berowne recruited to deliver his initial sonnet to Rosaline) **11 fool** (referring to himself) **pin** bit **12 three** (referring to the King, Longaville, and Dumaine, who along with Berowne vowed to forsake the company of women) **in** in the same sort of predicament, i.e., in love

(4)                  **BEROWNE**                [IV.III.149]

SCENE: The King of Navarre's park

*{As Berowne was reading over his latest sonnet created for Rosaline, who should happen by but the King, Longaville, and Dumaine. One by one and in quick succession, each reveals their respective infatuations, oblivious to the fact that they are being observed by the others. Finally Berowne has seen enough. Playing the innocent, he leaps from the bushes to chide his lovesick companions.}*

| | |
|---|---:|
| Now step I forth to whip hypocrisy. *[Showing himself.]* | 1 |
| Ah, good my liege, I pray thee, pardon me. | |
| Good heart, what grace hast thou thus to reprove | |
| These worms for loving, that art most in love? | |
| Your eyes do make no coaches; in your tears | 5 |
| There is no certain princess that appears; | |
| You'll not be perjur'd, 'tis a hateful thing— | |
| Tush, none but the minstrels like of sonneting! | |
| But are you not asham'd? Nay, are you not, | |
| All three of you, to be thus much o'ershot? | 10 |
| *[To Dumaine.]* You found his mote; | |
| *[To Longaville.]* the King your mote did see; | |
| But I a beam do find in each of three. | |
| O, what a scene of fool'ry have I seen; | |
| Of sighs, of groans, of sorrow, and of teen! | 15 |
| O me, with what strict patience have I sat, | |
| To see a king transformed to a gnat! | |
| To see great Hercules whipping a gig, | |
| And profound Solomon to tune a jig, | |
| And Nestor play at push-pin with the boys, | 20 |
| And critic Timon laugh at idle toys! | |
| Where lies the grief, O tell me, good Dumaine? | |
| And, gentle Longaville, where lies thy pain? | |
| And where my liege's? All about the breast. | |
| A caudle, ho! [Ay], bitter is my jest. | 25 |
| I, that am honest, I, that hold it sin | |

To break the vow I am engaged in,
I am betrayed by keeping company
With men like you, men of inconstancy.
30    When shall you see me write a thing in rhyme?
Or groan for love? Or spend a minute's time
In pruning me? When shall you hear that I
Will praise a hand, a foot, a face, an eye,
A gait, a state, a brow, a breast, a waist,
35    A leg, a limb?

**4 These worms** (The King, unaware that his own versifying had been overheard by Berowne, has just finished berating Longaville and Dumaine for their own passionate displays.)   **5–6 Your...appears** (alludes to imagery in the King's sonnet that Berowne overheard; see VI.iii.23)   **8 Tush** (an interjection used to convey disdain)   **like of** approve of, are fond of   **sonneting** sonnet-writing   **10 o'ershot** in error   **11 his** (referring to Dumaine's)   **mote** speck of dust (figuratively, any tiny flaw or blemish)   **13 beam** (figuratively, a large defect)   **14 fool'ry** foolishness   **15 teen** grief   **16 strict** extreme   **17 to a gnat** i.e., into an insignificant creature   **18 whipping a gig** playing with a toy top   **19 tune** play   **20 Nestor** revered in the days of the Trojan war as the oldest and wisest of the Greeks   **push-pin** a child's game   **21 Timon** Timon of Athens, notorious for his misanthropy   **laugh...toys** take delight in mindless trifles   **24 breast** heart   **25 caudle** a warm, soothing drink given to the sick   **27 engaged in** sworn to   **32 pruning** preening   **34 state** bearing, demeanor

(5)                          **BEROWNE**                          [IV.III.287]

SCENE: The King of Navarre's park

*{As far as Berowne is concerned, the time has come to drop all this nonsense about forswearing the company of women. At the behest of his king and the other frustrated lovers, he proceeds to make a case for doing just that.}*

1    Consider what you first did swear unto:
To fast, to study, and to see no woman—
Flat treason 'gainst the kingly state of youth.
Say, can you fast? Your stomachs are too young,
5    And abstinence engenders maladies.
O, we have made a vow to study, lords,
And in that vow we have forsworn our books.
For when would you, my liege, or you, or you,

In leaden contemplation have found out
Such fiery numbers as the prompting eyes                              10
Of beauty's tutors have enrich'd you with?
Other slow arts entirely keep the brain,
And therefore, finding barren practicers,
Scarce show a harvest of their heavy toil.
But love, first learned in a lady's eyes,                            15
Lives not alone immured in the brain,
But, with the motion of all elements,
Courses as swift as thought in every power,
And gives to every power a double power,
Above their functions and their offices.                             20
It adds a precious seeing to the eye:
A lover's eyes will gaze an eagle blind,
A lover's ear will hear the lowest sound,
When the suspicious head of theft is stopp'd.
Love's feeling is more soft and sensible                             25
Than are the tender horns of cockled snails.
Love's tongue proves dainty Bacchus gross in taste.
For valor, is not Love a Hercules,
Still climbing trees in the Hesperides?
Subtle as Sphinx, as sweet and musical                               30
As bright Apollo's lute, strung with his hair.
And when Love speaks, the voice of all the gods
Make heaven drowsy with the harmony.
Never durst poet touch a pen to write
Until his ink were temp'red with Love's sighs.                       35
O, then his lines would ravish savage ears
And plant in tyrants mild humility.
From women's eyes this doctrine I derive:
They sparkle still the right Promethean fire;
They are the books, the arts, the academes,                          40
That show, contain, and nourish all the world;
Else none at all in aught proves excellent.
Then fools you were these women to forswear,
Or, keeping what is sworn, you will prove fools.
For wisdom's sake, a word that all men love,                         45
Or for love's sake, a word that loves all men,
Or for men's sake, the authors of these women,
Or women's sake, by whom we men are men,
Let us once lose our oaths to find ourselves,
Or else we lose ourselves to keep our oaths.                         50
It is religion to be thus forsworn,
For charity itself fulfills the law,
And who can sever love from charity?

**7 our books** i.e., our women's faces    **8 you, or you** (referring to Longaville
and Dumaine, respectively)    **9 leaden** dull    **10 numbers** verses
**prompting** inspiring    **12 slow** serious, dull    **arts** areas of study    **keep**
reside within    **16 immured** imprisoned    **17 elements** earth, air, fire, and
water    **18 power** faculty, capability    **20 Above . . . offices** over and above
their usual functions    **22 gaze . . . blind** (Berowne's point being that such a
feat would be most impressive, in that eagles were believed to be able to
stare directly at the sun)    **23 lowest** softest    **24 When . . . stopp'd** i.e.,
when even the thief, so cautiously alert, can hear nothing    **25 sensible**
sensitive    **26 horns** antennae    **cockled** shell-bearing    **27 dainty** refined
**Bacchus** Greek god of wine and revelry    **29 Still** continually    **Hesperides**
(One of Hercules's twelve labors was to gain the golden apples of the trees
of Hesperides.)    **30 Subtle** treacherous, cunning    **Sphinx** a monster of
Greek mythology    **31 Apollo** the sun god    **32 voice** singing    **34 durst**
dared    **37 mild** gentle    **39 sparkle . . . right** continuously emit sparks of
the true    **Promethean fire** sacred fire (from the legend of Prometheus,
who stole fire from heaven and gave it to mankind)    **40 academes**
academies    **42 aught** anything    **44 prove** turn out to be    **46 loves all
men** inspires all men with love    **47 authors** fathers    **49 once** for once,
this once    **lose** forgo, relinquish    **51 religion** faithful, religious    **thus
forsworn** to go back on our oaths    **52 For . . . law** (alludes to the biblical
passage, "for he that loveth another hath fulfilled the law")

(6)                          ARMADO                          [V.i.87]

SCENE: The King of Navarre's park

*{In his own inimitable way, Armado solicits from Holofernes some assistance in
staging an evening's entertainment for the Princess and her ladies.}*

1    Sir, it is the King's most sweet pleasure and affection to congratulate the
     Princess at her pavilion in the posteriors of this day, which the rude multitude
     call the afternoon. The King is a noble gentleman, and my familiar, I do assure ye,
     very good friend. For what is inward between us, let it pass. I do beseech thee,
5    remember thy courtesy; I beseech thee, apparel thy head. And among other
     importunate and most serious designs, and of great import indeed, too—but
     let that pass; for I must tell thee, it will please his Grace, by the world, sometime
     to lean upon my poor shoulder, and with his royal finger, thus, dally with my
     excrement, with my mustachio; but, sweet heart, let that pass. By the world,
10   I recount no fable! Some certain special honors it pleaseth his greatness to
     impart to Armado, a soldier, a man of travel, that hath seen the world; but let
     that pass. The very all of all is—but, sweet heart, I do implore secrecy—that the

King would have me present the Princess, sweet chuck, with some delightful ostentation, or show, or pageant, or antic, or firework. Now, understanding that the curate and your sweet self are good at such eruptions and sudden   15 breaking out of mirth, as it were, I have acquainted you withal, to the end to crave your assistance.

**1 affection** inclination, disposition   **2 pavilion** (referring to the spacious tents that have been set up to accommodate the Princess and her entourage) **posteriors** (Armado's whimsical way of saying "the latter part")   **rude** common   **3 familiar** close friend   **4 inward** private   **let it pass** never mind about that   **5 remember ... head** (Holofernes removed his hat as a courtesy upon first meeting Armado; Armado is now reminding him of that fact and encouraging him to once again cover, or "apparel," his head.) **6 importunate** urgent   **7 will ... Grace** pleases the King   **8 poor** insignificant   **9 excrement** outgrowth (of hair)   **12 all of all** sum total, point of all (of this)   **13 chuck** chick (a term of endearment) **14 ostentation** spectacular display   **antic** pageant or similar show featuring outlandish costumes   **15 curate** (referring to Holofernes's companion, Sir Nathaniel)   **16 withal** with this   **17 crave** request

**ALTERNATE**
Boyet   [V.ii.81–118]

# MACBETH

On his way home from a successful military campaign, Macbeth encounters three witches who hail him as Thane of Cawdor and "king hereafter." When word soon arrives that King Duncan has in fact named Macbeth as the new Thane of Cawdor, Macbeth starts to thinking. Before long, his lust for the crown—not to mention Lady Macbeth's prodding—have turned those thoughts to murder. After weathering a few fleeting pangs of conscience, Macbeth slays Duncan in his sleep, and is crowned king.

Though Duncan's sons, Malcolm and Donalbain, are initially suspected of the King's murder, it isn't long before Macbeth emerges as the true culprit. When Macbeth's former comrade, Macduff, convinces Malcolm to fight for his rightful place on the Scottish throne, Macbeth's fate seems all but sealed.

Left twisting in the wind by his friends and Lady Macbeth (who descends into madness and kills herself), Macbeth is eventually set upon by Macduff in the fields of Dunsinane, and is slain. Soon thereafter, Malcolm is hailed as the new King of Scotland.

**DUNCAN,** King of Scotland
**MALCOLM,** son to Duncan
**DONALBAIN,** son to Duncan
**MACBETH,** a general of the King's army
**BANQUO,** a general of the King's army
**MACDUFF,** a Scottish noble and officer of the King's army

**LADY MACBETH,** wife to Macbeth
**HECATE,** mistress of witches
**WITCHES,** underlings to Hecate

(1)                         **MACBETH**                    [I.VII.1]

SCENE: An inner courtyard of Macbeth's castle

*{While all around him preparations are being made for a banquet in Duncan's honor, Macbeth pauses to reconsider his less-than-hospitable designs on the King's life.}*

| | |
|---|---:|
| If it were done when 'tis done, then 'twere well | 1 |
| It were done quickly. If th' assassination | |
| Could trammel up the consequence, and catch | |
| With his surcease success; that but this blow | |
| Might be the be-all and the end-all—here, | 5 |
| But here, upon this bank and shoal of time, | |
| We'd jump the life to come. But in these cases | |
| We still have judgment here, that we but teach | |
| Bloody instructions, which, being taught, return | |
| To plague th' inventor. This even-handed justice | 10 |
| Commends th' ingredience of our poisoned chalice | |
| To our own lips. He's here in double trust: | |
| First, as I am his kinsman and his subject, | |
| Strong both against the deed; then, as his host, | |
| Who should against his murderer shut the door, | 15 |
| Not bear the knife myself. Besides, this Duncan | |
| Hath borne his faculties so meek, hath been | |
| So clear in his great office, that his virtues | |
| Will plead like angels, trumpet-tongu'd, against | |
| The deep damnation of his taking-off; | 20 |
| And pity, like a naked new-born babe, | |
| Striding the blast, or heaven's cherubins, hors'd | |
| Upon the sightless couriers of the air, | |
| Shall blow the horrid deed in every eye, | |
| That tears shall drown the wind. I have no spur | 25 |
| To prick the sides of my intent, but only | |
| Vaulting ambition, which o'erleaps itself | |
| And falls on th' other. | |

**3 trammel . . . consequence** entangle in a net, and thereby prevent, the consequences (of Duncan's assassination)   **4 his surcease** i.e., Duncan's death **success** that which follows   **5 here** in this world   **7 jump** risk **8 still have judgment** are always punished **that** in that   **11 Commends** offers **ingredience** ingredients   **17 faculties so meek** royal powers so mercifully   **18 clear** blameless, free of taint   **20 deep** profound **taking-off** murder   **22 Striding** bestriding **blast** uproar bound to result from

Duncan's muder (?) **cherubins** cherubim **hors'd** mounted   **23 sightless couriers** invisible runners (i.e., the winds)   **28 other** other side (like a rider "vaulting" onto his horse, only to "o'erleap" the saddle and tumble down the other side)

(2)                                  MACBETH                                  [II.1.33]

SCENE: Macbeth's castle

*{The die is cast, and the fateful hour of Duncan's assassination has arrived. Even as he struggles to fend off the occasional hallucination, Macbeth braces himself for the foul deed yet to be done.}*

|     |                                                                 |
|-----|-----------------------------------------------------------------|
| 1   | Is this a dagger which I see before me,                         |
|     | The handle toward my hand? Come, let me clutch thee.            |
|     | I have thee not, and yet I see thee still.                      |
|     | Art thou not, fatal vision, sensible                            |
| 5   | To feeling as to sight? Or art thou but                         |
|     | A dagger of the mind, a false creation,                         |
|     | Proceeding from the heat-oppressed brain?                       |
|     | I see thee yet, in form as palpable                             |
|     | As this which I draw. [*Draws his dagger.*]                     |
| 10  | Thou marshall'st me the way that I was going,                   |
|     | And such an instrument I was to use.                            |
|     | Mine eyes are made the fools o' th' other senses,               |
|     | Or else worth all the rest. I see thee still,                   |
|     | And on thy blade and dudgeon gouts of blood,                    |
| 15  | Which was not so before. There's no such thing;                 |
|     | It is the bloody business which informs                         |
|     | Thus to mine eyes. Now o'er the one half-world                  |
|     | Nature seems dead, and wicked dreams abuse                      |
|     | The curtain'd sleep; witchcraft celebrates                      |
| 20  | Pale Hecate's off'rings; and wither'd murder—                   |
|     | Alarum'd by his sentinel, the wolf,                             |
|     | Whose howl's his watch—thus with his stealthy pace,             |
|     | With Tarquin's ravishing strides, towards his design            |
|     | Moves like a ghost. Thou sure and firm-set earth,               |
| 25  | Hear not my steps, which way they walk, for fear                |
|     | Thy very stones prate of my whereabout,                         |
|     | And take the present horror from the time,                      |
|     | Which now suits with it. Whiles I threat, he lives;             |
|     | Words, to the heat of deeds, too cold breath gives.             |

30

[*A bell rings.*]
I go, and it is done; the bell invites me.
Hear it not, Duncan, for it is a knell
That summons thee to heaven or to hell.

**3 have thee not** cannot take hold of you   **4 sensible** as perceptible
**7 heat-oppressed** fever-stricken   **10 marshall'st** leads   **14 dudgeon**
handle   **gouts** drops   **16 informs** takes shape   **17 half-world** hemisphere
**18 abuse** deceive   **19 curtain'd** encircled by bed curtains   **20 Pale
Hecate's** (Hecate was the goddess of witchcraft as well as the moon
goddess, hence the "pale" imagery.)   **off'rings** rituals   **21 Alarum'd** stirred
to action   **22 watch** hourly call (like that of a night watchman)
**23 Tarquin's** (It was the Roman, Tarquin, who raped ["ravished"] Lucrece.)
**design** undertaking, objective   **27 horror** ominous silence   **28 suits with**
is so suited to   **threat** threaten (murder)

(3)                         MACBETH                    [II.ii.14]

SCENE: Macbeth's castle

*{Duncan is no more. Returning from the King's bedchamber with bloody daggers
in hand, a dazed Macbeth rejoins his wife to reflect upon his horrific night's
work.}*

I have done the deed. This is a sorry sight.                          1
There's one did laugh in 's sleep, and one cried "Murder!"
That they did wake each other. I stood and heard them.
But they did say their prayers, and address'd them
Again to sleep.                                                      5
One cried "God bless us!" and "Amen!" the other,
As they had seen me with these hangman's hands.
List'ning their fear, I could not say "Amen,"
When they did say "God bless us!"
Wherefore could I not pronounce "Amen?"                             10
I had most need of blessing, and "Amen"
Stuck in my throat.
Methought I heard a voice cry "Sleep no more,
Macbeth does murder sleep!"—the innocent sleep,
Sleep that knits up the ravel'd sleave of care,                     15
The death of each day's life, sore labor's bath,
Balm of hurt minds, great nature's second course,
Chief nourisher in life's feast—

Still it cried "Sleep no more!" to all the house;
20    "Glamis hath murder'd sleep, and therefore Cawdor
Shall sleep no more; Macbeth shall sleep no more."
I am afraid to think what I have done.
[*A knock is heard within.*]
Whence is that knocking?
25    How is 't with me, when every noise appalls me?
What hands are here? Ha! They pluck out mine eyes.
Will all great Neptune's ocean wash this blood
Clean from my hand? No, this my hand will rather
The multitudinous seas incarnadine,
30    Making the green one red. [*There is another knock.*]
Wake Duncan with thy knocking! I would thou couldst!

**1 sorry sight** (referring to his blood-stained hands)   **2 one** (referring to
Duncan's attendants)   **3 That** so that   **4 address'd them** prepared
themselves   **7 As** as if   **hangman's** i.e., bloody (The hangman would
normally draw and quarter his victim, and thereby end up with
blood-covered hands.)   **15 knit's up** ties together   **ravel'd sleave** unraveled
or tangled threads   **17 second course** (Feasts customarily consisted of two
courses, the second of which was the main, or "chief nourisher.")   **19 Still**
constantly   **20 Glamis, Cawdor** (Macbeth holds two titles, Thane of
Glamis and Thane of Cawdor.)   **24 Whence** from what place or source
**25 appalls** instills with fear, dismays   **29 multitudinous** vast   **incarnadine**
turn red   **30 green** green ocean   **one red** one entire body of red

(4)                          MALCOLM                          [IV.III.39]

SCENE: The King of England's palace

*{Macduff has been trying to convince Malcolm that, as rightful heir, Malcolm
should depose Macbeth and assume the Scottish throne. But Malcolm wasn't
born yesterday. Suspecting that something sinister may be afoot—Macduff and
Macbeth were once close comrades, after all—Malcolm concocts a litany of
personal shortcomings in order to test Macduff's sincerity and resolve.}*

1    I think our country sinks beneath the yoke;
It weeps, it bleeds, and each new day a gash
Is added to her wounds. I think withal
There would be hands uplifted in my right;
5    And here from gracious England have I offer
Of goodly thousands. But, for all this,

When I shall tread upon the tyrant's head,
Or wear it on my sword, yet my poor country
Shall have more vices than it had before,
More suffer, and more sundry ways than ever,                    10
By him that shall succeed.
It is myself I mean, in whom I know
All the particulars of vice so grafted
That, when they shall be open'd, black Macbeth
Will seem as pure as snow, and the poor state                   15
Esteem him as a lamb, being compar'd
With my confineless harms. I grant him bloody,
Luxurious, avaricious, false, deceitful,
Sudden, malicious, smacking of every sin
That has a name. But there's no bottom, none,                   20
In my voluptuousness. Your wives, your daughters,
Your matrons, and your maids could not fill up
The cistern of my lust, and my desire
All continent impediments would o'erbear
That did oppose my will. With this there grows                  25
In my most ill-compos'd affection such
A stanchless avarice that, were I king,
I should cut off the nobles for their lands,
Desire his jewels, and this other's house;
And my more-having would be as a sauce                          30
To make me hunger more, that I should forge
Quarrels unjust against the good and loyal,
Destroying them for wealth. The king-becoming graces,
As justice, verity, temp'rance, stableness,
Bounty, perseverance, mercy, lowliness,                         35
Devotion, patience, courage, fortitude,
I have no relish of them, but abound
In the division of each several crime,
Acting it many ways. Nay, had I pow'r, I should
Pour the sweet milk of concord into hell,                       40
Uproar the universal peace, confound
All unity on earth. If such a one be
Fit to govern, speak. I am as I have spoken.

**I think** am aware that   **3 withal** at the same time, besides   **4 right** i.e., to
the Scottish throne   **5 England** the King of England   **10 More...more**
shall suffer more, and in more   **11 succeed** follow   **13 particulars**
varieties  **grafted** embedded   **14 open'd** disclosed, revealed   **17 my**
**confineless harms** the limitless damage I would cause  **him** you that he's
**18 Luxurious** lustful   **19 Sudden** rash, violent   **21 In** to
**voluptuousness** sensual appetite, self-indulgence   **22 matrons** respectable

elderly women   **24 continent** restraining, restrictive   **o'erbear** overwhelm
**26 ill-compos'd affection** evil character   **27 stanchless** insatiable
**28 cut off** do away with, destroy   **29 his** i.e., one man's   **34 verity**
truthfulness   **35 Bounty** generosity, benevolence   **lowliness** humility
**37 relish** trace   **38 division** various aspects   **several** separate, particular
**crime** sin   **39 Acting it** manifesting it, acting it out   **40 concord** harmony
**41 Uproar** disrupt, throw into chaos   **universal peace** world's orderliness
**confound** bring to ruin

**ALTERNATES**
Macbeth   [III.i.47–71]
Macbeth   [III.i.74–141]

# MEASURE FOR MEASURE

Duke Vincentio has made known his intention to leave Vienna and turn control of the city over to his deputy, Angelo. But in fact, it's all a ruse. After merely pretending to leave town, the Duke adopts the guise of a friar so that he might clandestinely observe local events as they unfold.

Suddenly flush with power, Deputy Angelo immediately sets about addressing what he views as the city's declining morality. First up is the sentencing of young Claudio to death for impregnating his girlfriend, Juliet, before the two could be legally married. When Claudio's sister, Isabella, appears before Angelo to beg that he spare her brother's life, Angelo agrees to do just that—if she agrees to be his mistress. Unable to compromise her honor, Isabella spurns the deputy's vile offer and informs Claudio that she cannot save him.

Just in the nick of time, reenter Duke Vincentio. After orchestrating a bit of intrigue that involved Angelo's former betrothed, Mariana, the Duke dispenses with his friar disguise, spares Claudio's life, condemns Angelo's hypocrisy (even as he compels him to wed Mariana), and to top things off, requests for himself Isabella's hand in marriage.

**VINCENTIO,** the Duke of Vienna

**ANGELO,** deputy to the Duke Vincentio

**CLAUDIO,** a young gentleman, brother to Isabella

**ISABELLA,** sister to Claudio

**MARIANA,** betrothed to Angelo

(1)                    ANGELO                    [II.ii.162]

SCENE: Angelo's home

*{Isabella's plea for her brother's life appears to have moved Angelo—but in a way that neither she nor Angelo could have anticipated. With Isabella gone, the Deputy marvels over this curious twist of fate.}*

1    What's this, what's this? Is this her fault or mine?
     The tempter or the tempted; who sins most, ha?
     Not she, nor doth she tempt; but it is I
     That, lying by the violet in the sun,
5    Do as the carrion does, not as the flow'r,
     Corrupt with virtuous season. Can it be
     That modesty may more betray our sense
     Than woman's lightness? Having waste ground enough,
     Shall we desire to raze the sanctuary
10   And pitch our evils there? O, fie, fie, fie!
     What dost thou, or what art thou, Angelo?
     Dost thou desire her foully for those things
     That make her good? O, let her brother live!
     Thieves for their robbery have authority
15   When judges steal themselves. What, do I love her,
     That I desire to hear her speak again,
     And feast upon her eyes? What is 't I dream on?
     O cunning enemy that, to catch a saint,
     With saints dost bait thy hook! Most dangerous
20   Is that temptation that doth goad us on
     To sin in loving virtue. Never could the strumpet,
     With all her double vigor, art, and nature,
     Once stir my temper; but this virtuous maid
     Subdues me quite. Ever till now,
25   When men were fond, I smil'd and wond'red how.

**6 Corrupt** putrefy, decay  **with virtuous season** i.e., alongside of that which is virtuous and flourishing (The sense here is that, despite Isabella's goodness and purity, Angelo's misguided infatuation with her is resulting in his own moral decline.)  **7 betray our sense** reveal our sensual nature and desires  **8 lightness** wanton behavior  **10 pitch our evils** build our outhouses  **14 authority** justification  **16 That** in that  **22 double vigor** deceitful power  **art** skill (as a prostitute)  **nature** sensual nature, sexual appeal  **23 stir my temper** disrupt my mental composure  **24 Subdues** overwhelms  **25 were fond** acted foolishly (due to love), became infatuated

(2)                    **DUKE VINCENTIO**                    [III.1.5]

SCENE: A prison cell in Vienna

*{The Duke, disguised as a friar, pays a call on Claudio in hopes of reconciling
the young man to what (for the moment at least) appears to be his inevitable
fate.}*

Be absolute for death: either death or life                      1
Shall thereby be the sweeter. Reason thus with life:
If I do lose thee, I do lose a thing
That none but fools would keep. A breath thou art,
Servile to all the skyey influences                             5
That dost this habitation where thou keep'st
Hourly afflict. Merely, thou art death's fool,
For him thou labor'st by thy flight to shun,
And yet runn'st toward him still. Thou art not noble,
For all th' accommodations that thou bear'st                   10
Are nurs'd by baseness. Thou 'rt by no means valiant,
For thou dost fear the soft and tender fork
Of a poor worm. Thy best of rest is sleep,
And that thou oft provok'st, yet grossly fear'st
Thy death, which is no more. Thou art not thyself,            15
For thou exists on many a thousand grains
That issue out of dust. Happy thou art not,
For what thou hast not, still thou striv'st to get,
And what thou hast, forget'st. Thou art not certain,
For thy complexion shifts to strange effects,                 20
After the moon. If thou art rich, thou 'rt poor;
For, like an ass whose back with ingots bows,
Thou bear'st thy heavy riches but a journey,
And death unloads thee. Friend hast thou none,
For thine own bowels, which do call thee sire—                25
The mere effusion of thy proper loins—
Do curse the gout, serpigo, and the rheum
For ending thee no sooner. Thou hast nor youth nor age,
But as it were an after-dinner's sleep,
Dreaming on both, for all thy blessed youth                   30
Becomes as aged, and doth beg the alms
Of palsied eld; and when thou art old and rich,
Thou hast neither heat, affection, limb, nor beauty,
To make thy riches pleasant. What's yet in this
That bears the name of life? Yet in this life                 35
Lie hid moe thousand deaths; yet death we fear,
That makes these odds all even.

**1 absolute for** resolute toward   **5 skyey** atmospheric, celestial
**6 habitation** (1) the body (2) the Earth   **keep'st** dwell   **7 Merely**
completely, utterly   **fool** amusement, plaything   **8 flight to shun** running to
flee from him   **10 accommodations** worldly comforts   **11 nurs'd**
fostered   **12 fork** forked tongue (which at the time was thought to be the
cause of the snake's stinging bite)   **13 worm** snake   **14 provok'st** induce
**grossly** ignorantly   **15 no more** (than sleep)   **thyself** self-contained, an
independent entity   **19 certain** steadfast   **20 complexion** disposition,
temperament   **shifts ... effects** takes on different appearances   **21 After** in
accordance with, the same as   **25 bowels** i.e., offspring   **26 mere** very
**proper** own   **27 gout, serpigo, rheum** various afflictions commonly
associated with advanced age   **28 nor youth** neither youth
**29 after-dinner's sleep** afternoon's nap   **31 as aged** like old age
(i.e., helpless and dependent on the care of others)   **32 eld** old people
**33 heat** vitality   **affection** passion   **limb** i.e., effective use of your limbs
**35 Yet** still   **36 moe** more   **37 makes ... even** relieves us of all these ills


ALTERNATE
Duke Vincentio   [III.ii.261–282]

# THE MERCHANT OF VENICE

Bassanio wants in the worst way to travel to Belmont and court the heiress Portia, but he needs money to do so. Upon looking to his merchant friend Antonio for financial assistance, Bassanio learns that he too is cash-poor at the moment. Even so, Antonio manages to secure a loan from the money-lender Shylock—but only by agreeing to a most severe condition: if Antonio defaults, he must forfeit to Shylock a pound of his own flesh.

In Belmont, Portia is bound by her late father's will to marry the first suitor who can choose correctly from among three chests made of gold, silver, and lead, respectively. When Bassanio arrives on the scene, he quickly manages to succeed where all others before him have failed—the lead chest it is. Portia is elated by Bassanio's winning guess, and the two lovers are soon married.

Joy is short-lived, however, as word arrives that Antonio's ships have wrecked at sea; unable to repay the loan, the merchant is now faced with meeting Shylock's demand for a pound of his flesh. Bassanio rushes off to his friend's aid, followed shortly thereafter by Portia, who, disguised as a male lawyer, proves to be instrumental in saving Antonio's hide. In court it is determined that the conditions of Shylock's loan are not only pernicious, but virtually impossible to enforce. Antonio is thus spared (and so, it turns out, were his ships), while Shylock is sent off to a life of Christianity.

**PRINCE OF MOROCCO,** suitor to Portia
**ANTONIO,** a merchant of Venice
**BASSANIO,** friend to Antonio, suitor to Portia
**SHYLOCK,** a Jewish moneylender
**LAUNCELOT GOBBO,** servant to Shylock
**BALTHASAR,** servant to Portia

**PORTIA,** a rich heiress
**NERISSA,** a gentlewoman attending on Portia

(1)                           **SHYLOCK**                    [I.III.106]

SCENE: A street in Venice

*{Though they've long been adversaries, Antonio is compelled by present circum-
stances to approach Shylock for a short-term loan. The irony of such a request
does not pass unappreciated.}*

| | |
|---|---|
| 1 | Signior Antonio, many a time and oft |
| | In the Rialto you have rated me |
| | About my moneys and my usances. |
| | Still have I borne it with a patient shrug, |
| 5 | For suff'rance is the badge of all our tribe. |
| | You call me misbeliever, cut-throat dog, |
| | And spit upon my Jewish gaberdine, |
| | And all for use of that which is mine own. |
| | Well then, it now appears you need my help: |
| 10 | Go to, then. You come to me, and you say |
| | "Shylock, we would have moneys"—you say so— |
| | You, that did void your rheum upon my beard |
| | And foot me as you spurn a stranger cur |
| | Over your threshold! Moneys is your suit. |
| 15 | What should I say to you? Should I not say |
| | "Hath a dog money? Is it possible |
| | A cur can lend three thousand ducats?" Or |
| | Shall I bend low and in a bondman's key, |
| | With bated breath and whisp'ring humbleness, |
| 20 | Say this: |
| | "Fair sir, you spit on me on Wednesday last, |
| | You spurn'd me such a day, another time |
| | You call'd me dog, and for these courtesies |
| | I'll lend you thus much moneys?" |

**2 Rialto** an island and district in Venice  **rated** berated, reviled  **3 usances**
usury  **4 Still** always  **5 suff'rance** forbearance  **badge** mark  **tribe** i.e.,
the Jews  **7 gaberdine** long and loose-fitting upper garment  **10 Go to**
(an exclamation similar to "come now" that was commonly used to express
disapproval or impatience)  **12 void your rheum** cast your spittle
**13 foot** kick  **spurn** kick  **17 ducats** gold coins  **18 a bondman's key** the
manner of a slave

(2)                    LAUNCELOT GOBBO                    [II.ii.1]

SCENE: A street in Venice

*{To run or not to run . . . that is the question which Launcelot now faces. Whether 'tis nobler to flee from Shylock's grasp, or to stay put and suffer yet more abuse at the hands of his merciless employer.}*

Certainly my conscience will serve me to run from this Jew my master. The     1
fiend is at mine elbow and tempts me, saying to me "Gobbo, Launcelot Gobbo,
good Launcelot," or "good Gobbo," or "good Launcelot Gobbo, use your legs,
take the start, run away." My conscience says, "No; take heed, honest Launcelot,
take heed, honest Gobbo," or, as aforesaid, "honest Launcelot Gobbo, do not     5
run; scorn running with thy heels." Well, the most courageous fiend bids me
pack. "Fia!" says the fiend; "away!" says the fiend; "for the heavens, rouse up
a brave mind," says the fiend, "and run!" Well, my conscience, hanging about
the neck of my heart, says very wisely to me, "My honest friend Launcelot,
being an honest man's son,"—or rather an honest woman's son, for indeed, my     10
father did something smack, something grow to, he had a kind of taste; well,
my conscience says, "Launcelot, budge not." "Budge," says the fiend. "Budge
not," says my conscience. "Conscience," say I, "you counsel well." "Fiend," say
I, "you counsel well." To be rul'd by my conscience, I should stay with the Jew
my master, who, God bless the mark, is a kind of devil; and to run away from     15
the Jew, I should be rul'd by the fiend, who, saving your reverence, is the devil
himself. Certainly the Jew is the very devil incarnation; and, in my conscience,
my conscience is but a kind of hard conscience, to offer to counsel me to stay
with the Jew. The fiend gives the more friendly counsel. I will run, fiend; my
heels are at your commandment. I will run.     20

**1 serve** encourage, allow   **1–2 The fiend** the Devil   **4 take the start**
make haste, journey forth immediately   **5 aforesaid** was said before
**6 courageous** spirited, animated   **7 pack** depart   **Fia** get along, away   **for
the heavens** for heaven's sake   **11 smack, grow to, kind of taste**
(Launcelot, in his own delicate way, is suggesting that his father had a
proclivity for lecherous behavior.)   **15 God . . . mark** (an expression that in
effect begs forgiveness if any offense is taken over what is about to be uttered,
just as does the "saving your reverence" that follows)   **17 incarnation**
(Launcelot's corruption of "incarnate") **in** by   **18 hard** harsh, merciless

(3)                    PRINCE OF MOROCCO                [II.VII.13]

SCENE: Portia's house

*{Morocco is here to take his best shot at winning Portia's hand in marriage. He knows the rules of the game; all that remains is to weigh his three options.}*

| | |
|---|---|
| 1 | Some god direct my judgment! Let me see; |
| | I will survey th' inscriptions back again. |
| | What says this leaden casket? |
| | "Who chooseth me must give and hazard all he hath." |
| 5 | Must give—for what? For lead? Hazard for lead? |
| | This casket threatens. Men that hazard all |
| | Do it in hope of fair advantages; |
| | A golden mind stoops not to shows of dross. |
| | I'll then nor give nor hazard aught for lead. |
| 10 | What says the silver with her virgin hue? |
| | "Who chooseth me shall get as much as he deserves." |
| | As much as he deserves. Pause there, Morocco, |
| | And weigh thy value with an even hand. |
| | If thou be'st rated by thy estimation, |
| 15 | Thou dost deserve enough; and yet enough |
| | May not extend so far as to the lady; |
| | And yet to be afeared of my deserving |
| | Were but a weak disabling of myself. |
| | As much as I deserve; why, that's the lady! |
| 20 | I do in birth deserve her, and in fortunes, |
| | In graces, and in qualities of breeding; |
| | But more than these, in love I do deserve. |
| | What if I stray'd no farther, but chose here? |
| | Let's see once more this saying grav'd in gold: |
| 25 | "Who chooseth me shall gain what many men desire." |
| | Why, that's the lady; all the world desires her. |
| | From the four corners of the earth they come |
| | To kiss this shrine, this mortal breathing saint. |
| | The Hyrcanian deserts and the vasty wilds |
| 30 | Of wide Arabia are as throughfares now |
| | For princes to come view fair Portia. |
| | The watery kingdom, whose ambitious head |
| | Spits in the face of heaven, is no bar |
| | To stop the foreign spirits, but they come, |
| 35 | As o'er a brook, to see fair Portia. |
| | One of these three contains her heavenly picture. |
| | Is 't like that lead contains her? 'Twere damnation |
| | To think so base a thought; it were too gross |

To rib her cerecloth in the obscure grave.
Or shall I think in silver she's immur'd,                                    40
Being ten times undervalued to tried gold?
O sinful thought! Never so rich a gem
Was set in worse than gold. They have in England
A coin that bears the figure of an angel
Stamp'd in gold, but that's insculp'd upon;                                  45
But here an angel in a golden bed
Lies all within. Deliver me the key.
Here do I choose, and thrive I as I may!

**2 survey** carefully observe   **4 hazard** put at risk   **7 advantages** returns,
profits   **8 of dross** of no value   **9 nor give** neither give   **aught** anything
**10 virgin** pure, natural   **13 even** impartial   **14 rated** valued   **estimation**
worth   **18 disabling** underrating, disparagement   **20 birth** noble lineage
**24 grav'd** engraved   **29 Hyrcanian** (Hyrcania was a country noted for its
wild and desolate environs.)   **deserts** uninhabited areas   **vasty** vast
**30 throughfares** thoroughfares   **32 watery kingdom** ocean   **37 like**
likely   **39 rib** enclose   **cerecloth** burial shroud   **40 immur'd** entombed
**41 undervalued to** less in value than   **tried** refined   **45 insculp'd upon**
engraved on the surface   **46 an angel** i.e., a likeness of Portia

(4)                              SHYLOCK                              [III.1.44]

SCENE: A street in Venice

*{The word around town is that one of Antonio's cargo ships has been lost at sea.
If true, it would mean that the merchant is suddenly knee deep in financial
trouble. When a couple of Antonio's friends pump Shylock for whatever light
he can shed on the subject, Shylock snaps back with a peevish reply.}*

There I have another bad match! A bankrupt, a prodigal, who dare scarce        1
show his head on the Rialto; a beggar, that was us'd to come so smug upon the
mart! Let him look to his bond. He was wont to call me usurer; let him look to
his bond. He was wont to lend money for a Christian cur'sy; let him look to his
bond. [For] if he forfeit, I [will] take his flesh; if it will feed nothing else, it will   5
feed my revenge. He hath disgrac'd me, and hind'red me half a million, laugh'd at
my losses, mock'd at my gains, scorn'd my nation, thwarted my bargains, cool'd
my friends, heated mine enemies. And what's his reason? I am a Jew. Hath
not a Jew eyes? Hath not a Jew hands, organs, dimensions, senses, affections,
passions? Fed with the same food, hurt with the same weapons, subject to the   10
same diseases, heal'd by the same means, warm'd and cool'd by the same winter

and summer, as a Christian is? If you prick us, do we not bleed? If you tickle us, do we not laugh? If you poison us, do we not die? And if you wrong us, shall we not revenge? If we are like you in the rest, we will resemble you in that. If a Jew wrong a Christian, what is his humility? Revenge. If a Christian wrong a Jew, what should his sufferance be by Christian example? Why, revenge. The villainy you teach me, I will execute, and it shall go hard but I will better the instruction.

**1 match** bargain   **2 Rialto** a district of Venice, and center of the city's commercial activity **smug** neat, trim   **3 bond** promissory note **wont** accustomed   **4 for a** out of **cur'sy** courtesy   **5 take his flesh** (see I.iii.146) **7 nation** i.e., the Jewish people   **9 dimensions** bodily proportions **14 revenge** seek vengeance   **15 his humility** the Christian's benevolence (in response)   **16 his sufferance** the Jew's forbearance   **17 and...will** and rest assured but that I will

(5)                          SHYLOCK                     [IV.i.35]

SCENE: A court of justice

*{Shylock's day in court has finally arrived. When the Duke of Venice suggests, as the presiding authority, that Shylock show mercy by not pursuing his legal entitlement of a pound of Antonio's flesh, Shylock proves less than amenable to the idea.}*

1    I have possess'd your Grace of what I purpose,
     And by our holy Sabbath have I sworn
     To have the due and forfeit of my bond.
     If you deny it, let the danger light
5    Upon your charter and your city's freedom.
     You'll ask me why I rather choose to have
     A weight of carrion flesh than to receive
     Three thousand ducats. I'll not answer that;
     But, say, it is my humor—is it answer'd?
10   What if my house be troubled with a rat
     And I be pleas'd to give ten thousand ducats
     To have it ban'd? What, are you answer'd yet?
     Some men there are love not a gaping pig,
     Some that are mad if they behold a cat,
15   And others, when the bagpipe sings i' th' nose,
     Cannot contain their urine; for affection,
     Mistress of passion, sways it to the mood

Of what it likes or loathes. Now, for your answer:
As there is no firm reason to be rend'red
Why he cannot abide a gaping pig,                                    20
Why he a harmless necessary cat,
Why he a woolen bagpipe, but of force
Must yield to such inevitable shame
As to offend, himself being offended;
So can I give no reason, nor I will not,                             25
More than a lodg'd hate and a certain loathing
I bear Antonio, that I follow thus
A losing suit against him. Are you answered?

**1 possess'd** informed  **purpose** intend   **4 danger** damage   **5 Upon...
freedom** (Shylock is assuring the Duke that, should Antonio not be forced
to meet his contractual obligations, Venice's reputation among merchants—
and thus its economic viability—will most certainly suffer as a result.)
**7 carrion flesh** (Shylock refers disparagingly to the terms of his loan to
Antonio; see I.iii.146.)   **8 ducats** gold coins   **9 humor** fancy, whim
**12 ban'd** poisoned   **13 gaping pig** roasted pig served whole and with its
mouth open   **16 affection** disposition, inclination   **20–22 he, he, he** one
person, another, still another   **26 lodg'd** deep-seated, steadfast   **27 follow**
pursue   **28 losing** financially unprofitable

**ALTERNATES**

| | |
|---|---|
| Gratiano | [I.i.73–104] |
| Bassanio | [I.i.122–176] |
| Prince of Arragon | [II.ix.19–79] |
| Bassanio | [III.ii.73–148] |

# THE MERRY WIVES OF WINDSOR

In dire need of some cash, Falstaff decides to court Mistresses Ford and Page, hoping he can thereby gain access to their husbands' purses. The ladies are understandably revolted by Falstaff's amorous overtures, but decide to lead him on anyway just for the fun of it. Employing Mistress Quickly as their go-between, the two wives begin their intrigue by arranging separate assignations with the clueless Sir John.

Elsewhere, a disgruntled pair of Falstaff's followers have alerted Masters Ford and Page to Falstaff's designs on their wives. Unlike Page, Ford takes the warning to heart, but is frustrated in his two attempts to catch his wife and Sir John in the act.

After Mistresses Ford and Page finally inform one and all of their shenanigans with Falstaff, everyone agrees it would be swell to stage one last, elaborate humiliation of the fat knight. The plan comes off swimmingly, of course, and afterwards the conspirators all saunter over to Page's house for a bit of country cheer.

SIR JOHN FALSTAFF, a roguish knight
MASTER FORD, a gentleman of Windsor
MASTER PAGE, a gentleman of Windsor
SIR HUGH EVANS, a Welsh parson
NYM, follower of Falstaff
PISTOL, follower of Falstaff

MISTRESS FORD, wife to Ford
MISTRESS PAGE, wife to Page
MISTRESS QUICKLY, confidante to Mistresses Ford and Page

(1)                           FALSTAFF                        [I.III.38]

SCENE: A room in the Garter Inn

*{Having faced up to the fact that his coffers are almost empty, Sir John informs his underworld operatives, Nym and Pistol, of his plan to rectify this unfortunate situation.}*

My honest lads, I will tell you what I am about. Indeed, I am in the waist two         1
yards about; but I am now about no waste; I am about thrift. Briefly, I do mean
to make love to Ford's wife. I spy entertainment in her. She discourses, she
carves, she gives the leer of invitation. I can construe the action of her familiar
style; and the hardest voice of her behavior, to be English'd rightly, is, "I am       5
Sir John Falstaff's." Now, the report goes she has all the rule of her husband's
purse. He hath a legion of angels. [*Showing a pair of letters.*] I have writ me
here a letter to her; and here another to Page's wife, who even now gave me
good eyes too, examin'd my parts with most judicious oeillades. Sometimes
the beam of her view gilded my foot, sometimes my portly belly. O, she did       10
so course o'er my exteriors with such a greedy intention, that the appetite of
her eye did seem to scorch me up like a burning-glass! Here's another letter
to her. She bears the purse too; she is a region in Guiana, all gold and bounty. I
will be cheaters to them both, and they shall be exchequers to me. They shall
be my East and West Indies, and I will trade to them both. [*Giving the letters*      15
*to Pistol and Nym.*] Go, bear thou this letter to Mistress Page; and thou this to
Mistress Ford. We will thrive, lads, we will thrive.

**1 about** up to   **2 yards about** yards around   **4 carves** conveys ease and
friendliness by making affected gestures with the hand   **construe** interpret
**5 hardest** harshest   **English'd** put into plain English   **6 all the rule**
complete control   **7 angels** gold coins bearing the image of an angel
**9 oeillades** amorous glances   **10 gilded** shined on (as if a "beam" of
sunlight)   **12 burning-glass** magnifying glass (used to focus the rays of the
sun)   **13 Guiana** (Possibly a reference to *The Discovery of the Large, Rich,
and Beautiful Empire of Guiana*, a 1596 account of Sir Walter Raleigh's South
American travels.)   **14 cheaters** escheators (who were officers appointed
to oversee property that was forfeited to the king; Falstaff plays on the more
familiar "deceiver" sense of the word as well)   **exchequers** treasuries (The
escheator was an official of the Exchequer.)

(2)                            FORD                    [II.ii.287]

SCENE: A room in the Garter Inn

*{Ford suspects Mistress Ford of being unfaithful to him. In order to catch her red-handed, he has come here to the Garter, disguised as "Master Brook," to employ Falstaff in the seduction of his wife. But when, in agreeing to take on the job, Sir John reveals that Mistress Ford has already made overtures to him anyway, Ford can barely wait until Falstaff exits before unleashing his indignation.}*

1    What a damn'd Epicurean rascal is this! My heart is ready to crack with impatience. Who says this is improvident jealousy? My wife hath sent to him, the hour is fix'd, the match is made. Would any man have thought this? See the hell of having a false woman! My bed shall be abus'd, my coffers ransack'd,

5    my reputation gnawn at; and I shall not only receive this villainous wrong, but stand under the adoption of abominable terms, and by him that does me this wrong. Terms! Names! Amaimon sounds well; Lucifer, well; Barbason, well; yet they are the devils' additions, the names of fiends. But Cuckold! Wittol!— Cuckold! The devil himself hath not such a name. Page is an ass, a secure ass.

10   He will trust his wife; he will not be jealous. I will rather trust a Fleming with my butter, Parson Hugh the Welshman with my cheese, an Irishman with my aqua-vitae bottle, or a thief to walk my ambling gelding, than my wife with herself. Then she plots, then she ruminates, then she devises; and what they think in their hearts they may effect, they will break their hearts but they will

15   effect. God be prais'd for my jealousy! Eleven o'clock the hour. I will prevent this, detect my wife, be reveng'd on Falstaff, and laugh at Page. I will about it; better three hours too soon than a minute too late. Fie, fie, fie! Cuckold, cuckold, cuckold!

**1 Epicurean** sensual   **2 improvident** rash   **6 stand ... terms** stand to assume some hideous titles (like "cuckold")   **7 Amaimon, Lucifer, Barbason** various names for the Devil   **8 additions** titles   **Wittol** one who is resigned to the fact that his wife is unfaithful to him   **9 secure** overconfident   **10–12 Fleming ... bottle** (alluding to popular stereotypes of the day, namely that the Flemish love butter, the Welsh eat a lot of cheese, and the Irish are fond of strong drink)   **12 walk** exercise   **14 effect** bring about, accomplish   **15 prevent** anticipate, forestall   **16–17 about it** get moving

(3)                        FORD                        [III.ii.30]

SCENE: A street in Windsor

*{Convinced that his wife is stepping out on him, Ford seems truly stunned when Master Page, just prior to strolling off, blithely dismisses the notion that something similarly sinister may be unfolding in his own household.}*

Has Page any brains? Hath he any eyes? Hath he any thinking? Sure, they sleep;    1
he hath no use of them. Why, this boy will carry a letter twenty mile as
easy as a cannon will shoot point-blank twelve score. He pieces out his wife's
inclination; he gives her folly motion and advantage. And now she's going to
my wife, and Falstaff's boy with her. A man may hear this show'r sing in the    5
wind. And Falstaff's boy with her! Good plots, they are laid: and our revolted
wives share damnation together. Well, I will take him, then torture my wife,
pluck the borrow'd veil of modesty from the so-seeming Mistress Page, divulge
Page himself for a secure and willful Actaeon; and to these violent proceedings
all my neighbors shall cry aim. [*A clock is heard.*] The clock gives me my cue,    10
and my assurance bids me search. There I shall find Falstaff. I shall be rather
prais'd for this than mock'd, for it is as positive as the earth is firm that Falstaff
is there. I will go.

**1 sure** surely, certainly   **2 this boy** (Ford has just seen Mistress Page
walking with Robin, a youth employed by Falstaff.)   **3 twelve score** i.e.,
twelve score (240) paces from the target   **pieces out** adds to   **4 motion**
instigation, prompting   **advantage** favorable opportunity   **5–6 hear . . .
wind** tell by the wind that a rain shower is brewing (figuratively, that trouble
is ahead)   **6 Good** sound, well-considered   **7 him** (referring to Falstaff)
**8 borrow'd** assumed, counterfeit   **9 secure** unsuspecting   **Actaeon** a
noted cuckold of mythology   **10 cry aim** a phrase from archery more or
less equivalent to "good shot"

(4)                      FALSTAFF                      [III.v.61]

SCENE: A room in the Garter Inn

*{Earlier on, Ford adopted the guise of "Master Brook" and recruited Falstaff to seduce Mistress Ford (see entry [2]). Now, "Brook" returns for a progress report.}*

Now, Master Brook, you come to know what hath pass'd between me and    1
Ford's wife. Master Brook, I will not lie to you. I was at her house the hour

she appointed me. But the peaking cornuto her husband, Master Brook,
dwelling in a continual 'larum of jealousy, comes me in the instant of our

5   encounter, after we had embrac'd, kiss'd, protested, and, as it were, spoke the
prologue of our comedy; and at his heels a rabble of his companions, thither
provok'd and instigated by his distemper, and forsooth, to search his house for
his wife's love. As good luck would have it, comes in one Mistress Page, gives
intelligence of Ford's approach, and, in her invention, and Ford's wife's distrac-

10  tion, they convey'd me into a buck-basket. By the Lord, a buck-basket! Ramm'd
me in with foul shirts and smocks, socks, foul stockings, greasy napkins, that,
Master Brook, there was the rankest compound of villainous smell that ever
offended nostril. You shall hear, Master Brook, what I have suffer'd to bring
this woman to evil for your good. Being thus cramm'd in the basket, a couple

15  of Ford's knaves, his hinds, were call'd forth by their mistress to carry me in
the name of foul clothes to Datchet Lane. They took me on their shoulders,
met the jealous knave their master in the door, who ask'd them once or twice
what they had in their basket. I quak'd for fear, lest the lunatic knave would
have search'd it; but fate, ordaining he should be a cuckold, held his hand. Well,

20  on went he for a search, and away went I for foul clothes. But mark the sequel,
Master Brook. I suffer'd the pangs of three several deaths: first, an intolerable
fright, to be detected with a jealous rotten bell-wether; next, to be compass'd,
like a good bilbo, in the circumference of a peck, hilt to point, heel to head; and
then, to be stopp'd in, like a strong distillation, with stinking clothes that fretted

25  in their own grease. Think of that—a man of my kidney. Think of that—that
am as subject to heat as butter; a man of continual dissolution and thaw. It was
a miracle to scape suffocation. And in the height of this bath, when I was more
than half stew'd in grease, like a Dutch dish, to be thrown in the Thames,
and cool'd, glowing hot, in that surge, like a horse-shoe! Think of that—

30  hissing hot—think of that, Master Brook!

**3 peaking cornuto** sneaking cuckold   **4 'larum** alarm, excited state
**5 protested** declared our love   **7 forsooth** truly   **9 intelligence** news   **in
her invention** owing to her inventiveness   **9–10 distraction** i.e.,
distraction of her husband   **10 buck-basket** basket used for carrying dirty
laundry   **15 hinds** servants   **19 held his hand** guided him   **21 several**
separate, different   **22 with** by   **bell-wether** loud, clamorous person (The
bell-wether sheep was at the front of the flock, around whose neck a bell
was usually hung.)   **compass'd** enclosed   **23 bilbo** a sword crafted in
Bilbao, Spain, noted for its exceptional quality   **peck** container holding a
quarter of a bushel; that is, a very small space   **hilt...head** (Falstaff was
evidently bent in half inside the basket; a fine sword like a bilbo can be
similarly bent without breaking.)   **24 stopp'd** shut   **fretted** decayed
**25 kidney** temperament, condition   **26 subject** vulnerable   **dissolution**
dissolving   **27 scape** escape   **28 Dutch dish** (Dutch cuisine was thought to
be particularly greasy.)   **29 surge** i.e., the turbulent Thames river

(5)                           FORD                      [III.v.139]

SCENE: A room in the Garter Inn

*{Though Ford failed to catch his wife committing adultery with Falstaff the first time around, he remains a man on a mission. Having just sent Sir John off to another assignation with his wife, Ford stands as determined as ever to evade the cuckold's horns.}*

Hum, ha! Is this a vision? Is this a dream? Do I sleep? Master Ford, awake!    1
Awake, Master Ford! There's a hole made in your best coat, Master Ford. This
'tis to be married! This 'tis to have linen and buck-baskets! Well, I will proclaim
myself what I am. I will now take the lecher; he is at my house. He cannot
scape me; 'tis impossible he should. He cannot creep into a halfpenny purse,    5
nor into a pepper box. But, lest the devil that guides him should aid him, I will
search impossible places. Though what I am I cannot avoid, yet to be what I
would not shall not make me tame. If I have horns to make one mad, let the
proverb go with me: I'll be horn-mad!

**3 buck-baskets** baskets used for carrying dirty laundry   **5 scape** escape
**halfpenny purse** small purse designed to hold tiny halfpenny coins
**7 impossible places** i.e., places (like a pepperbox) in which Falstaff could
not possibly hide   **what I am** i.e., a cuckold   **8 would not** wish not to be
**horns** (of a cuckold)   **9 horn-mad** raving mad, furious (with a play on the
cuckold's horns)

(6)                         FALSTAFF                      [V.v.1]

SCENE: Windsor Park

*{Falstaff has once again been duped by the Windsor wives (see IV.iv.27 for an account of their plan). It's midnight in Windsor Park, and as instructed, Sir John has arrived fully decked out as Herne the hunter, with nary a clue as to the ignoble fate that awaits him.}*

The Windsor bell hath struck twelve; the minute draws on. Now, the hot-    1
blooded gods assist me! Remember, Jove, thou wast a bull for thy Europa; love
set on thy horns. O powerful love, that, in some respects makes a beast a
man; in some other, a man a beast. You were also, Jupiter, a swan for the love
of Leda. O omnipotent Love, how near the god drew to the complexion of    5
a goose! A fault done first in the form of a beast—O Jove, a beastly fault!—

and then another fault in the semblance of a fowl; think on 't, Jove, a foul fault! When gods have hot backs, what shall poor men do? For me, I am here a Windsor stag, and the fattest, I think, I' th' forest. Send me a cool rut-time,

10    Jove, or who can blame me to piss my tallow? Who comes here? My doe? [*Enter Mistresses Ford and Page.*] My doe with the black scut! Let the sky rain potatoes; let it thunder to the tune of "Greensleeves," hail kissing-comfits, and snow eringoes; let there come a tempest of provocation, I will shelter me here. [What], Mistress Page is come with you? Divide me like a brib'd buck, each

15    a haunch. I will keep my sides to myself, my shoulders for the fellow of this walk, and my horns I bequeath your husbands. Am I a woodman, ha? Speak I like Herne the hunter? Why, now is Cupid a child of conscience; he makes restitution. As I am a true spirit, welcome!

**2–5 Jove...Europa, Jupiter...Leda** (refers to earthly guises adopted by Jupiter in order to indulge his prodigious sexual appetite)    **5 complexion** temperament    **6 fault** sin, wrongdoing    **8 hot** lecherous (with, perhaps, a play on the heat generated during carnal activity)    **9 rut-time** mating season for deer    **10 piss my tallow** sweat off excess fat, in the manner of a stag during mating season    **11 scut** tail    **12 potatoes** sweet potatoes (which were thought to be an aphrodisiac)    **"Greensleeves"** (A popular song of the day.)    **kissing-comfits** sweetmeats used to sweeten one's breath    **13 eringoes** candied roots (a supposed aphrodisiac)    **provocation** sexual arousal    **14 brib'd** stolen (It was common practice for poachers to immediately cut up and divide among themselves a fallen deer.)    **15–16 fellow...walk** keeper of this forest    **16 horns** (with a play on the cuckold's horns)    **woodman** hunter (of women)    **17 Herne** (For more on Herne the hunter, see IV.iv.28)    **Cupid...conscience** i.e., Cupid is behaving honorably toward me    **17–18 he makes restitution** (i.e., he grants me the amorous pleasures he formerly withheld.)

**ALTERNATES**
Ford    [II.ii.154–251]
Fenton    [IV.vi.8–55]

# A MIDSUMMER NIGHT'S DREAM

Helena loves Demetrius, but Demetrius only has eyes for Hermia. Hermia, on the other hand, has just run off with Lysander. Before long, all four lovers end up in a forest outside Athens.

In these very same woods reside the King and Queen of the Fairies, Oberon and Titania, who have recently locked horns over the services of a young boy. Determined that he shall be the one who employs the lad, Oberon manages to anoint Titania's eyes with a potion which will induce her to fall in love with the first creature she sees. If Oberon's plot unfolds as intended, Titania will be so humiliated she will be forced to relinquish the boy to him.

For good measure, Oberon instructs his servant, Puck, to similarly enchant Demetrius, whose heartless rejection of Helena the fairy King has just witnessed. Puck botches the job, however, and ends up sprinkling both Demetrius and Lysander with the potion, thereby inducing them to passionately pursue a bewildered Helena.

Meanwhile, a bewitched Titania is in hot pursuit herself. The object of her lust is a local simpleton named Bottom—this despite the fact that Bottom's head has of late been changed into that of an ass, courtesy of the impish Puck. Mayhem ensues, of course, until Oberon finally sets things right by releasing Lysander, Bottom, and Titania from their spells.

By story's end, marriages and merriment are everywhere, as one and all gather to enjoy an unforgettable performance of "Pyramus And Thisby," courtesy of Bottom and his fellow players.

**THESEUS,** Duke of Athens
**LYSANDER,** in love with Hermia
**DEMETRIUS,** in love with Hermia
**BOTTOM,** a weaver and would-be actor
**OBERON,** King of the Fairies
**PUCK,** aide to Oberon

**HERMIA,** in love with Lysander
**HELENA,** in love with Demetrius
**TITANIA,** Queen of the Fairies

(1)                          OBERON                          [II.1.148]

SCENE: A wooded area near Athens

*{Oberon covets the services of a young boy in Titania's retinue, but so far the Queen of the Fairies has steadfastly refused to relinquish the lad. Oberon has therefore devised a plan to break down Titania's resistance—a scheme he now shares with his trusty assistant, Puck.}*

| | |
|---|---|
| 1 | My gentle Puck, come hither. Thou rememb'rest |
| | Since once I sat upon a promontory, |
| | And heard a mermaid on a dolphin's back |
| | Uttering such dulcet and harmonious breath |
| 5 | That the rude sea grew civil at her song |
| | And certain stars shot madly from their spheres, |
| | To hear the sea-maid's music. |
| | That very time I saw, but thou couldst not, |
| | Flying between the cold moon and the earth, |
| 10 | Cupid all arm'd. A certain aim he took |
| | At a fair vestal throned by the west, |
| | And loos'd his love-shaft smartly from his bow, |
| | As it should pierce a hundred thousand hearts; |
| | But I might see young Cupid's fiery shaft |
| 15 | Quench'd in the chaste beams of the wat'ry moon, |
| | And the imperial vot'ress passed on |
| | In maiden meditation, fancy-free. |
| | Yet mark'd I where the bolt of Cupid fell: |
| | It fell upon a little western flower, |
| 20 | Before milk-white, now purple with love's wound, |
| | And maidens call it love-in-idleness. |
| | Fetch me that flow'r; the herb I show'd thee once. |
| | The juice of it on sleeping eyelids laid |
| | Will make or man or woman madly dote |
| 25 | Upon the next live creature that it sees. |
| | Fetch me this herb, and be thou here again |
| | Ere the leviathan can swim a league. [*Puck exits.*] |
| | Having once this juice, |
| | I'll watch Titania when she is asleep, |
| 30 | And drop the liquor of it in her eyes. |
| | The next thing then she waking looks upon, |
| | Be it on lion, bear, or wolf, or bull, |
| | On meddling monkey, or on busy ape, |
| | She shall pursue it with the soul of love. |

And ere I take this charm from off her sight,                                              35
As I can take it with another herb,
I'll make her render up her page to me.
But who comes here? I am invisible,
And I will overhear their conference.

**2 Since** when   **4 breath** voice   **5 rude** rough, turbulent   **6 spheres**
(It was once believed that invisible spheres carried stars and other celestial
bodies as they revolved around the earth.)   **10 all** fully   **11 vestal** vestal
virgin   **throned...west** (Shakespeare's affectionate allusion to England's
monarch at the time, Queen Elizabeth)   **12 loos'd** let loose   **13 As** as if
**14 might** could   **15 moon** (referring to Diana, the moon goddess and
goddess of chastity)   **16 vot'ress** female who has taken a vow
**17 fancy-free** free from the spell of love   **24 or man** either man
**27 leviathan** whale   **33 meddling** pestering   **busy** bothering   **37 page**
(referring to the boy in question)   **38 I am invisible** (Traditionally, Oberon
delivers this aside to explain how he is able to eavesdrop undetected.)
**39 conference** conversation

(2)                              BOTTOM                              [IV.i.200]

SCENE: A wooded area near Athens

*{Alas, Bottom's love affair with Titania has come to an end, for Oberon has
removed his magic spell. As he slowly gathers his wits, Bottom struggles to make
sense of a whirlwind romance (and the ass's head that went with it) that he
hopes was no more than a midsummer night's dream.}*

When my cue comes, call me, and I will answer. My next is, "Most fair              1
Pyramus." Heigh-ho! Peter Quince! Flute, the bellows mender! Snout, the
tinker! Starveling! God's my life, stol'n hence, and left me asleep! I have had a
most rare vision. I have had a dream, past the wit of man to say what dream
it was. Man is but an ass, if he go about to expound this dream. Methought I      5
was—there is no man can tell what. Methought I was—and methought I had—
but man is but a patch'd fool, if he will offer to say what methought I had. The
eye of man hath not heard, the ear of man hath not seen, man's hand is not
able to taste, his tongue to conceive, nor his heart to report, what my dream
was. I will get Peter Quince to write a ballad of this dream. It shall be call'd     10
"Bottom's Dream," because it hath no bottom; and I will sing it in the latter
end of a play, before the Duke. Peradventure, to make it the more gracious, I
shall sing it at her death.

**2 Heigh-ho!** (an exclamation on the order of "yoo-hoo" utilized to beckon someone)   **2–3 Peter Quince . . . Starveling** (along with Bottom, all are members of the troupe of would-be actors)   **3 God's** God save   **4 wit** mental capacity   **5 go about** makes it a point, attempts   **7 patch'd fool** motley-clad jester (Motley, a multi-colored patchwork cloth, made up the traditional costume of the professional fool.)   **11 hath no bottom** is all tangled up (A "bottom" was the wooden spool upon which a weaver wound his wool.)   **12 Peradventure** perhaps **gracious** attractive   **13 her** (referring to Thisby, who dies at the end of Bottom's play, "Pyramus and Thisby")

(3)                              BOTTOM                          [V.i.272]

SCENE: The palace of Theseus

*{Theseus selected Bottom and his fellow actors to provide the evening's entertainment, a presentation of the playlet "Pyramus and Thisby." Though intended as tragedy, the story takes on a decidedly comic flavor in the hands of these rustic players. As the climax nears, Pyramus discovers what he believes to be evidence of his beloved Thisby's demise—her bloodstained mantle. For better or worse, Bottom pulls out all the stops in his vivid interpretation of the scene.}*

1      Sweet Moon, I thank thee for thy sunny beams;
           I thank thee, Moon, for shining now so bright;
       For, by thy gracious, golden, glittering gleams,
           I trust to take of truest Thisby sight.
5                  But stay, O spite!
                   But mark, poor knight,
               What dreadful dole is here!
                   Eyes, do you see?
                   How can it be?
10             O dainty duck! O dear!
                   Thy mantle good,
                   What, stain'd with blood?
               Approach, ye Furies fell!
                   O Fates, come, come,
15                 Cut thread and thrum,
                   Quail, crush, conclude, and quell!
       O wherefore, Nature, didst thou lions frame?
           Since lion vile hath here deflow'r'd my dear,
       Which is—no, no—which was the fairest dame
20         That liv'd, that lov'd, that lik'd, that look'd with cheer.

Come, tears, confound,
    Out, sword, and wound
The pap of Pyramus;
    Ay, that left pap,
    Where heart doth hop. [*Stabs himself.*]                25
Thus die I, thus, thus, thus.
    Now am I dead,
    Now am I fled;
My soul is in the sky.
    Tongue, lose thy sight;                                  30
    Moon, take thy flight.
Now, die, die, die, die, die. [*He dies.*]

**5 spite** distressing or malicious stroke of fortune   **7 dole** woeful thing,
sorrowful sight   **13 Furies** grotesque creatures of Greek mythology who
punished sinners   **fell** cruel   **15 thread and thrum** i.e., everything, the
good and the bad together   **16 Quail** overpower   **quell** slay, destroy
**17 frame** create   **23 pap** empty remains   **24 left** remaining   **25 hop** beat,
flutter   **30–31 Tongue, Moon** (Apparently caught up in his moment of
passion, Bottom has inadvertently reversed "Tongue" and "Moon." Death
actually would result in Pyramus's tongue taking "flight"—being
silenced—and his losing "sight" of the moon.)

(4)                          PUCK                          [V.I.371]

SCENE: The palace of Theseus

*{"Pyramus and Thisby" has reached its moving conclusion (see preceding entry),
and the evening is spent. All that remains is for Puck to bid the audience adieu.}*

Now the hungry lion roars,                                  1
And the wolf behowls the moon,
Whilst the heavy ploughman snores,
All with weary task fordone.
Now the wasted brands do glow,                              5
Whilst the screech-owl, screeching loud,
Puts the wretch that lies in woe
In remembrance of a shroud.
Now it is the time of night
That the graves, all gaping wide,                           10
Every one lets forth his sprite,
In the churchway paths to glide.

And we fairies, that do run
By the triple Hecate's team
15   From the presence of the sun,
Following darkness like a dream,
Now are frolic. Not a mouse
Shall disturb this hallowed house.
I am sent with broom before,
20   To sweep the dust behind the door.
If we shadows have offended,
Think but this, and all is mended,
That you have but slumb'red here,
While these visions did appear.
25   And this weak and idle theme,
No more yielding but a dream,
Gentles, do not reprehend;
If you pardon, we will mend.
And, as I am an honest Puck,
30   If we have unearned luck
Now to scape the serpent's tongue,
We will make amends ere long;
Else the Puck a liar call.
So, good night unto you all.
35   Give me your hands, if we be friends,
And Robin shall restore amends.

**2 behowls** howls at   **3 heavy** sleepy   **4 fordone** exhausted   **5 wasted brands** logs consumed by fire   **11 sprite** ghost   **14 triple Hecate's** (Hecate ruled in three separate capacities; as Luna in heaven, as Diana on earth and as Proserpina in the underworld.)   **17 frolic** merry   **20 behind** from behind (Puck is also known as "Robin Goodfellow," a household spirit who, despite his mischievous nature, was known to help housekeepers from time to time.)   **21 shadows** fairies   **23 slumb'red** dreamt   **25 idle** silly   **26 No...but** yielding nothing more than   **27 Gentles** gentlefolk   **28 mend** do better (next time)   **31 scape** escape   **the serpent's tongue** i.e., hissing   **35 hands** applause   **36 restore amends** make amends later on

### Alternates

Oberon                          [IV.i.46–75]
Quince (as "Prologue")   [V.i.108–151]

# MUCH ADO ABOUT NOTHING

Benedick is no fan of Beatrice, while Beatrice has little but scorn for Benedick. It's a bit surprising then that "friends" of each are soon conspiring to convince both Benedick and Beatrice that one is madly in love with the other.

Elsewhere in Messina, another plot unfolds. Because Don John resents the close friendship forged between his brother Don Pedro and young Claudio, he has decided to undermine Claudio's plans to marry Hero, daughter to Leonato.

Don John's scheme plays out precisely as planned when Claudio and Don Pedro happen to glimpse a servant disguised as Hero dallying with another man in Hero's bedroom window. Thus convinced that he's been betrayed by his betrothed, Claudio publicly humiliates Hero at the altar by refusing her hand in marriage.

Everything appears to have completely unraveled when, thanks in part to some dubious police work by Constable Dogberry, Don John's villainy is revealed and Claudio and Hero are reunited. As for Beatrice and Benedick, they eventually tumble to the fact that their would-be romance was founded on their friends' machinations, but even so resign themselves to the bonds of matrimony.

DON PEDRO, Prince of Arragon
DON JOHN, bastard brother to Don Pedro
CLAUDIO, a young lord of Florence
BENEDICK, a young lord of Padua
LEONATO, governor of Messina
ANTONIO, brother to Leonato
DOGBERRY, a constable

HERO, daughter to Leonato
BEATRICE, niece to Leonato
URSULA, a gentlewoman attending on Hero

**(1)**                               **BENEDICK**                          **[II.1.239]**

SCENE: A hall in Leonato's house

*{In the midst of a masked ball, Don Pedro informs Benedick that Lady Beatrice "hath a quarrel" with him. To Beatrice's complaint that she has been "much wrong'd" by him, Benedick is quick to retort that the feelings are mutual.}*

1      O, she misus'd me past the endurance of a block! An oak but with one green
       leaf on it would have answer'd her. My very visor began to assume life and
       scold with her. She told me, not thinking I had been myself, that I was the
       Prince's jester, that I was duller than a great thaw; huddling jest upon jest with
5      such impossible conveyance upon me that I stood like a man at a mark, with
       a whole army shooting at me. She speaks poniards, and every word stabs. If
       her breath were as terrible as her terminations, there were no living near her;
       she would infect to the north star. I would not marry her, though she were
       endow'd with all that Adam had left him before he transgress'd. She would
10     have made Hercules have turn'd spit, yea, and have cleft his club to make the
       fire too. Come, talk not of her; you shall find her the infernal Ate in good
       apparel. I would to God some scholar would conjure her, for certainly, while
       she is here, a man may live as quiet in hell as in a sanctuary, and people sin
       upon purpose because they would go thither; so indeed all disquiet, horror,
15     and perturbation follow her. [*Beatrice approaches.*] Look, here she comes. Will
       your Grace command me any service to the world's end? I will go on the
       slightest errand now to the Antipodes that you can devise to send me on; I
       will fetch you a toothpicker now from the furthest inch of Asia, bring you the
       length of Prester John's foot, fetch you a hair off the great Cham's beard, do
20     you any embassage to the Pigmies, rather than hold three words' conference
       with this harpy! O God, sir, here's a dish I love not! I cannot endure my Lady
       Tongue.

**1–2 misus'd** abused  **but . . . it** i.e., with but the least little bit of life left in it
**2 visor** mask  **3 scold** quarrel  **not . . . myself** not realizing who I was (due
to the mask he wore)  **4 a great thaw** i.e., that part of the year when
roads are muddy and impassable, thus forcing one to forgo the customary
social activities  **huddling** heaping up  **5 impossible conveyance**
incredible adeptness  **at a mark** used as a target  **6 poniards** daggers
**terminations** words, expressions  **7 were** would be  **8 north star**
(considered the most distant star)  **9 left** bestowed upon  **10 Hercules . . .**
**spit** (Turning a spit over the fire was considered to be work of the most
menial kind.)  **11 Ate** the goddess of discord and mischief  **12 scholar**
i.e., one who was knowledgeable in the Latin formulas used to exorcise evil
spirits  **14 upon** on  **would** desire to  **thither** (referring to hell)
**15 perturbation** agitation  **17 Antipodes** opposite ends of the earth

**18 toothpicker** toothpick    **19 Prester John** a legendary ruler of the Far East    **Cham** Khan, ruler of the Mongols    **20 embassage** errand, mission    **Pigmies** legendary race of small people believed to inhabit the mountains of India    **21 harpy** mythical monster, having a woman's face and body, and the wings and claws of a bird

(2)                         BENEDICK                         [II.iii.7]

SCENE: Leonato's orchard

*{Claudio has fallen in love with Hero, and no one is more surprised by the sudden turn of events than Claudio's close friend and confirmed bachelor, Benedick.}*

I do much wonder that one man, seeing how much another man is a fool when    1
he dedicates his behaviors to love, will, after he hath laugh'd at such shallow
follies in others, become the argument of his own scorn by falling in love; and
such a man is Claudio. I have known when there was no music with him but
the drum and the fife; and now had he rather hear the tabor and the pipe. I    5
have known when he would have walk'd ten mile afoot to see a good armor;
and now will he lie ten nights awake, carving the fashion of a new doublet. He
was wont to speak plain and to the purpose, like an honest man and a soldier;
and now is he turn'd orthography—his words are a very fantastical banquet,
just so many strange dishes. May I be so converted and see with these eyes?    10
I cannot tell; I think not. I will not be sworn but love may transform me to
an oyster; but I'll take my oath on it, till he have made an oyster of me, he
shall never make me such a fool. One woman is fair, yet I am well; another
is wise, yet I am well; another virtuous, yet I am well; but till all graces be in
one woman, one woman shall not come in my grace. Rich she shall be, that's    15
certain; wise, or I'll none; virtuous, or I'll never cheapen her; fair, or I'll never
look on her; mild, or come not near me; noble, or not I for an angel; of good
discourse, an excellent musician, and her hair shall be of what color it please
God. [*Sees Don Pedro and Claudio.*] Ha! The Prince and Monsieur Love! I will
hide me in the arbor.    20

**3 argument** subject    **5 drum, fife** (instruments typically heard on the battlefield)    **tabor, pipe** (musical instruments symbolic of peaceful merriment)    **6 armor** suit of armor    **7 carving** contemplating, planning    **doublet** close-fitting jacket or vest-type garment    **9 orthography** orthographer (i.e., one who is studied or affected in his use of words)    **10 converted** transformed, altered    **14 graces** pleasing qualities    **15 grace** favor, good opinion    **16 I'll none** I'll have none of her company    **cheapen** bargain for    **17 for an angel** (1) though she be an angel (2) for ten shillings ("Angel" was the common term for a ten-shilling coin bearing the image of the archangel Michael. A "noble" was also a coin, thus the double play on words.)

(3)                    **BENEDICK**                    [II.III.220]

SCENE: Leonato's orchard

*{Benedick has just overheard a conversation (staged expressly for his benefit) in which it was reported that Beatrice has fallen madly in love with him. Even for a steadfast critic of love like himself, such news is cause for a bit of reassessment.}*

1    This can be no trick; the conference was sadly borne. They have the truth of this from Hero. They seem to pity the lady. It seems her affections have their full bent. Love me? Why, it must be requited. I hear how I am censur'd. They say I will bear myself proudly, if I perceive the love come from her; they say
5    too that she will rather die than give any sign of affection. I did never think to marry. I must not seem proud; happy are they that hear their detractions and can put them to mending. They say the lady is fair—'tis a truth, I can bear them witness; and virtuous; 'tis so, I cannot reprove it; and wise, but for loving me; by my troth, it is no addition to her wit, nor no great argument of her folly,
10    for I will be horribly in love with her. I may chance have some odd quirks and remnants of wit broken on me, because I have rail'd so long against marriage. But doth not the appetite alter? A man loves the meat in his youth that he cannot endure in his age. Shall quips and sentences and these paper bullets of the brain awe a man from the career of his humor? No, the world must be
15    peopled. When I said I would die a bachelor, I did not think I should live till I were married. [*Sees Beatrice approaching.*] Here comes Beatrice. By this day, she's a fair lady! I do spy some marks of love in her.

**1 sadly borne** seriously conducted   **2–3 have ... bent** are stretched to their limit   **6 their detractions** of their faults   **8 reprove** deny, disprove **but** if only   **9 by my troth** (a common affirmation of the day on the order of "I'll say this," or "I declare")   **10 chance** possibly   **quirks** jests, witticisms **13 quips** sarcastic remarks   **sentences** maxims   **paper bullets** verbal salvos   **14 awe** deter   **career ... humor** pursuit of his fancy   **16 marks** outward signs

(4)                    **DOGBERRY**                [III.III.22]

SCENE: A street in Messina

*{Master Constable Dogberry is about to turn over the watch to the evening crew.*
*But first there is the matter of selecting a night constable, as well as the issuance*
*of a few final instructions.}*

Neighbor Seacole, you are thought here to be the most senseless and fit man          1
for the constable of the watch; therefore bear you the lantern. This is your
charge: you shall comprehend all vagrom men; you are to bid any man stand,
in the Prince's name. If 'a will not stand, why then take no note of him, but
let him go, and presently call the rest of the watch together and thank God          5
you are rid of a knave. You shall also make no noise in the streets; for, for the
watch to babble and to talk is most tolerable and not to be endur'd. Rather
you [should] sleep than talk, for I cannot see how sleeping should offend—only
have a care that your bills be not stol'n. Well, you are to call at all the alehouses,
and bid those that are drunk get them to bed. If they will not, why then let         10
them alone till they are sober. If they make you not then the better answer,
you may say they are not the men you took them for. If you meet a thief, you
may suspect him, by virtue of your office, to be no true man; and, for such kind
of men, the less you meddle or make with them, why, the more is for your
honesty. If you know him to be a thief, by your office you may lay hands on        15
him; but I think they that touch pitch will be defil'd. The most peaceable way
for you, if you do take a thief, is to let him show himself what he is and steal
out of your company. If you hear a child cry in the night, you must call to the
nurse and bid her still it. If the nurse be asleep and will not hear you, why then
depart in peace, and let the child wake her with crying; for the ewe that will       20
not hear her lamb when it baes will never answer a calf when he bleats. This is
the end of the charge: you, constable, are to present the Prince's own person.
If you meet the Prince in the night, you may stay him—five shillings to one on
't with any man that knows his statues, you may stay him—marry, not without
the Prince be willing, for indeed, the watch ought to offend no man, and it is an    25
offense to stay a man against his will. Ha, ah, ha! Well, masters, good night. An
there be any matter of weight chances, call up me. Keep your fellows' counsels
and your own, and good night. Adieu. Be vigitant, I beseech you.

**1 senseless** (Dogberry's malapropism for "sensible")   **2–3 This…charge**
these are your instructions   **3 comprehend** (i.e., "apprehend")   **vagrom**
(i.e., "vagrant")   **stand** stop   **7 tolerable** (i.e., "intolerable")   **9 bills**
hooked blades or axes fastened onto long poles   **11 the better answer** a
more acceptable reply   **13 true** honest   **14 is** it is   **16 touch…defil'd**
(see Ecclesiasticus 13:1)   **19 still** quiet   **21 baes, bleats** (Dogberry has
gotten his baby animal cries confused; in fact it's the calf that baes and the

lamb that bleats.)  **22 present** represent  **23 stay** detain  **24 statues**
(i.e., "statutes")  **26 An** if  **27 chances** (that) comes up, occurs
**28 vigitant** (i.e., "vigilant")

(5)                              **LEONATO**                        [V.1.3]

SCENE: Before Leonato's house

*{Distraught over his daughter's recent public humiliation, Leonato lashes out when his brother Antonio suggests that he try to put the whole unfortunate affair behind him.}*

| | |
|---|---|
| 1 | I pray thee, cease thy counsel, |
| | Which falls into mine ears as profitless |
| | As water in a sieve. Give not me counsel, |
| | Nor let no comforter delight mine ear |
| 5 | But such a one whose wrongs do suit with mine. |
| | Bring me a father that so lov'd his child, |
| | Whose joy of her is overwhelm'd like mine, |
| | And bid him speak of patience; |
| | Measure his woe the length and breadth of mine, |
| 10 | And let it answer every strain for strain, |
| | And thus for thus, and such a grief for such, |
| | In every lineament, branch, shape, and form; |
| | If such a one will smile and stroke his beard, |
| | Bid sorrow wag, cry "hem!" when he should groan, |
| 15 | Patch grief with proverbs, make misfortune drunk |
| | With candle-wasters, bring him yet to me, |
| | And I of him will gather patience. |
| | But there is no such man. For, brother, men |
| | Can counsel and speak comfort to that grief |
| 20 | Which they themselves not feel; but, tasting it, |
| | Their counsel turns to passion, which before |
| | Would give preceptial med'cine to rage, |
| | Fetter strong madness in a silken thread, |
| | Charm ache with air and agony with words. |
| 25 | No, no, 'tis all men's office to speak patience |
| | To those that wring under the load of sorrow, |
| | But no man's virtue nor sufficiency |
| | To be so moral when he shall endure |
| | The like himself. Therefore give me no counsel. |
| 30 | For there was never yet philosopher |

That could endure the toothache patiently,
However they may have writ the style of gods
And made a push at chance and sufferance.

**4 delight** (attempt to) soothe, please   **5 wrongs** injuries, losses   **suit with match**   **9 Measure his woe** let his woe match in size and scope   **10 strain** deep feeling, strong emotion   **12 lineament** feature   **14 wag** move on   **cry "hem!"** merely clear his throat   **15 patch** cover over   **drunk** insensible to pain, numb   **16 candle-wasters** those who waste candles with late night study (such as moral philosophers)   **22 preceptial med'cine** treatment consisting merely of axioms and precepts   **23 Fetter** restrain   **24 air** breath (i.e., mere words)   **25 all men's office** every man's proper function   **26 wring** writhe   **27 sufficiency** ability   **28 moral** prone to moralizing   **32 writ** written in   **33 made...at** faced up to, withstood   **sufferance** suffering

## Alternates

Leonato       [IV.i.120–143]
Friar Francis   [IV.i.200–243]

# OTHELLO

Othello and Desdemona fell in love and were secretly married, much to the chagrin of the bride's father, Brabantio. Othello's subsequent appearance before the Duke of Venice to defend his conduct is interrupted by news of an impending attack on Cyprus by the Turks. The Moor is sent to defend the island, and Desdemona is permitted to accompany him.

Enter Iago. Recently passed over for promotion to lieutenant in favor of the dashing Cassio, Iago vowed revenge on all concerned. Through a series of intricate machinations, he manages to make good on his word. First he secures Cassio's professional disgrace by getting the lieutenant drunk while on duty. Next, Iago contrives a plot to convince Othello that his wife and Cassio are having an affair.

While Cassio manages to survive an attempt on his life by Roderigo (a dupe of Iago's who also loves Desdemona), Othello's beloved wife is not so lucky. Consumed by jealousy, the Moor slinks into Desdemona's bedchamber and smothers her in her sleep.

When Iago's villainy is finally revealed, an enraged Othello attempts to slay him, but failing that, slays himself instead. Iago is then arrested and led off to his just rewards.

**OTHELLO,** a Moorish noble and officer

**BRABANTIO,** a senator, father to Desdemona

**CASSIO,** lieutenant to Othello

**IAGO,** ensign to Othello

**RODERIGO,** unsuccessful suitor to Desdemona

**DESDEMONA,** wife to Othello

**EMILIA,** wife to Iago

(1)                    **OTHELLO**                    [I.III.76]

SCENE: A chamber of Venice's Senate House

*{Brabantio was incensed by his daughter's elopement with Othello—so much
so that he accused the Moor of beguiling his daughter with witchcraft and love
potions. Now Othello gets to have his say. Having been summoned before the
Duke of Venice, he confidently steps forward to defend his actions.}* [Line 24
also makes for an effective starting point.]

Most potent, grave, and reverend signiors,                      1
My very noble and approv'd good masters;
That I have ta'en away this old man's daughter,
It is most true; true, I have married her.
The very head and front of my offending                         5
Hath this extent, no more. Rude am I in my speech,
And little bless'd with the soft phrase of peace;
For since these arms of mine had seven years' pith,
Till now some nine moons wasted, they have us'd
Their dearest action in the tented field;                       10
And little of this great world can I speak
More than pertains to feats of broil and battle,
And therefore little shall I grace my cause
In speaking for myself. Yet, by your gracious patience,
I will a round unvarnish'd tale deliver                         15
Of my whole course of love; what drugs, what charms,
What conjuration, and what mighty magic—
For such proceeding I am charg'd withal—
I won his daughter. As truly as to heaven
I do confess the vices of my blood,                             20
So justly to your grave ears I'll present
How I did thrive in this fair lady's love,
And she in mine.
Her father lov'd me, oft invited me;
Still question'd me the story of my life,                        25
From year to year; the battles, sieges, fortunes,
That I have pass'd.
I ran it through, even from my boyish days
To th' very moment that he bade me tell it,
Wherein I spoke of most disastrous chances,                     30
Of moving accidents by flood and field,
Of hair-breadth scapes i' th' imminent deadly breach,
Of being taken by the insolent foe
And sold to slavery, of my redemption thence,

35    And portance in my travels' history;
      Wherein of antres vast and deserts idle,
      Rough quarries, rocks, and hills whose heads touch heaven,
      It was my hint to speak—such was my process—
      And of the Cannibals that each other eat,
40    The Anthropophagi, and men whose heads
      Do grow beneath their shoulders. This to hear
      Would Desdemona seriously incline;
      But still the house-affairs would draw her thence,
      Which ever as she could with haste dispatch
45    She'd come again, and with a greedy ear
      Devour up my discourse. Which I observing,
      Took once a pliant hour, and found good means
      To draw from her a prayer of earnest heart
      That I would all my pilgrimage dilate,
50    Whereof by parcels she had something heard,
      But not intentively. I did consent,
      And often did beguile her of her tears,
      When I did speak of some distressful stroke
      That my youth suffer'd. My story being done,
55    She gave me for my pains a world of sighs.
      She swore, in faith, 'twas strange, 'twas passing strange,
      'Twas pitiful, 'twas wondrous pitiful,
      She wish'd she had not heard it, yet she wish'd
      That heaven had made her such a man. She thank'd me,
60    And bade me, if I had a friend that lov'd her,
      I should but teach him how to tell my story,
      And that would woo her. Upon this hint I spake.
      She lov'd me for the dangers I had pass'd,
      And I lov'd her that she did pity them.
65    This only is the witchcraft I have us'd.
      Here comes the lady; let her witness it.

**1 grave** respected, worthy  **signiors** gentlemen   **2 approv'd** tested and proved   **5 head and front** height and breadth, sum total   **6 Rude** rough, unpolished   **8 pith** strength   **9 Till … wasted** Till nine months ago (during which time he's apparently been away from the battlefield)  **us'd** expended **10 dearest** most valued, most significant  **tented** (Scores of tents housing men and supplies was a common sight on the battlefield.)  **12 broil** brawling   **15 round** honest, straightforward   **18 proceeding** actions **withal** with   **20 the … blood** my human failings   **21 justly** truthfully **25 Still** continually   **27 pass'd** experienced, endured   **31 accidents** events **flood** sea   **32 scapes** escapes   **imminent deadly** death-threatening **breach** a trench or other gap that is made in a fortification   **35 portance** behavior, conduct   **36 antres** caverns   **idle** barren   **38 hint** opportunity, cue   **process** story, course of events   **40 Anthropophagi** man-eaters

**42 seriously incline** be earnestly disposed   **47 pliant hour** opportune moment   **49 dilate** relate in detail   **50 by parcels** in a piecemeal fashion **51 intentively** attentively   **54 my youth** in my youth I   **56 faith** truth **passing** extremely   **66 witness** confirm, testify to

(2)                          IAGO                          [I.III.319]

SCENE: A chamber in Venice's Senate House

*{Roderigo is so distraught over his failure to win Desdemona's affections that he is contemplating drowning himself. For strictly self-serving reasons, Iago takes it upon himself to buoy the poor man's spirits.}*

Virtue? A fig! 'Tis in ourselves that we are thus or thus. Our bodies are our     1
gardens, to the which our wills are gardeners; so that if we will plant nettles or
sow lettuce, set hyssop and weed up thyme, supply it with one gender of herbs
or distract it with many, either to have it sterile with idleness or manur'd with
industry—why, the power and corrigible authority of this lies in our wills. If the     5
balance of our lives had not one scale of reason to poise another of sensuality,
the blood and baseness of our natures would conduct us to most prepost'rous
conclusions. But we have reason to cool our raging motions, our carnal stings,
our unbitted lusts, whereof I take this that you call love to be a sect or scion.
It is merely a lust of the blood and a permission of the will. Come, be a man.     10
Drown thyself? Drown cats and blind puppies. I have profess'd me thy friend,
and I confess me knit to thy deserving with cables of perdurable toughness. I
could never better stead thee than now. Put money in thy purse. Follow thou
the wars; defeat thy favor with an usurp'd beard. I say, put money in thy purse.
It cannot be long that Desdemona should continue her love to the Moor—put     15
money in thy purse—nor he his to her. It was a violent commencement in
her, and thou shalt see an answerable sequestration—put but money in thy
purse. These Moors are changeable in their wills—fill thy purse with money.
The food that to him now is as luscious as locusts shall be to him shortly as
bitter as coloquintida. She must change for youth; when she is sated with his     20
body, she will find the error of her choice. She must have change, she must.
Therefore put money in thy purse. If thou wilt needs damn thyself, do it a more
delicate way than drowning. Make all the money thou canst. If sanctimony and
a frail vow betwixt an erring barbarian and a super-subtle Venetian be not
too hard for my wits and all the tribe of hell, thou shalt enjoy her. Therefore     25
make money. A pox of drowning thyself! It is clean out of the way. Seek thou
rather to be hang'd in compassing thy joy than to be drown'd and go without
her. Go, make money. I have told thee often, and I retell thee again and again,
I hate the Moor. My cause is hearted; thine hath no less reason. Let us be
conjunctive in our revenge against him. If thou canst cuckold him, thou dost     30

thyself a pleasure, me a sport. There are many events in the womb of time which will be deliver'd. Traverse, go, provide thy money. We will have more of this tomorrow. Adieu.

1 **Virtue** (Roderigo has just stated that it is simply not in his virtue (i.e., nature) to overcome this infatuation he has with Desdemona.) **fig** i.e., worthless or contemptible thing    3 **set** put in, plant **hyssop** an herb **weed up** clear the weeds from **supply it** i.e., plant the garden **gender** sort 4 **distract it** divide it up **with idleness** for lack of cultivation    5 **corrigible authority of** ability to correct    6 **poise** counterbalance    7 **blood** carnal appetite    8 **motions** desires, emotions    9 **unbitted** unbridled **sect or scion** offshoot    10 **It** i.e., love    11 **Drown cats** i.e., better that you should drown cats    12 **knit** committed, bound closely **thy deserving** that which you deserve, your just reward **perdurable** lasting, durable    13 **stead** be of use to, serve **Put...purse** (For some time now Iago has had easy access to Roderigo's purse, ostensibly to facilitate the winning of Desdemona's affections [see I.i.2–3]. The truth is, though, that Roderigo has been swindled; gold and jewels intended as gifts for Desdemona were in fact kept by Iago for himself [see V.i.14–17].)    14 **defeat thy favor** alter your appearance **usurp'd** false    16 **violent commencement** emotional undertaking, rash action    17 **answerable sequestration** i.e., correspondingly abrupt separation    19 **locusts** fruit of the carob tree    20 **coloquintida** a bitter apple used as a purgative **for** on account of    23 **delicate** noble, refined **Make** raise **sanctimony** the bond of matrimony    24 **erring** vagabond, wandering **super-subtle** highly refined and delicate    26 **pox of** curse on **clean** completely    27 **compassing** obtaining, achieving    29 **hearted** rooted in my heart, deeply felt    30 **conjunctive** united    31 **sport** amusement    32 **Traverse** march, onward (a military term)

(3)                          IAGO                          [I.III.383]

SCENE: A chamber in Venice's Senate House

*{Iago has just finished tranquilizing Roderigo (see preceding entry), and now contemplates his next foul scheme—a plot designed to convince Othello that Cassio is dallying with his Desdemona.}*

1    Thus do I ever make my fool my purse;
     For I mine own gain'd knowledge should profane
     If I would time expend with such a snipe
     But for my sport and profit. I hate the Moor,
5    And it is thought abroad that 'twixt my sheets
     H'as done my office. I know not if 't be true;
     But I, for mere suspicion in that kind,

Will do as if for surety. He holds me well;
The better shall my purpose work on him.
Cassio's a proper man. Let me see now:                                    10
To get his place and to plume up my will
In double knavery—How, how?—Let's see:
After some time, to abuse Othello's ears
That he is too familiar with his wife.
He hath a person and a smooth dispose                                     15
To be suspected, fram'd to make women false.
The Moor is of a free and open nature,
That thinks men honest that but seem to be so,
And will as tenderly be led by th' nose
As asses are.                                                             20
I have 't—it is engend'red. Hell and night
Must bring this monstrous birth to the world's light.

**1 fool** (referring to Roderigo)   **3 snipe** simpleton   **5 it...abroad** there is
widespread rumor   **6 office** business, assigned duty   **8 do...surety** act as
if I knew it for a fact   **holds me well** thinks well of me   **10 proper**
handsome   **11 plume...will** glorify myself   **14 he** (referring to Cassio)
**15 dispose** manner   **16 fram'd** designed   **17 free** noble, generous
**19 tenderly** readily   **21 It is engend'red** the plot is conceived

(4)                              IAGO                          [II.1.214]

SCENE: An open place near a harbor in Cyprus

*{Iago's machinations continue unabated as he attempts to persuade Roderigo
that it is the handsome young Cassio, and not Othello, who is his chief rival for
Desdemona's love.}*

If thou be'st valiant—as, they say, base men being in love have then a nobil-    1
ity in their natures more than is native to them—list me, and let thy soul be
instructed. Mark me with what violence she first lov'd the Moor, but for bragging and telling her fantastical lies. And will she love him still for prating? Let not
thy discreet heart think it. Her eye must be fed; and what delight shall she have    5
to look on the devil? When the blood is made dull with the act of sport, there
should be, again to inflame it and to give satiety a fresh appetite, loveliness in
favor, sympathy in years, manners, and beauties—all which the Moor is defective in. Now, for want of these requir'd conveniences, her delicate tenderness
will find itself abus'd, begin to heave the gorge, disrelish and abhor the Moor.    10
Very nature will instruct her in it and compel her to some second choice. Now,
sir, this granted—as it is a most pregnant and unforc'd position—who stands
so eminent in the degree of this fortune as Cassio does? A knave very voluble;

15    no further conscionable than in putting on the mere form of civil and humane
seeming, for the better compassing of his salt and most hidden loose affection?
Why, none, why, none—a slipper and subtle knave, a finder of occasions, that
has an eye can stamp and counterfeit advantages, though true advantage never
present itself; a devilish knave. Besides, the knave is handsome, young, and
hath all those requisites in him that folly and green minds look after. A pestilent
20    complete knave, and the woman hath found him already. Didst thou not see her
paddle with the palm of his hand? Didst not mark that? They met so near with
their lips that their breaths embrac'd together. Villainous thoughts, Roderigo!
When these mutualities so marshal the way, hard at hand comes the master
and main exercise, th' incorporate conclusion.

**2 list** listen to   **3 violence** passion  **she** (referring to Desdemona)  **but**
simply, just   **4 still** always  **prating** speaking boastfully   **5 discreet**
discerning   **6 blood** sensual appetite  **sport** sexual intercourse   **8 favor**
appearance  **sympathy** similarity   **9 conveniences** compatibilities
**10 heave the gorge** feel nauseous   **12 pregnant and unforc'd** obvious
and believable   **13 voluble** well-spoken glib   **14 humane** courteous
**15 compassing** winning, achieving  **salt** lecherous, wanton  **loose**
**affection** undisciplined passion   **16 slipper** slippery  **occasions**
opportunities   **17 stamp...advantages** create promising situations (as in
sexual opportunities)   **19 folly** wantonness  **green** youthful   **20 complete**
accomplished  **found** taken note of   **21 paddle with** fondle, caress
**23 mutualities** intimate exchanges  **hard at hand** right behind
**23–24 the...exercise** i.e., the sexual act   **24 incorporate** carnal

(5)                          I A G O                          [II.1.286]

SCENE: An open place near a harbor in Cyprus

*{Having successfully duped Roderigo (see preceding entry), Iago pauses to rejoice
in and reflect upon his sinister methods.}*

1    That Cassio loves her, I do well believe 't:
That she loves him, 'tis apt and of great credit.
The Moor—howbeit that I endure him not—
Is of a constant, loving, noble nature,
5    And I dare think he'll prove to Desdemona
A most dear husband. Now, I do love her too,
Not out of absolute lust, though peradventure
I stand accountant for as great as sin,
But partly led to diet my revenge,
10    For that I do suspect the lusty Moor
Hath leap'd into my seat; the thought whereof

Doth, like a poisonous mineral, gnaw my inwards.
And nothing can or shall content my soul
Till I am even'd with him, wife for wife;
Or failing so, yet that I put the Moor                               15
At least into a jealousy so strong
That judgment cannot cure. Which thing to do,
If this poor trash of Venice, whom I trash
For his quick hunting, stand the putting on,
I'll have our Michael Cassio on the hip,                             20
Abuse him to the Moor in the rank garb—
For I fear Cassio with my night-cap too—
Make the Moor thank me, love me, and reward me
For making him egregiously an ass
And practicing upon his peace and quiet,                             25
Even to madness. 'Tis here, but yet confus'd.
Knavery's plain face is never seen till us'd.

**1 her** (referring to Desdemona)   **2 apt** natural, likely  **of great credit**
highly credible   **3 howbeit...not** although I personally cannot tolerate him
**7 peradventure** perhaps   **8 accountant** accountable   **9 diet** feed
**11 leap'd...seat** assumed what is properly my role (Without any clear
reason, Iago believes Othello may have cuckolded him.)   **12 inwards** innards
**18 poor...Venice** (referring to Roderigo)  **trash** restrain, check (It is not
certain what imagery is intended here. To "trash" a hunting dog meant to
hang weights on his back, thereby keeping him from hunting too quickly and
[as with Roderigo?] making him even more eager to capture his prey.)
**19 stand...on** responds appropriately when I urge him to fight (see
II.i.263–280)   **20 on the hip** at a disadvantage, at my mercy (The term
comes from the sport of wrestling.)   **21 Abuse** slander  **the rank garb** an
offensive manner   **22 night-cap** i.e., bed-partner, wife   **25 practicing**
**upon** plotting against

(6)                        OTHELLO                      [III.III.335]

SCENE: A garden outside Othello's castle

*{Iago's scheme to smear Desdemona and Cassio (see preceding entry) has almost*
*reached fruition. Here, a tormented Othello lashes out at Iago as he grapples with*
*both his need to know the truth and his desire to remain blissfully ignorant.}*

Avaunt! Be gone! Thou hast set me on the rack.                       1
I swear 'tis better to be much abus'd
Than but to know 't a little.
What sense had I of her stol'n hours of lust?

5    I saw 't not, thought it not, it harm'd not me.
     I slept the next night well, fed well, was free and merry;
     I found not Cassio's kisses on her lips.
     He that is robb'd, not wanting what is stol'n,
     Let him not know 't, and he's not robb'd at all.
10   I had been happy if the general camp,
     Pioners and all, had tasted her sweet body,
     So I had nothing known. O, now, forever
     Farewell the tranquil mind! Farewell content!
     Farewell the plumed troop, and the big wars
15   That makes ambition virtue! O, farewell!
     Farewell the neighing steed, and the shrill trump,
     The spirit-stirring drum, th' ear-piercing fife,
     The royal banner, and all quality,
     Pride, pomp and circumstance of glorious war!
20   And O you mortal engines, whose rude throats
     Th' immortal Jove's dread clamors counterfeit,
     Farewell! Othello's occupation's gone.
     Villain, be sure thou prove my love a whore!
     Be sure of it! Give me the ocular proof,
25   Or, by the worth of mine eternal soul,
     Thou hadst been better have been born a dog
     Than answer my wak'd wrath! Make me to see 't,
     That the probation bear no hinge nor loop
     To hang a doubt on; or woe upon thy life!
30   If thou dost slander her and torture me,
     Never pray more; abandon all remorse;
     On horror's head horrors accumulate;
     Do deeds to make heaven weep, all earth amaz'd;
     For nothing canst thou to damnation add
35   Greater than that. Her name, that was as fresh
     As Dian's visage, is now begrim'd and black
     As mine own face. If there be cords, or knives,
     Poison, or fire, or suffocating streams,
     I'll not endure it. Would I were satisfied!

**1 Avaunt** away   **6 free** carefree   **8 wanting** missing   **11 Pioners** the
lowest grade of soldiers, employed primarily in jobs such as digging and
mining   **16 trump** trumpet, bugle   **19 Pride** magnificence **circumstance**
ceremony   **20 mortal engines** deadly instruments of war, cannons **rude**
brutal, discordant   **21 counterfeit** imitate, copy   **24 ocular** visible
**28 probation** proof   **31 remorse** compassion   **32 horrors accumulate**
heap on even more atrocities   **33 all** i.e., all those inhabiting   **34 to** to your
**36 Dian** Diana, the moon goddess and goddess of chastity **visage**

appearance, face   **37 If** even if   **39 it** i.e., the slandering of her name and reputation   **satisfied** convinced, made certain

(7)                                    IAGO                                    [III.III.391]

SCENE: A garden outside Othello's castle

*{Iago responds to Othello's demand for unmistakable proof of Desdemona's infidelity (see preceding entry).}*

| | |
|---|---:|
| I see, sir, you are eaten up with passion. | 1 |
| I do repent me that I put it to you. | |
| You would be satisfied? But how, my lord? | |
| Would you, the supervisor, grossly gape on? | |
| Behold her topp'd? | 5 |
| It were a tedious difficulty, I think, | |
| To bring them to that prospect; damn them then, | |
| If ever mortal eyes do see them bolster | |
| More than their own. What then? How then? | |
| What shall I say? Where's satisfaction? | 10 |
| It is impossible you should see this, | |
| Were they as prime as goats, as hot as monkeys, | |
| As salt as wolves in pride, and fools as gross | |
| As ignorance made drunk. But yet, I say, | |
| If imputation and strong circumstances | 15 |
| Which lead directly to the door of truth | |
| Will give you satisfaction, you might have 't. | |
| I do not like this office; | |
| But sith I am ent'red in this cause so far, | |
| Prick'd to 't by foolish honesty and love, | |
| I will go on. I lay with Cassio lately; | 20 |
| And, being troubled with a raging tooth, | |
| I could not sleep. There are a kind of men | |
| So loose of soul that in their sleeps will mutter | |
| Their affairs. One of this kind is Cassio. | 25 |
| In sleep I heard him say, "Sweet Desdemona, | |
| Let us be wary, let us hide our loves." | |
| And then, sir, would he gripe and wring my hand; | |
| Cry, "O sweet creature!" and then kiss me hard, | |
| As if he pluck'd up kisses by the roots | 30 |
| That grew upon my lips; then laid his leg | |

Over my thigh, and sigh'd, and kiss'd, and then
Cried, "Cursed fate that gave thee to the Moor!"
[Though] this was but his dream, it may help to
35    Thicken other proofs that do demonstrate thinly.
But be wise. Yet we see nothing done.
She may be honest yet.

**3 satisfied** convinced, made certain (of Desdemona's infidelity)
**4 supervisor** observer, onlooker  **grossly** stupidly  **5 topp'd** copulated
with  **7 prospect** scene, situation  **7–9 damn . . . own** i.e., to condemn
them only if human eyes other than their own see them in bed together
**11 see** (manage to) witness  **12 prime** lustful  **13 salt** lecherous  **pride**
heat  **15 imputation** report  **18 office** task  **19 sith** since  **24 loose**
undisciplined, lacking in restraint  **28 gripe** grab, grip  **35 Thicken**
substantiate, bolster

(8)                                OTHELLO                        [V.II.I]

SCENE: A bedchamber in Othello's castle

*{Othello has entered Desdemona's room, where she lies fast asleep. Though he's
come here to do away with his beloved for her supposed infidelity, it's evident
that the Moor is very much a torn man.}*

1    It is the cause, it is the cause, my soul.
Let me not name it to you, you chaste stars!
It is the cause. Yet I'll not shed her blood,
Nor scar that whiter skin of hers than snow,
5    And smooth as monumental alabaster.
Yet she must die, else she'll betray more men.
Put out the light, and then put out the light.
If I quench thee, thou flaming minister,
I can again thy former light restore,
10    Should I repent me; but once put out thy light,
Thou cunning'st pattern of excelling nature,
I know not where is that Promethean heat
That can thy light relume. When I have pluck'd the rose,
I cannot give it vital growth again;
15    It needs must wither. I'll smell thee on the tree.
[*He draws near, and kisses her.*]
O balmy breath, that dost almost persuade
Justice to break her sword! One more, one more.

Be thus when thou art dead, and I will kill thee,
And love thee after. One more, and that's the last.                    20
So sweet was ne'er so fatal. I must weep,
But they are cruel tears. This sorrow's heavenly;
It strikes where it doth love. She wakes.

**1 cause** i.e., the cause of justice (Othello believes that the infidelity he
ascribes to Desdemona is tantamount to a crime; a transgression which, even
if he were to set aside the matter of his personal honor, he would still feel
duty-bound to punish.)   **7 the light ... light** the candle, and then end her
life   **11 cunning'st** most marvelous   **12 Promethean heat** life-giving fire
(alludes to the fire that Prometheus stole from heaven)   **13 relume** rekindle
**17 balmy** delightfully fragrant   **22–23 This ... love** (an allusion to the
biblical passage found at Hebrews 12:6)

### ALTERNATES

| | |
|---|---|
| Iago | [I.i.41–65] |
| Roderigo | [I.i.120–140] |
| Brabantio | [I.ii.62–81] |
| Othello | [III.iii.258–279] |
| Othello | [IV.ii.34–81] |
| Othello | [V.ii.259–282] |

# PERICLES

The trouble begins when Pericles realizes that the answer to a riddle posed by King Antiochus lies in the King's incestuous relationship with his daughter. Afraid of what having such knowledge might mean to his health, Pericles flees his native Tyre—landing first in Tharsus, before eventually settling in Pentapolis.

Shortly after marrying Thaisa, daughter to the King of Pentapolis, Pericles learns that Antiochus has died. Figuring it safe to return home, Pericles and the pregnant Thaisa set sail for Tyre. While at sea, Thaisa apparently dies while giving birth to a daughter, Marina. Thaisa's body is set adrift in a casket and eventually washes ashore in Ephesus, where wise old Cerimon manages to revive her. Pericles, meanwhile, stops by Tharsus to ask that Dionyza and Cleon raise his daughter Marina, and then continues on his way to Tyre.

Time passes, and the graces of an adolescent Marina come to so eclipse those of Dionyza's own daughter that Dionyza decides she must have Marina killed. But before the deed can be done, Marina is captured by pirates and ends up in a brothel in Mytilene. Rather than succumb there to a life of disrepute, Marina instead manages to become a noted teacher of the arts.

Eventually, Pericles and Marina find each other when Pericles happens to land in Mytilene. A vision Pericles has then compels him and Marina to travel to Ephesus, where the two are reunited with Thaisa, and everyone lives happily ever after.

**ANTIOCHUS,** King of Antioch
**PERICLES,** Prince of Tyre
**CLEON,** Governor of Tharsus
**CERIMON,** a lord of Ephesus

**DIONYZA,** wife to Cleon
**THAISA,** wife to Pericles
**MARINA,** daughter to Pericles and Thaisa

(1)                    PERICLES                [I.i.121]

SCENE: Antiochus's palace

*{Before he could take King Antiochus's daughter for his bride, Pericles first had to solve the King's riddle. Unfortunately, Pericles did just that. Astutely deciphering the brainteaser as a revelation of the incestuous relationship between his would-be wife and her father, Pericles now takes a moment alone to weigh carefully his next move.}*

How courtesy would seem to cover sin,                      1
When what is done is like an hypocrite,
The which is good in nothing but in sight!
If it be true that I interpret false,
Then were it certain you were not so bad                   5
As with foul incest to abuse your soul;
Where now you're both a father and a son,
By your uncomely claspings with your child—
Which pleasures fits a husband, not a father—
And she an eater of her mother's flesh,                   10
By the defiling of her parent's bed;
And both like serpents are, who, though they feed
On sweetest flowers, yet they poison breed.
Antioch, farewell, for wisdom sees those men
Blush not in actions blacker than the night              15
Will 'schew no course to keep them from the light.
One sin, I know, another doth provoke;
Murder's as near to lust as flame to smoke.
Poison and treason are the hands of sin,
Ay, and the targets to put off the shame.                20
Then lest my life be cropp'd to keep you clear,
By flight I'll shun the danger which I fear.

**1 courtesy** (In the interest of self-preservation, Pericles opted not to disclose the riddle's solution. Antiochus, fully aware that Pericles was on to him, "courteously" offered him another forty days to unravel the puzzle.) **would seem** falsely attempts   **3 sight** mere appearance   **8 uncomely** unseemly   **claspings** embraces   **10 eater...flesh** (The first two lines of the riddle read: "I am no viper, yet I feed / On mother's flesh which did me breed." It was thought that a viper's newborn ate their way out of the mother's body.)   **14 sees those men** understands that those men who **16 'schew** eschew   **20 targets** shields   **put off** fend off, deflect **21 cropp'd** cut off   **clear** undetected

(2)                          CERIMON                          [III.ii.49]

SCENE: Cerimon's house

*{During a storm at sea, Thaisa went into labor and apparently died during childbirth. Afterward, a sealed casket containing Thaisa was set adrift, eventually washing ashore near the home of Cerimon. As a man learned in the art of medicine, Cerimon's curiosity is aroused when his servants enter bearing the chest.}*

| | |
|---|---|
| 1 | What's that? Set it down, let's look upon it. |
| | 'Tis wondrous heavy. Wrench it open straight. |
| | If the sea's stomach be o'ercharg'd with gold, |
| | 'Tis a good constraint of fortune it belches upon us. |
| 5 | [*The chest is opened.*] |
| | O you most potent gods! What's here? A corse? |
| | Shrouded in cloth of state, balmed and entreasured |
| | With full bags of spices! A passport too! |
| | Apollo, perfect me in the characters! |
| 10 | [*Reads from a scroll.*] |
| | "Here I give to understand, |
| | If e'er this coffin drives a-land, |
| | I, King Pericles, have lost |
| | This queen, worth all our mundane cost. |
| 15 | Who finds her, give her burying; |
| | She was the daughter of a king. |
| | Besides this treasure for a fee, |
| | The gods requite his charity!" |
| | If thou livest, Pericles, thou hast a heart |
| 20 | That even cracks for woe! This chanc'd tonight, |
| | For look how fresh she looks! They were too rough |
| | That threw her in the sea. Make a fire within. |
| | Fetch hither all my boxes in my closet. |
| | Death may usurp on nature many hours, |
| 25 | And yet the fire of life kindle again |
| | The o'erpress'd spirits. I heard of an Egyptian |
| | That had nine hours lien dead, |
| | Who was by good appliance recovered. |
| | [*A servant enters with boxes, cloths and fire.*] |
| 30 | Well said, well said! The fire and cloths. |
| | The rough and woeful music that we have, |
| | Cause it to sound, beseech you. [*Music is heard.*] |
| | The viol once more. How thou stirr'st, thou block! |
| | The music there!—I pray you, give her air. |

Gentlemen, this queen will live! Nature awakes;                    35
A warmth breathes out of her. She hath not been
Entranc'd above five hours. See how she gins
To blow into life's flower again! Behold,
Her eyelids, cases to those heavenly jewels
Which Pericles hath lost, begin to part                            40
Their fringes of bright gold. The diamonds
Of a most praised water doth appear,
To make the world twice rich. Live, and make
Us weep to hear your fate, fair creature,
Rare as you seem to be.                                            45

**2 straight** straightaway, at once   **3 o'ercharg'd** overloaded   **4 constraint**
forced or compulsive act (such as a belch)   **6 corse** corpse   **7 of state** i.e.,
befitting royalty   **balmed** anointed with fragrant oils   **8 passport** (Pericles
enclosed in the casket a scroll identifying Thaisa. It is to this "passport" that
Cerimon refers.)   **9 perfect . . . characters** enable me to read the words
(Apollo was the patron of scholars.)   **14 mundane cost** worldly treasures
**17 this treasure** (refers to jewels that Peicles also enclosed in the casket)
**18 his** i.e., he who buries Thaisa   **20 even** quite, fully   **chanc'd** happened
**tonight** last night   **21 rough** hasty   **24 usurp on** encroach upon
**26 o'erpress'd** weighed down, overcome (as with grief or pain)   **27 lien**
lain   **28 good appliance** skillful medical treatment   **recovered** brought
back to life   **30 Well said** well done   **31 rough** unrefined, harsh   **33 viol**
(The viol was a popular stringed instrument of the day, made in various sizes
and played with a bow.)   **How thou stirr'st** how quickly you move (said
ironically)   **37 Entranc'd above** unconscious more than   **gins** begins
**38 blow** blossom   **42 praised water** esteemed luster

# RICHARD II

Unable to settle a dispute between Bolingbroke and Mowbray concerning the Duke of Gloucester's murder, Richard instead elects to exile them. Mowbray is gone for good, while Bolingbroke is banished for six years.

Before long, however, Bolingbroke has returned to England—with a vengeance. His mission is to reclaim lands belonging to his family which Richard unduly seized upon the death of Bolingbroke's father, John of Gaunt.

Shortly after Richard arrives in Wales to squelch an Irish uprising, he learns of Bolingbroke's brazen reappearance on English soil. Fearing the worst, the King retires to nearby Flint Castle, where Bolingbroke and his army soon show up and take Richard into custody.

Once all concerned have resurfaced in London, Richard appears before Bolingbroke and agrees to relinquish the throne. After Bolingbroke is crowned King Henry IV, the new King makes known his desire to see the ex-King eliminated from the scene. Henry's implicit wish is granted when a band of assassins slip into Pomfret Castle and murder Richard in his cell.

**KING RICHARD II**

**JOHN OF GAUNT,** Duke of Lancaster, uncle to King Richard

**BOLINGBROKE,** Duke of Hereford, afterward King Henry IV

**DUKE OF AUMERLE,** An English noble loyal to King Richard

**EARL OF NORTHUMBERLAND,** an English noble in league with Bolingbroke

**BISHOP OF CARLISLE**

**DUCHESS OF GLOUCESTER,** sister-in-law to John of Gaunt

(1)                    **KING RICHARD**              [III.ii.144]

SCENE: The coast of Wales

*{Richard and his followers arrived here intending to quash a minor rebellion in nearby Ireland. The King's spirits were uncharacteristically high upon setting ashore, but soon deteriorate into utter despair when he learns that his key supporters back home have either been subdued or seduced by his archrival, Bolingbroke.}*

Of comfort no man speak!                                          1
Let's talk of graves, of worms, and epitaphs,
Make dust our paper, and with rainy eyes
Write sorrow on the bosom of the earth.
Let's choose executors and talk of wills.                         5
And yet not so, for what can we bequeath
Save our deposed bodies to the ground?
Our lands, our lives, and all are Bolingbroke's,
And nothing can we call our own but death
And that small model of the barren earth                         10
Which serves as paste and cover to our bones.
For God's sake, let us sit upon the ground
And tell sad stories of the death of kings:
How some have been depos'd, some slain in war,
Some haunted by the ghosts they have depos'd,                    15
Some poisoned by their wives, some sleeping kill'd—
All murdered; for within the hollow crown
That rounds the mortal temples of a king
Keeps Death his court, and there the antic sits,
Scoffing his state and grinning at his pomp,                     20
Allowing him a breath, a little scene,
To monarchize, be fear'd, and kill with looks,
Infusing him with self and vain conceit,
As if this flesh which walls about our life
Were brass impregnable; and humor'd thus                         25
Comes at the last and with a little pin
Bores through his castle wall, and farewell king!
Cover your heads, and mock not flesh and blood
With solemn reverence. Throw away respect,
Tradition, form, and ceremonious duty;                           30
For you have but mistook me all this while.
I live with bread like you, feel want,
Taste grief, need friends. Subjected thus,
How can you say to me I am a king?

**3 dust** earth, the ground   **10 model...earth** i.e., mound of dirt that covers a grave, which is shaped like (a "model" of) the body beneath **11 Which** the "model," i.e., the outer body   **paste** piecrust   **15 ghosts** i.e., ghosts of kings   **16 sleeping kill'd** killed in their sleep   **18 rounds** encircles   **19 antic** jester   **20 Scoffing his state** scoffing at the king's regal manner   **pomp** royal splendor   **21 breath** brief moment   **22 monarchize** rule, play the monarch   **23 self** self-importance   **25 humor'd thus** having thus amused himself (referring to Death)   **27 his** i.e., the king's   **28 Cover your heads** i.e., pay no respect (Richard refers to the practice of showing respect by removing one's hat when in the presence of royalty.) **33 Subjected thus** subject to such common human needs and wants as I am

(2)                     KING RICHARD                     [III.iii.72]

SCENE: Before Flint Castle

*{Sequestered inside Flint Castle, a dispirited Richard could only watch as Bolingbroke's forces massed in the fields below. But when Bolingbroke's emissary, the Earl of Northumberland, approaches to negotiate a settlement, Richard summons up what little remains of the old Lancaster fire and puts forth a convincingly bold front.}*

1   We are amaz'd, and thus long have we stood
    To watch the fearful bending of thy knee,
    Because we thought ourself thy lawful king.
    And if we be, how dare thy joints forget
5   To pay their aweful duty to our presence?
    If we be not, show us the hand of God
    That hath dismiss'd us from our stewardship;
    For well we know, no hand of blood and bone
    Can gripe the sacred handle of our scepter,
10  Unless he do profane, steal, or usurp.
    And though you think that all, as you have done,
    Have torn their souls by turning them from us,
    And we are barren and bereft of friends,
    Yet know, my master, God omnipotent,
15  Is mustering in his clouds on our behalf
    Armies of pestilence; and they shall strike
    Your children yet unborn and unbegot,
    That lift your vassal hands against my head
    And threat the glory of my precious crown.
20  Tell Bolingbroke—for yon methinks he stands—
    That every stride he makes upon my land

Is dangerous treason. He is come to open
The purple testament of bleeding war;
But ere the crown he looks for live in peace,
Ten thousand bloody crowns of mothers' sons                    25
Shall ill become the flower of England's face,
Change the complexion of her maid-pale peace
To scarlet indignation, and bedew
Her pastures' grass with faithful English blood.

**1 We are** I am (Richard is employing the royal plural)   **2 watch** watch for
**fearful** deferential   **5 aweful** reverential   **9 gripe** clutch, grip   **14 know**
know that   **18 That** of you that   **19 threat** threaten   **20 yon** yonder, over
there (referring to the fields that surround Flint Castle)   **23 purple**
blood-red   **25 crowns** heads   **26 flower** bloom, beauty   **27 maid-pale**
white-complexioned

(3)                    KING RICHARD                    [III.iii.143]

SCENE: Before Flint Castle

*{As the writing on the wall grows more unmistakable by the minute (see previous
entry), Richard edges closer and closer toward surrender.}*

What must the King do now? Must he submit?                    1
The King shall do it. Must he be depos'd?
The King shall be contented. Must he lose
The name of king? A' God's name, let it go.
I'll give my jewels for a set of beads,                    5
My gorgeous palace for a hermitage,
My gay apparel for an almsman's gown,
My figur'd goblets for a dish of wood,
My scepter for a palmer's walking-staff,
My subjects for a pair of carved saints,                    10
And my large kingdom for a little grave,
A little little grave, an obscure grave;
Or I'll be buried in the king's highway,
Some way of common trade, where subjects' feet
May hourly trample on their sovereign's head;                    15
For on my heart they tread now whilst I live,
And, buried once, why not upon my head?
Aumerle, thou weep'st, my tender-hearted cousin!
We'll make foul weather with despised tears;
Our sighs and they shall lodge the summer corn,                    20
And make a dearth in this revolting land.

Or shall we play the wantons with our woes,
And make some pretty match with shedding tears?
As thus, to drop them still upon one place,
25    Till they have fretted us a pair of graves
Within the earth; and, therein laid, there lies
Two kinsmen digg'd their graves with weeping eyes.
Would not this ill do well? Well, well, I see
I talk but idly, and you laugh at me.
30    Most mighty prince, my Lord Northumberland,
What says King Bolingbroke? Will his Majesty
Give Richard leave to live till Richard die?

**4 A'** in   **5 set of beads** rosary   **7 almsman's** one who lives on charity
**8 figur'd** ornamented   **9 palmer's** pilgrim's   **14 way** road   **trade** traffic,
activity   **18 Aumerle** (The Duke of Aumerle is by Richard's side.)
**20 lodge** beat down, flatten   **corn** i.e., grain   **21 dearth** famine   **22 play
the wantons** sport, frolic   **23 match** contest, game   **24 still** continually
**25 fretted us** worn away for us   **27 digg'd** who dug   **28 ill** suffering, ill
fortune   **31 King, Majesty** (Richard is speaking ironically.)

(4)                    **BISHOP OF CARLISLE**                    [IV.i.115]

SCENE: Westminster Hall

*{Carlisle proves himself a rare commodity around England these days—a man
of both courage and principle. Refusing to simply stand aside while Bolingbroke
ascends the throne unchallenged, the Bishop steps forth from the toadies around
him and boldly speaks his mind.}*

1    Worst in this royal presence may I speak,
Yet best beseeming me to speak the truth.
Would God that any in this noble presence
Were enough noble to be upright judge
5    Of noble Richard! Then true noblesse would
Learn him forbearance from so foul a wrong.
What subject can give sentence on his king?
And who sits here that is not Richard's subject?
Thieves are not judg'd but they are by to hear,
10    Although apparent guilt be seen in them;
And shall the figure of God's majesty,
His captain, steward, deputy elect,
Anointed, crowned, planted many years,
Be judg'd by subject and inferior breath,
15    And he himself not present? O forfend it, God,

That in a Christian climate, souls refin'd
Should show so heinous, black, obscene a deed!
I speak to subjects, and a subject speaks,
Stirr'd up by God, thus boldly for his king.
My Lord of Hereford here, whom you call king,                    20
Is a foul traitor to proud Hereford's king.
And if you crown him, let me prophesy:
The blood of English shall manure the ground,
And future ages groan for this foul act;
Peace shall go sleep with Turks and infidels,                    25
And in this seat of peace tumultuous wars
Shall kin with kin and kind with kind confound;
Disorder, horror, fear, and mutiny
Shall here inhabit, and this land be call'd
The field of Golgotha and dead men's skulls.                     30
O, if you raise this house against this house,
It will the woefullest division prove
That ever fell upon this cursed earth.
Prevent it, resist it, let it not be so,
Lest child, child's children, cry against you "woe!"            35

1 **Worst...speak** though it may be that I speak here as the lowest in rank among this noble company   2 **Yet...me** yet it best becomes me (as a clergyman)   4 **upright** righteous, moral   5 **noblesse** nobility   6 **Learn** teach   **forbearance** to refrain   9 **by to hear** present to hear (testimony given against them)   10 **apparent** clear, obvious   13 **planted** established (as king) for   15 **forfend** forbid   16 **climate** country   18 **subjects** i.e., of Richard's   21 **Hereford's** (referring here to the county, not the lord)   23 **manure** fertilize   27 **with** by means of   **confound** destroy   30 **Golgotha** site outside of ancient Jerusalem where Christ was crucified   31 **house...house** (referring to the houses of Lancaster and York, respectively)

(5)                    **KING RICHARD**                    [IV.i.162]

SCENE: Westminster Hall

*{Figuratively and literally, Bolingbroke has just assumed the English throne. All that remains is the mere formality of King Richard's official abdication. Having been summoned for that very reason, Richard enters and addresses the court.}*

Alack, why am I sent for to a king                               1
Before I have shook off the regal thoughts
Wherewith I reign'd? I hardly yet have learn'd

To insinuate, flatter, bow, and bend my knee.
5      Give sorrow leave awhile to tutor me
To this submission. Yet I well remember
The favors of these men. Were they not mine?
Did they not sometime cry, "All hail!" to me?
So Judas did to Christ. But he, in twelve,
10     Found truth in all but one; I, in twelve thousand, none.
God save the King! Will no man say amen?
Am I both priest and clerk? Well then, amen.
God save the King, although I be not he;
And yet, amen, if heaven do think him me.
15     Give me the crown. [He takes the crown.]
Here, cousin, seize the crown. Here, cousin,
On this side my hand, and on that side thine.
Now is this golden crown like a deep well
That owes two buckets, filling one another,
20     The emptier ever dancing in the air,
The other down, unseen, and full of water.
That bucket down and full of tears am I,
Drinking my griefs, whilst you mount up on high.
My crown I [resign], but still my griefs are mine.
25     You may my glories and my state depose,
But not my griefs. Still am I king of those.
Your cares set up do not pluck my cares down.
My care is loss of care, by old care done;
Your care is gain of care, by new care won.
30     The cares I give I have, though given away;
They tend the crown, yet still with me they stay.
Now mark me how I will undo myself:
[He surrenders his crown and scepter.]
I give this heavy weight from off my head
35     And this unwieldy scepter from my hand,
The pride of kingly sway from out my heart;
With mine own tears I wash away my balm,
With mine own hands I give away my crown,
With mine own tongue deny my sacred state,
40     With mine own breath release all duteous oaths.
All pomp and majesty I do forswear;
My manors, rents, revenues I forgo;
My acts, decrees, and statutes I deny.
God pardon all oaths that are broke to me!
45     God keep all vows unbroke are made to thee!
Make me, that nothing have, with nothing griev'd,
And thou with all pleas'd, that hast all achiev'd!
Long mayst thou live in Richard's seat to sit,

And soon lie Richard in an earthy pit!
God save King Henry, unking'd Richard says,                                    50
And send him many years of sunshine days!

**3 Wherewith** by means of which    **4 insinuate** ingratiate myself    **6 Yet** still
**7 favors** faces  **men** (referring to the nobility present)    **9 he, in twelve**
Christ, among his twelve disciples    **12 priest and clerk** (It was the custom
in religious services of the day for the clerk to say "amen" to the priest's
prayers.)    **19 owes** has, owns    **25 state** royal status    **27–31 Your...stay**
i.e., your assuming the cares of state does not signal the end of my sorrows.
My grief is the loss of my royal responsibilities, brought about by my feeble
carelessness; your concern is the gain of such royal responsibilities, won by
you through zealous effort. The anxieties that I bequeath to you I continue to
possess, even though I've given them away; though they accompany the
crown, they remain with me as well.    **37 balm** fragrant oils    **39 sacred
state** divine right to rule    **43 deny** disown, cancel    **44 oaths** (of allegiance)
**45 are** that are    **48 seat** throne

(6)                          **KING RICHARD**                          [V.v.1]

SCENE: Pomfret Castle

*{Sitting alone in his dungeon cell, a recently-dethroned Richard engages in a
spot of soulful introspection.}*

I have been studying how I may compare                                          1
This prison where I live unto the world;
And, for because the world is populous,
And here is not a creature but myself,
I cannot do it. Yet I'll hammer it out.                                         5
My brain I'll prove the female to my soul,
My soul the father, and these two beget
A generation of still-breeding thoughts;
And these same thoughts people this little world,
In humors like the people of this world,                                       10
For no thought is contented. The better sort,
As thoughts of things divine, are intermix'd
With scruples and do set the word itself
Against the word,
As thus, "Come, little ones," and then again,                                  15
"It is as hard to come as for a camel
To thread the postern of a small needle's eye."
Thoughts tending to ambition, they do plot

Unlikely wonders—how these vain weak nails
20  May tear a passage through the flinty ribs
Of this hard world, my ragged prison walls,
And, for they cannot, die in their own pride.
Thoughts tending to content flatter themselves
That they are not the first of fortune's slaves,
25  Nor shall not be the last—like seely beggars
Who, sitting in the stocks, refuge their shame
That many have and others must sit there;
And in this thought they find a kind of ease,
Bearing their own misfortunes on the back
30  Of such as have before endur'd the like.
Thus play I in one person many people,
And none contented. Sometimes am I king;
Then treasons make me wish myself a beggar,
And so I am. Then crushing penury
35  Persuades me I was better when a king;
Then I am king'd again, and by and by
Think that I am unking'd by Bolingbroke,
And straight am nothing. But whate'er I be,
Nor I nor any man, that but man is,
40  With nothing shall be pleas'd, till he be eas'd
With being nothing. [*Music is heard.*] Music do I hear?
Ha, ha, keep time! How sour sweet music is,
When time is broke and no proportion kept!
So is it in the music of men's lives.
45  And here have I the daintiness of ear
To check time broke in a disordered string;
But for the concord of my state and time
Had not an ear to hear my true time broke.
I wasted time, and now doth time waste me;
50  For now hath time made me his numb'ring clock.
My thoughts are minutes, and with sighs they jar
Their watches on unto mine eyes, the outward watch,
Whereto my finger, like a dial's point,
Is pointing still, in cleansing them from tears.
55  Now sir, the sound that tells what hour it is
Are clamorous groans, which strike upon my heart,
Which is the bell. So sighs and tears and groans
Show minutes, times, and hours. But my time
Runs posting on in Bolingbroke's proud joy,
60  While I stand fooling here, his Jack of the clock.
This music mads me. Let it sound no more,
For though it have holp madmen to their wits,
In me it seems it will make wise men mad.

Yet blessing on his heart that gives it me!
For 'tis a sign of love; and love to Richard                                65
Is a strange brooch in this all-hating world.

**8 still-breeding** continually breeding   **10 humors** moods, temperaments
**this world** i.e., the actual, material world   **13 scruples** doubts
**13–14 set . . . word** place one scriptural passage in opposition to another
(that is, cite excerpts from Scripture that appear to contradict each other)
**15–17 "Come . . . eye."** (alludes to Matthew 19:14 and 19:24)   **19 vain**
ineffectual   **21 ragged** rough   **22 for** because   **pride** glory   **23 content**
contentment   **25 seely** silly   **26 refuge their shame** seek refuge from
their disgrace (by acknowledging)   **38 straight** immediately   **39 Nor**
neither   **41 nothing** i.e., dead   **43 proportion** musical rhythm   **46 check**
chide, reprove   **47 concord** harmony   **50 numb'ring clock** i.e., clock that
numbers hours and minutes (as opposed to an hourglass)   **51–52 jar . . .**
**watch** tick away, marking the passage of time in my eyes, which are as a
clock-face   **53 Whereto** to which   **dial's point** clock hand   **58 times**
half-hours   **59 posting** racing, speeding   **proud joy** (time of) proud joy
**60 Jack . . . clock** the manikin in some older clocks that marks the passage of
the hour by popping out and striking a bell   **61 mads** maddens   **62 have . . .**
**to** has helped madmen to regain   **66 strange** remarkable, rare   **brooch**
ornament, jewel

**ALTERNATES**

John of Gaunt    [II.i.5–68]
King Richard    [III.ii.4–26]
Bolingbroke    [III.iii.31–61]
King Richard    [IV.i.228–291]

# RICHARD III

Though a bevy of would-be royal heirs stands between Richard and the throne of England, he is bound and determined to be the man who succeeds his ailing brother, King Edward IV. Even as Richard somehow manages to woo and wed the fair Lady Anne—this despite the fact that he killed her betrothed, the Prince of Wales—he embarks in earnest upon his plan to usurp the crown.

First of the potential successors to be eliminated from contention is Richard's brother the Duke of Clarence, who, at Richard's behest, is slain while imprisoned in the Tower of London. With Clarence out of the way, the death of King Edward enables Richard to finagle his way to the throne, which he quickly does through a series of subtle and not-so-subtle machinations.

To make sure he stays on top, Richard proceeds to tie up a few loose ends. For one thing, he sees to it that Edward's two young sons (and rightful heirs to the crown) are murdered. Next up: Richard's wife, Lady Anne, is neatly disposed of so that Richard can woo the late King Edward's daughter—a match that would further tighten his grip on the crown.

But when forces led by the Earl of Richmond arrive to do battle with the royal army at Bosworth Field, King Richard's day of reckoning comes at last. Richard's army goes down to defeat, while the King himself (sans horse) is slain by Richmond in hand-to-hand combat. The Wars of the Roses are finally over, and Richmond is hailed as King Henry VII.

**KING EDWARD IV**
**GEORGE, DUKE OF CLARENCE,** brother to Richard
**RICHARD, DUKE OF GLOUCESTER,** afterward King Richard III
**HENRY, EARL OF RICHMOND,** afterward King Henry VII
**LORD STANLEY,** an English noble

**QUEEN MARGARET,** widow of King Henry VI
**LADY ANNE,** daughter-in-law to King Henry VI, afterward wife to Richard

(1)          RICHARD, DUKE OF GLOUCESTER          [I.i.i]

SCENE: A street in London

*{Richard unveils the very essence of his being.}*

| | |
|---|---|
| Now is the winter of our discontent | 1 |

Now is the winter of our discontent                                        1
Made glorious summer by this son of York;
And all the clouds that low'r'd upon our house
In the deep bosom of the ocean buried.
Now are our brows bound with victorious wreaths,          5
Our bruised arms hung up for monuments,
Our stern alarums chang'd to merry meetings,
Our dreadful marches to delightful measures.
Grim-visag'd war hath smooth'd his wrinkled front;
And now, instead of mounting barbed steeds                    10
To fright the souls of fearful adversaries,
He capers nimbly in a lady's chamber
To the lascivious pleasing of a lute.
But I, that am not shap'd for sportive tricks,
Nor made to court an amorous looking-glass;                    15
I, that am rudely stamp'd, and want love's majesty
To strut before a wanton ambling nymph;
I, that am curtail'd of this fair proportion,
Cheated of feature by dissembling nature,
Deform'd, unfinish'd, sent before my time                          20
Into this breathing world, scarce half made up,
And that so lamely and unfashionable
That dogs bark at me as I halt by them—
Why, I, in this weak piping time of peace,
Have no delight to pass away the time,                                25
Unless to see my shadow in the sun
And descant on mine own deformity.
And therefore, since I cannot prove a lover
To entertain these fair well-spoken days,
I am determined to prove a villain                                       30
And hate the idle pleasures of these days.
Plots have I laid, inductions dangerous,
By drunken prophesies, libels, and dreams,
To set my brother Clarence and the King
In deadly hate the one against the other.                           35
And if King Edward be as true and just

As I am subtle, false, and treacherous,
This day should Clarence closely be mew'd up
About a prophesy, which says that G
40   of Edward's heirs the murderer shall be.
Dive, thoughts, down to my soul; here Clarence comes.

**2 son of York** i.e., King Edward IV (with a play on "sun," three of which formed Edward's badge)   **3 low'r'd** looked angrily, scowled   **4 In** are in   **6 bruised** dented   **arms** armour   **for monuments** as testaments, as trophies   **7 alarums** calls to arms   **8 measures** dances   **9 visag'd** appearing, looking   **front** forehead, brow   **10 barbed** armoured   **11 fearful** frightened   **14 sportive** amorous   **16 rudely** with crude or unskillful workmanship   **stamp'd** formed   **want** lack   **17 ambling** walking in an affected and alluring manner   **18 curtail'd** deprived   **proportion** shape, form   **19 feature** shapeliness, physical beauty   **dissembling** deceitful   **22 that** at that, even then   **unfashionable** poorly made   **23 halt** limp   **24 piping time** i.e., a time when the soft music of pipes is heard (rather than the drum and fife, instruments emblematic of war)   **27 descant** (1) discourse, comment (2) intone, warble   **29 entertain** while away   **31 idle** shallow, foolish   **32 inductions** preparations, initial steps of a plan   **37 subtle** sly, cunning   **38 closely** in close confinement   **mew'd up** caged (a term from falconry)   **39 About** concerning   **G** (The Duke of Clarence's given name was "George.")

(2)          RICHARD, DUKE OF GLOUCESTER          [I.ii.227]

SCENE: A street in London

*{Against all odds, Richard has not only managed to abate Lady Anne's fury, but has apparently won her affections to boot. Even Gloucester himself stands amazed.}*

1   Was ever woman in this humor woo'd?
Was ever woman in this humor won?
I'll have her, but I will not keep her long.
What? I, that kill'd her husband and his father,
5   To take her in her heart's extremest hate,
With curses in her mouth, tears in her eyes,
The bleeding witness of my hatred by,
Having God, her conscience, and these bars against me,

And I no friends to back my suit withal,
But the plain devil and dissembling looks?        10
And yet to win her! All the world to nothing!
Ha!
Hath she forgot already that brave prince,
Edward, her lord, whom I, some three months since,
Stabb'd in my angry mood at Tewkesbury?        15
A sweeter and a lovlier gentleman,
Fram'd in the prodigality of nature,
Young, valiant, wise, and no doubt, right royal,
The spacious world cannot again afford.
And will she yet abase her eyes on me,        20
That cropp'd the golden prime of this sweet prince,
And made her widow to a woeful bed?
On me, whose all not equals Edward's moi'ty?
On me, that halts and am misshapen thus?
My dukedom to a beggarly denier,        25
I do mistake my person all this while!
Upon my life, she finds—although I cannot—
Myself to be a marv'lous proper man.
I'll be at charges for a looking-glass,
And entertain a score or two of tailors        30
To study fashions to adorn my body.
Since I am crept in favor with myself,
I will maintain it with some little cost.
But first I'll turn yon fellow in his grave,
And then return lamenting to my love.        35
Shine out, fair sun, till I have bought a glass,
That I may see my shadow as I pass.

**1 humor** mood, state of mind (The background on Lady Anne's relationship
with Richard begins unfolding at I.ii.1.)   **7 bleeding witness** (referring to
Henry's corpse) **by** nearby   **8 bars** obstacles   **9 withal** besides
**10 dissembling looks** false appearances   **11 All...nothing** i.e., against
the worst of odds   **15 Stabb'd...Tewkesbury** (see Henry VI, 3, V.v.41)
**17 Fram'd** produced   **prodigality** abundance, lavishness   **19 afford** yield,
bring forth   **20 abase** lower   **21 cropp'd** cut short   **23 moi'ty** half
**24 halts** limps   **25 denier** small copper coin, valued at one-tenth of an
English cent   **26 mistake** misjudge   **person** bodily figure, external
appearance   **28 proper** good-looking   **29 be...for** purchase
**30 entertain** employ   **34 yon fellow** (referring to Henry's corpse)
**in** into

(3)                    **DUKE OF CLARENCE**                [I.IV.2]

SCENE: The Tower of London

*{Imprisoned in the Tower as a result of Richard's machinations, Clarence re-counts to his jailer an unsettling—and foretelling—dream from which he's just escaped.}*

| | |
|---|---|
| 1 | O, I have pass'd a miserable night, |
| | So full of fearful dreams, of ugly sights, |
| | That, as I am a Christian faithful man, |
| | I would not spend another such a night |
| 5 | Though 'twere to buy a world of happy days, |
| | So full of dismal terror was the time! |
| | Methoughts that I had broken from the Tower, |
| | And was embark'd to cross to Burgundy, |
| | And in my company my brother Gloucester, |
| 10 | Who from my cabin tempted me to walk |
| | Upon the hatches. Thence we look'd toward England, |
| | And cited up a thousand heavy times, |
| | During the wars of York and Lancaster, |
| | That had befall'n us. As we pac'd along |
| 15 | Upon the giddy footing of the hatches, |
| | Methought that Gloucester stumbled, and, in falling, |
| | Struck me, that thought to stay him, overboard |
| | Into the tumbling billows of the main. |
| | O Lord, methought what a pain it was to drown! |
| 20 | What dreadful noise of water in mine ears! |
| | What sights of ugly death within mine eyes! |
| | Methoughts I saw a thousand fearful wracks; |
| | A thousand men that fishes gnaw'd upon; |
| | Wedges of gold, great anchors, heaps of pearl, |
| 25 | Inestimable stones, unvalued jewels— |
| | All scatt'red in the bottom of the sea. |
| | Some lay in dead men's skulls; and in the holes |
| | Where eyes did once inhabit, there were crept, |
| | As 'twere in scorn of eyes, reflecting gems |
| 30 | That woo'd the slimy bottom of the deep, |
| | And mock'd the dead bones that lay scatt'red by. |
| | Methought I had, and often did I strive, |
| | To yield the ghost; but still the envious flood |
| | Stopp'd in my soul, and would not let it forth |
| 35 | To find the empty, vast, and wand'ring air, |
| | But smother'd it within my panting bulk, |

Who almost burst to belch it in the sea.
O, then began the tempest to my soul!
I pass'd, methought, the melancholy flood,
With that sour ferryman which poets write of,                    40
Unto the kingdom of perpetual night.
The first that there did greet my stranger soul
Was my great father-in-law, renowned Warwick,
Who spake aloud, "What scourge for perjury
Can this dark monarchy afford false Clarence?"                    45
And so he vanish'd. Then came wand'ring by
A shadow like an angel, with bright hair
Dabbled in blood, and he shriek'd out aloud,
"Clarence is come—false, fleeting, perjur'd Clarence,
That stabb'd me in the field by Tewkesbury.                       50
Seize on him, Furies, take him unto torment!"
With that, methought, a legion of foul fiends
Environ'd me, and howled in mine ears
Such hideous cries that with the very noise
I trembling wak'd, and for a season after                        55
Could not believe but that I was in hell,
Such terrible impression made my dream.
Ah, keeper, keeper, I have done these things,
That now give evidence against my soul,
For Edward's sake; and see how he requites me!                   60
O God, if my deep pray'rs cannot appease thee,
But thou wilt be aveng'd on my misdeeds,
Yet execute thy wrath in me alone!
O, spare my guiltless wife and my poor children!
Keeper, I prithee sit by me awhile.                               65
My soul is heavy, and I fain would sleep.

**2 fearful** frightening   **7 Methoughts** it seemed to me   **8 Burgundy**
province in eastern France (Clarence and Richard were sent to Burgundy for
safekeeping after the death of their father, the Duke of York.)   **11 hatches**
movable planks that form the deck of a ship   **Thence** from there   **12 cited
up** recalled   **15 giddy** precarious   **17 thought** intended, meant   **stay**
steady   **18 main** ocean   **22 wracks** wreckages   **25 Inestimable** valuable
and numerous beyond measure   **unvalued** priceless   **33 ghost** illusion,
phantasm   **envious** malicious   **34 Stopp'd in** enclosed, shut in   **36 bulk**
body   **39 melancholy flood** (refers to the River Styx, which in Greek
mythology was the main river to the underworld)   **40 sour ferryman**
(refers to Charon, who ferried souls across the River Styx to Hades)
**41 kingdom...night** i.e., Hades   **44 scourge** punishment   **45 dark
monarchy** i.e., Hades   **afford** give to   **47 shadow...angel** i.e., the ghost
of Prince Edward (see Henry VI, 3, V.v)   **49 fleeting** fickle   **perjur'd**

forsworn  **51 Furies** goddesses sent from hell to punish wrongdoers
**53 Environ'd** surrounded  **58 keeper** jailer  **61 deep** grave  **65 prithee**
beg of you  **66 fain** gladly

(4)                       KING EDWARD                    [II.1.103]

SCENE: The royal palace

*{Moments after Edward decided to pardon his brother Clarence for his alleged*
*crimes, word arrived that Clarence had in fact already been executed. When*
*an unwitting Lord Stanley subsequently enters to request that Edward pardon*
*one of Stanley's servants for a murder he's committed, the cutting irony of such*
*a juxtaposition is not lost on the King.}*

1       Have I a tongue to doom my brother's death,
        And shall that tongue give pardon to a slave?
        My brother kill'd no man; his fault was thought,
        And yet his punishment was bitter death.
5       Who sued to me for him? Who, in my wrath,
        Kneel'd at my feet and bid me be advis'd?
        Who spoke of brotherhood? Who spoke of love?
        Who told me how the poor soul did forsake
        The mighty Warwick, and did fight for me?
10      Who told me, in the field at Tewkesbury,
        When Oxford had me down, he rescued me,
        And said, "Dear brother, live, and be a king?"
        Who told me, when we both lay in the field
        Frozen almost to death, how he did lap me
15      Even in his garments, and did give himself,
        All thin and naked, to the numb cold night?
        All this from my remembrance brutish wrath
        Sinfully pluck'd, and not a man of you
        Had so much grace to put it in my mind.
20      But when your carters or your waiting vassals
        Have done a drunken slaughter, and defac'd
        The precious image of our dear Redeemer,
        You straight are on your knees for pardon, pardon;
        And I, unjustly too, must grant it you.
25      But for my brother not a man would speak;
        Nor I, ungracious, speak unto myself
        For him, poor soul. The proudest of you all
        Have been beholding to him in his life;

Yet none of you would once beg for his life.
O God, I fear thy justice will take hold                                    30
On me, and you, and mine, and yours for this!

**1 doom** decree   **6 be advis'd** think over things carefully   **14 lap** wrap
**20 carters...vassals** laborers or servants   **23 straight** immediately
**26 ungracious** unkind, merciless   **27 proudest** loftiest, most exalted

(5)                          KING RICHARD                          [V.III.177]

SCENE: Richard's camp near Tamworth

*{Richard is just now escaping from the clutches of a nightmare that featured
the ghosts of his many victims. One by one, the horror show's macabre actors
assured Richard that his end is only as far away as tomorrow's showdown on
the battlefield.}*

Give me another horse! Bind up my wounds!                                    1
Have mercy, Jesu!—Soft! I did but dream.
O coward conscience, how dost thou afflict me!
The lights burn blue. It is now dead midnight.
Cold fearful drops stand on my trembling flesh.                             5
What do I fear? Myself? There's none else by.
Richard loves Richard; that is, I am I.
Is there a murderer here? No. Yes, I am.
Then fly. What, from myself? Great reason why:
Lest I revenge. What, myself upon myself?                                    10
Alack, I love myself. Wherefore? For any good
That I myself have done unto myself?
O, no! Alas, I rather hate myself
For hateful deeds committed by myself!
I am a villain. Yet I lie, I am not.                                         15
Fool, of thyself speak well. Fool, do not flatter.
My conscience hath a thousand several tongues,
And every tongue brings in a several tale,
And every tale condemns me for a villain.
Perjury, perjury, in the highest degree;                                    20
Murder, stern murder, in the direst degree,
All several sins, all us'd in each degree,
Throng to the bar, crying all, "Guilty! Guilty!"
I shall despair. There is no creature loves me,
And if I die, no soul will pity me.                                          25

And wherefore should they, since that I myself
Find in myself no pity to myself?
Methought the souls of all that I had murder'd
Came to my tent, and every one did threat
30     Tomorrow's vengeance on the head of Richard.

**2 Soft** wait   **4 lights burn blue** (According to superstition, blue light
emanating from a torch or candle indicated that ghosts were present.)
**17 several** different, separate   **22 us'd** committed   **degree** i.e., degree of
evil, from bad to worst   **23 bar** court, tribunal   **28 Methought** it seemed
to me   **29 threat** threaten

(6)                    EARL OF RICHMOND                    [V.III.237]

SCENE: Richmond's camp near Tamworth

*{With the climactic battle against Richard's forces just around the corner,
Richmond exhorts his soldiers on to victory.}*

1     More than I have said, loving countrymen,
       The leisure and enforcement of the time
       Forbids to dwell upon. Yet remember this:
       God and our good cause fight upon our side.
5     The prayers of holy saints and wronged souls,
       Like high-rear'd bulwarks, stand before our faces.
       Richard except, those whom we fight against
       Had rather have us win than him they follow.
       For what is he they follow? Truly, gentlemen,
10    A bloody tyrant and a homicide;
       One rais'd in blood, and one in blood establish'd;
       One that made means to come by what he hath,
       And slaughtered those that were the means to help him;
       A base foul stone, made precious by the foil
15    Of England's chair, where he is falsely set;
       One that hath ever been God's enemy.
       Then, if you fight against God's enemy,
       God will in justice ward you as his soldiers;
       If you do sweat to put a tyrant down,
20    You sleep in peace, the tyrant being slain;
       If you do fight against your country's foes,
       Your country's fat shall pay your pains the hire;
       If you do fight in safeguard of your wives,
       Your wives shall welcome home the conquerors;
25    If you do free your children from the sword,

Your children's children quits it in your age.
Then, in the name of God and all these rights,
Advance your standards, draw your willing swords.
For me, the ransom of my bold attempt
Shall be this cold corpse on the earth's cold face;                    30
But if I thrive, the gain of my attempt
The least of you shall share his part thereof.
Sound drums and trumpets boldly and cheerfully;
God and Saint George! Richmond and victory!

**2 leisure** i.e., brief time allowed  **enforcement** compelling aspect
**3 Forbids** forbids us  **6 rear'd** raised erected  **7 Richard except** except
for Richard  **10 homicide** murderer  **11 in blood** by bloodshed
**establish'd** placed in power  **12 made means** created opportunity
**14 foul** ugly  **foil** thin backing of metal used to set off a jewel to advantage
**18 ward** guard, protect  **22 fat** abundance  **your...hire** the reward for
your labors  **25 sword** sword-wielding enemy  **26 quits** requites, repays
**age** lifetime  **29 ransom** (Important prisoners were commonly released in
exchange for the payment of a ransom. Richmond is vowing that, should his
efforts come up short on the battlefield, the only means of redemption for
him shall be through his death.)  **34 Saint George** patron saint of England

(7)                        KING RICHARD                    [V.III.314]

SCENE: Richard's camp near Tamworth

*{Across the field from Richmond's position (see preceding entry), Richard employs
his own method of stirring the troops.}*

What shall I say more than I have inferr'd?                            1
Remember whom you are to cope withal:
A sort of vagabonds, rascals, and runaways;
A scum of Britaines, and base lackey peasants,
Whom their o'ercloyed country vomits forth                            5
To desperate adventures and assur'd destruction.
You sleeping safe, they bring to you unrest;
You having lands, and blest with beauteous wives,
They would restrain the one, distain the other.
And who doth lead them but a paltry fellow,                          10
Long kept in Britaine at our mother's cost?
A milksop, one that never in his life
Felt so much cold as over shoes in snow?
Let's whip these stragglers o'er the seas again.
Lash hence these overweening rags of France,                        15

These famish'd beggars, weary of their lives,
Who, but for dreaming on this fond exploit,
For want of means, poor rats, had hang'd themselves.
If we be conquered, let men conquer us,
20    And not these bastard Britaines, whom our fathers
Have in their own land beaten, bobb'd, and thump'd
And in record left them the heirs of shame.
Shall these enjoy our lands? Lie with our wives?
Ravish our daughters? Hark! I hear their drum.
25    Fight, gentlemen of England! Fight, bold yeomen!
Draw, archers, draw your arrows to the head!
Spur your proud horses hard, and ride in blood!
Amaze the welkin with your broken staves!
A thousand hearts are great within my bosom.
30    Advance our standards, set upon our foes;
Our ancient word of courage, fair Saint George,
Inspire us with the spleen of fiery dragons!
Upon them! Victory sits on our helms!

**1 inferr'd** (already) asserted  **2 cope withal** fight with  **3 sort** gang
**runaways** deserters, cowards  **4 Britaines** Bretons, inhabitants of Brittany,
a province in the north of France  **5 o'ercloyed** gorged  **9 restrain** deprive
you of  **distain** dishonor, defile  **11 mother's** i.e., brother's, the Duke of
Burgundy's (This confusion of "mother's" for "brother's" results from a
misprint in Shakespeare's source material, Holinshed's *Chronicles*. Richard and
Richmond did not have the same mother. But while residing in Brittany,
Richmond had been supported by Richard's brother-in-law, the Duke of
Burgundy. "Brother's" is therefore the term that more accurately reflects
historical facts.)  **13 over ... snow** i.e., that of snow creeping in over his
shoe tops  **15 overweening** arrogant, presumptuous  **17 fond** foolish
**18 want of means** lack of money  **had** would have  **21 bobb'd** thrashed
**22 record** recorded history  **25 yeomen** minor landowners who made up
the bulk of the English infantry  **26 to the head** all the way back to the ears
**28 welkin** skies  **staves** lances  **31 word of courage** battle cry  **Saint
George** patron saint of England  **32 spleen** wrath  **33 helms** helmets

### ALTERNATES

Richard, Duke of Gloucester   [I.ii.149–183]
Sir James Tyrrel   [IV.iii.1–22]
King Richard   [IV.iv.291–336]

# ROMEO AND JULIET

It's love at first sight when Romeo and Juliet meet during a masked ball being held in the house of Capulet—this despite the fact that their families are embroiled in a protracted blood feud. By the next afternoon, the two are secretly wed by Friar Laurence.

It's not long after that when a street fight ends tragically with Romeo's friend, Mercutio, dead at the hands of Juliet's cousin, Tybalt—who in turn is then slain by Romeo. For his part in the brawl, Romeo is banished, and after spending the night with his new bride, he retreats to the nearby city of Mantua.

Meanwhile, unaware of his daughter's recent elopement, Capulet has arranged for Juliet to marry a young nobleman named Paris. When Juliet's resistance to the idea is overruled by her insistent parents, the desperate newlywed turns to Friar Laurence for help. The Friar's solution is to provide Juliet with a potion that will make her appear dead for forty-two hours. If all goes as planned, Romeo will arrive at the Capulet burial vault shortly after Juliet is laid to rest, and spirit her away from Verona.

But alas, all does not go as planned. Because a messenger fails to reach Romeo with word of the Friar's scheme, Romeo arrives at Juliet's tomb believing that she has actually died. No sooner does Romeo imbibe a lethal potion he had earlier procured, than Juliet awakens. Discovering her dead husband beside her, Juliet stabs herself, and dies.

**ESCALUS,** Prince of Verona

**PARIS,** a young noble of Verona

**CAPULET,** head of the house of Capulet

**ROMEO,** a young gentleman of Verona

**MERCUTIO,** friend to Romeo, kinsman to the Prince

**BENVOLIO,** cousin and friend to Romeo

**TYBALT,** cousin to Juliet

**FRIAR LAURENCE,** a Franciscan, confidant to Romeo and Juliet

**LADY CAPULET,** mother to Juliet, wife to Capulet

**JULIET,** daughter to Capulet

**NURSE,** nurse to Juliet

(1)                          MERCUTIO                          [I.iv.53]

SCENE: A street in London

*{No sooner does Romeo mention a dream he recently had than Mercutio seizes center stage and the opportunity to wax poetic.}*

1    O, then I see Queen Mab hath been with you.
     She is the fairies' midwife, and she comes
     In shape no bigger than an agate-stone
     On the forefinger of an alderman,
5    Drawn with a team of little atomi
     Over men's noses as they lie asleep.
     Her chariot is an empty hazel-nut,
     Made by the joiner squirrel or old grub,
     Time out o' mind the fairies' coachmakers.
10   Her wagon-spokes made of long spinners' legs,
     The cover of the wings of grasshoppers,
     Her traces of the smallest spider web,
     Her collars of the moonshine's wat'ry beams,
     Her whip of cricket's bone, the lash of film,
15   Her wagoner a small grey-coated gnat,
     Not half so big as a round little worm
     Prick'd from the lazy finger of a maid.
     And in this state she gallops night by night
     Through lovers' brains, and then they dream of love;
20   O'er courtiers' knees, that dream on cur'sies straight;
     O'er lawyers' fingers, who straight dream on fees;
     O'er ladies' lips, who straight on kisses dream,
     Which oft the angry Mab with blisters plagues,
     Because their breaths with sweetmeats tainted are.
25   Sometime she gallops o'er a courtier's nose,
     And then dreams he of smelling out a suit;
     And sometime comes she with a tithe-pig's tail
     Tickling a parson's nose as 'a lies asleep,
     Then dreams he of another benefice.
30   Sometime she driveth o'er a soldier's neck,
     And then dreams he of cutting foreign throats,
     Of breaches, ambuscadoes, Spanish blades,
     Of healths five-fathom deep; and then anon
     Drums in his ear, at which he starts and wakes,
35   And being thus frighted swears a prayer or two

And sleeps again. That is that very Mab
That plats the manes of horses in the night,
And bakes the elf-locks in foul sluttish hairs,
Which once untangled much misfortune bodes.
This is the hag, when maids lie on their backs,                                    40
That presses them and learns them first to bear,
Making them women of good carriage.
I talk of dreams,
Which are the children of an idle brain,
Begot of nothing but vain fantasy,                                                 45
Which is as thin of substance as the air
And more inconstant than the wind, who woos
Even now the frozen bosom of the north,
And, being anger'd, puffs away from thence,
Turning his side to the dew-dropping south,                                        50

**1 Queen Mab** (The character of Queen Mab appears to be Shakespeare's own creation, although the name itself may be of Celtic origin.)  **2 midwife** (in the sense that Mab assists in the "delivery" of dreams)  **3 agate-stone** (It was common practice to carve tiny figures into an agate stone prior to setting it in a piece of jewelry.)  **5 atomi** tiny creatures  **8 joiner** carpenter **grub** boring insect (portrayed here as a fellow carpenter to the "joiner squirrel")  **9 Time...mind** longer than recorded time  **10 spinners'** spiders'  **12 traces** lines of a harness that secure the animal to the vehicle **13 collars** harnesses  **14 film** gossamer thread  **17 Prick'd...maid** (alluding to the old wives tale that "worms breed in the fingers of the idle") **20 on** of  **straight** immediately  **24 sweetmeats** candied fruits **26 smelling...suit** discovering someone who will pay for his influence at court  **27 tithe-pig** (In lieu of money, a pig was sometimes given by a parishioner to the parson as payment of his tithe.)  **29 benefice** ecclesiastical office to which an endowment is attached (essentially, a religious position with a steady salary)  **32 breaches** breaks through fortifications **ambuscadoes** ambushes  **Spanish blades** (Swords made in the Spanish city of Toledo were considered to be the finest available.)  **33 healths** toasts to one's health and prosperity  **then anon** shortly thereafter **34 Drums** (like those heard on a battlefield)  **37 plats** tangles  **38 bakes** makes solid and tight  **elf-locks** tangled masses of hair (Superstition of the day held that such tangles were the work of elves, who would then wreak havoc if someone were to untangle their creations.)  **41 presses** weighs down on  **learns** teaches  **bear** (1) bear the weight of men during copulation (2) bear children  **42 good carriage** admirable demeanor (with a play on their ability to "bear")  **45 vain** silly, empty-headed  **49 anger'd** (over his lack of success in wooing the frigid northland)

(2)                        ROMEO                        [II.ii.1]

SCENE: Capulet's orchard

*{Mercutio and Benvolio have just strolled off, having finally had their fill of
needling the love-stricken Romeo. Left to wander alone among the trees of
Capulet's garden, young Montague suddenly finds himself but a stone's throw
away from his beloved Juliet's balcony and bedchamber.}*

1    He jests at scars that never felt a wound.
    [*A light appears in Juliet's window.*]
    But soft, what light through yonder window breaks?
    It is the east, and Juliet is the sun.
5    Arise, fair sun, and kill the envious moon,
    Who is already sick and pale with grief
    That thou, her maid, art far more fair than she.
    Be not her maid, since she is envious;
    Her vestal livery is but sick and green
10    And none but fools do wear it; cast it off.
    [*Juliet appears on the balcony.*]
    It is my lady; O, it is my love!
    O, that she knew she were!
    She speaks, yet she says nothing. What of that?
15    Her eye discourses; I will answer it.
    I am too bold, 'tis not to me she speaks.
    Two of the fairest stars in all the heaven,
    Having some business, do entreat her eyes
    To twinkle in their spheres till they return.
20    What if her eyes were there, they in her head?
    The brightness of her cheek would shame those stars,
    As daylight doth a lamp; her eyes in heaven
    Would through the airy region stream so bright
    That birds would sing and think it were not night.
25    See how she leans her cheek upon her hand.
    O, that I were a glove upon that hand,
    That I might touch that cheek. She speaks!
    O, speak again, bright angel, for thou art
    As glorious to this night, being o'er my head,
30    As is a winged messenger of heaven
    Unto the white-upturned wond'ring eyes
    Of mortals that fall back to gaze on him
    When he bestrides the lazy puffing clouds
    And sails upon the bosom of the air.

**1 He** (referring to Mercutio)  **that** who  **wound** i.e., of Cupid's arrow
**3 soft** stay, wait   **7 her maid** a devoted admirer of Diana (who was both
moon goddess and the patroness of virgins)   **9 sick and green** (It was
thought that a form of anemia called "the green sickness" commonly afflicted
young unmarried women.)   **19 spheres** transparent, hollow globes believed
to revolve around the earth carrying heavenly bodies such as moons, planets
and stars   **20 there** i.e., in the sky  **they** (the stars)   **23 stream** shine
**27 She speaks** (Juliet has just sighed a lamentful "Ay me.")
**31 white-upturned** looking upward so that the whites are prominent

(3)                           MERCUTIO                        [III.1.5]

SCENE: A public place in Verona

*{Sensing that a brawl might easily erupt on this sweltering afternoon, Benvolio*
*has urged Mercutio to join him indoors, away from potential trouble. The irony*
*of such a suggestion coming from the likes of Benvolio does not escape the amused*
*Mercutio.}*

Thou art like one of these fellows that when he enters the confines of a tavern,       1
claps me his sword upon the table and says, "God send me no need of thee!"
and by the operation of the second cup draws him on the drawer, when indeed
there is no need. Thou art as hot a Jack in thy mood as any in Italy, and as
soon mov'd to be moody, and as soon moody to be mov'd. An there were       5
two such, we should have none shortly, for one would kill the other. Thou!
Why, thou wilt quarrel with a man that hath a hair more or a hair less in his
beard than thou hast. Thou wilt quarrel with a man for cracking nuts, having
no other reason but because thou hast hazel eyes. What eye but such an eye
would spy out such a quarrel? Thy head is as full of quarrels as an egg is full       10
of meat, and yet thy head hath been beaten as addle as an egg for quarreling.
Thou hast quarrel'd with a man for coughing in the street, because he hath
waken'd thy dog that hath lain asleep in the sun. Didst thou not fall out with a
tailor for wearing his new doublet before Easter? With another, for tying his
new shoes with old riband? And yet thou wilt tutor me from quarreling!       15

**2 claps me** sets down with conviction   **3 by . . . cup** by the time the second
drink takes effect  **draws . . . drawer** draws his sword on the tapster
**4 Jack** knave, ill-mannered fellow   **5 moody** angry, peevish  **mov'd** (to take
action)  **An** if   **11 meat** i.e., edible matter  **addle** addled, mixed up
**14 doublet** a jacket-like garment   **15 riband** ribbon  **tutor . . .**
**quarreling** instruct me not to quarrel

(4)                          ROMEO                    [III.III.12]

SCENE: Friar Laurence's room

*{Friar Laurence has just given Romeo the good news: The Prince has mercifully decided to merely banish, and not execute, young Montague for his part in Tybalt's death. As might be expected, however, Romeo sees the Prince's edict in a somewhat different light.}*

| | |
|---|---|
| 1 | Banishment? Be merciful, say "death;" |
| | For exile hath more terror in his look, |
| | Much more than death. Do not say "banishment." |
| | There is no world without Verona's walls, |
| 5 | But purgatory, torture, hell itself. |
| | Hence "banished" is banish'd from the world, |
| | And world's exile is death; then "banished" |
| | is death mis-term'd. Calling death "banished," |
| | Thou cutt'st my head off with a golden axe, |
| 10 | And smilest upon the stroke that murders me. |
| | 'Tis torture, and not mercy. Heaven is here |
| | Where Juliet lives, and every cat and dog |
| | And little mouse, every unworthy thing, |
| | Live here in heaven and may look on her, |
| 15 | But Romeo may not. More validity, |
| | More honorable state, more courtship lives |
| | In carrion flies than Romeo. They may seize |
| | On the white wonder of dear Juliet's hand |
| | And steal immortal blessing from her lips, |
| 20 | Who, even in pure and vestal modesty, |
| | Still blush, as thinking their own kisses sin; |
| | But Romeo may not, he is banished. |
| | Flies may do this, but I from this must fly; |
| | They are free men, but I am banished. |
| 25 | And sayest thou yet that exile is not death? |
| | Hadst thou no poison mix'd, no sharp-ground knife, |
| | No sudden mean of death, though ne'er so mean, |
| | But "banished" to kill me? "Banished?" |
| | O friar, the damned use that word in hell; |
| 30 | Howling attends it. How hast thou the heart, |
| | Being a divine, a ghostly confessor, |
| | A sin-absolver, and my friend profess'd, |
| | To mangle me with that word "banished?" |

**4 without** outside   **13 unworthy thing** negligible creature   **15 validity**
value   **16 state** status   **courtship** opportunity for wooing   **20 Who**
(referring to Juliet's lips)   **vestal** chaste   **21 Still** continually   **their own**
**kisses** their touching one another   **27 sudden . . . so mean** swift and
immediate means of death, though it may be contemptible   **30 attends**
accompanies   **31 divine** priest   **ghostly** spiritual   **32 friend profess'd**
confirmed friend

(5)                    FRIAR LAURENCE                    [III.iii.108]

SCENE: Friar Laurence's room

*{Completely distraught over his banishment from Verona (see preceding entry),*
*Romeo has drawn his dagger and is threatening to do away with himself. In*
*steps the good Friar with a game attempt to talk some sense into the lad.}*

Hold thy desperate hand!                                           1
Art thou a man? Thy form cries out thou art;
Thy tears are womanish, thy wild acts denote
The unreasonable fury of a beast.
Unseemly woman in a seeming man,                                   5
And ill-beseeming beast in seeming both!
Thou hast amaz'd me. By my holy order,
I thought thy disposition better temper'd.
Hast thou slain Tybalt? Wilt thou slay thyself,
And slay thy lady that in thy life lives,                          10
By doing damned hate upon thyself?
Why railest thou on thy birth, the heaven, and earth,
Since birth, and heaven, and earth, all three do meet
In thee at once, which thou at once wouldst lose?
Fie, fie, thou shamest thy shape, thy love, thy wit,              15
Which, like a usurer, abound'st in all,
And usest none in that true use indeed
Which should bedeck thy shape, thy love, thy wit.
Thy noble shape is but a form of wax,
Digressing from the valor of a man;                               20
Thy dear love sworn but hollow perjury,
Killing that love which thou hast vow'd to cherish.
Thy wit, that ornament to shape and love,
Misshapen in the conduct of them both,
Like powder in a skilless soldier's flask                         25

Is set afire by thine own ignorance,
And thou dismemb'red with thine own defense.
What, rouse thee, man! Thy Juliet is alive,
For whose dear sake thou wast but lately dead;
30    There art thou happy. Tybalt would kill thee,
But thou slewest Tybalt; there art thou happy.
The law that threat'ned death becomes thy friend
And turns it to exile; there art thou happy.
A pack of blessings light upon thy back,
35    Happiness courts thee in her best array;
But, like a mishaved and sullen wench,
Thou pouts upon thy fortune and thy love.
Take heed, take heed, for such die miserable.
Go, get thee to thy love, as was decreed;
40    Ascend her chamber, hence and comfort her.
But look thou stay not till the watch be set,
For then thou canst not pass to Mantua,
Where there shalt live till we can find a time
To blaze your marriage, reconcile your friends,
45    Beg pardon of the Prince, and call thee back
With twenty hundred thousand times more joy
Than thou went'st forth in lamentation.
I'll find out your man, and he shall signify
From time to time every good hap to you
50    That chances here. 'Tis late. Farewell, good night.

**5 a seeming** (what is) seemingly a   **8 disposition** temperament
**temper'd** controlled, restrained   **13 heaven, and earth** i.e., body and
soul   **15 Fie** (an expression of disgust)   **shape** human form, body   **wit**
intellect   **16 Which** (you) who   **usurer** i.e., one who fails to appropriately
utilize his considerable assets   **all** all capabilities   **18 bedeck** adorn
**19 form of wax** waxwork figure   **20 Digressing** deviating   **22 that** i.e.,
Juliet's   **23 ornament** embellishment   **24 conduct** guidance   **25 skilless**
inexperienced   **flask** powder-horn   **27 thine own defense** that which
should serve as your defense, i.e., your "wit"   **29 lately** recently   **dead** (see
previous entry)   **30 happy** fortunate, blessed   **35 array** fashion
**36 mishaved** misbehaved   **39 decreed** (earlier) agreed upon   **41 watch
be set** the city's guards are at their posts   **44 blaze** proclaim   **friends**
relations   **48 find out** seek out, locate   **man** manservant   **signify** relate
**49 good hap** bit of good fortune   **50 chances** happens, comes about

(6)            **CAPULET**          [III.v.141]

SCENE: Juliet's bedchamber

*{Capulet has made plans to have his daughter wed the young nobleman, Paris. When his wife informs him that Juliet will have nothing to do with such an arrangement (hardly surprising, since Juliet was secretly married to Romeo earlier that day), Capulet lashes out at his unappreciative child.}* [By omitting lines 1–5 and 10–13, this entire piece can be directed toward Juliet.]

Soft, take me with you, take me with you, wife.      1
How? Will she none? Doth she not give us thanks?
Is she not proud? Doth she not count her blest,
Unworthy as she is, that we have wrought
So worthy a gentleman to be her bride?      5
Hang thee, young baggage! Disobedient wretch!
I tell thee what: get thee to church a' Thursday,
Or never after look me in the face.
Speak not, reply not, do not answer me!
My fingers itch. Wife, we scarce thought us blest      10
That God had lent us but this only child;
But now I see this one is one too much,
And that we have a curse in having her.
God's bread, it makes me mad!
Day, night, hour, tide, time, work, play,      15
Alone, in company, still my care hath been
To have her match'd; and having now provided
A gentleman of noble parentage,
Of fair demesnes, youthful, and nobly lien'd,
Stuff'd, as they say, with honorable parts,      20
Proportion'd as one's thought would wish a man—
And then to have a wretched puling fool,
A whining mammet, in her fortune's tender,
To answer, "I'll not wed, I cannot love,
I am too young; I pray you, pardon me."      25
But, an you will not wed, I'll pardon you;
Graze where you will, you shall not house with me.
Look to 't, think on 't, I do not use to jest.
Thursday is near. Lay hand on heart; advise.
As you be mine, I'll give you to my friend;      30
An you be not, hang, beg, starve, die in the streets,
For, by my soul, I'll ne'er acknowledge thee,
Nor what is mine shall never do thee good.
Trust to 't, bethink you; I'll not be forsworn.

**1 Soft** wait a moment  **take . . . you** let me be sure I understand you
**2 none** have none of it, i.e., the arranged marriage   **3 proud** ecstatic
**count her blest** consider herself blessed   **4 wrought** procured, obtained
**5 bride** bridegroom   **6 baggage** a term of general contempt similar to
"good-for-nothing" (Note that Capulet now addresses Juliet.)   **7 Thursday**
i.e., the assigned day of the wedding   **10 scarce** scarcely, hardly   **14 God's**
**bread** (a mild oath used to convey exasperation)   **15 tide** season   **16 still**
always   **care** concern   **19 demesnes** lands, estates   **nobly lien'd** of noble
birth   **22 wretched** loathsome   **puling** whimpering   **23 mammet** doll,
puppet   **in . . . tender** when good fortune is offered to her   **26 an** if
**pardon you** grant your release, permit you to leave (Capulet is intentionally
corrupting Juliet's meaning when she asked that she be "pardoned.")
**28 I . . . use** it is not my custom   **29 advise** consider well, weigh matters
carefully   **30 friend** (referring to Paris)   **34 Trust to 't** believe it, count on
it   **bethink you** think about it

ALTERNATES

Friar Laurence   [II.iii.1–30]
Romeo             [V.i.34–57]
Romeo             [V.iii.74–120]

# THE TAMING OF THE SHREW

Baptista has declared that, despite her many suitors, his younger daughter Bianca can be courted only after his older, shrewish one, Katharina, is first married off.

Attracted by the prospect of her sizable dowry, Petruchio gamely embraces the challenge of wooing Kate. A series of fiery confrontations between the two ensue, until Petruchio at last manages to both wed and tame the recalcitrant Kate.

**BAPTISTA,** a rich gentleman of Padua
**LUCENTIO,** a young gentleman of Pisa, suitor to Bianca
**PETRUCHIO,** a gentleman of Verona, suitor to Katharina
**GRUMIO,** servant to Petruchio

**KATHARINA,** daughter to Baptista
**BIANCA,** daughter to Baptista

(1)                           **PETRUCHIO**                    [II.1.243]

SCENE: Baptista's house

*{Though Katharina has yet to be the least bit impressed with her suitor, Petruchio will not be denied. Refusing to acknowledge her verbal barbs and contrary ways, he instead takes pains to assure Kate that her fate is already sealed.}*

'Twas told me you were rough and coy and sullen,                    1
And now I find report a very liar;
For thou art pleasant, gamesome, passing courteous,
But slow in speech, yet sweet as spring-time flowers.
Thou canst not frown, thou canst not look askance,                 5
Nor bite the lip, as angry wenches will,
Nor hast thou pleasure to be cross in talk;
But thou with mildness entertain'st thy wooers
With gentle conference, soft and affable.
Why does the world report that Kate doth limp?                    10

O sland'rous world! Kate like the hazel-twig
Is straight and slender, and as brown in hue
As hazel nuts, and sweeter than the kernels.
O, let me see thee walk. Thou dost not halt.
15   Did ever Dian so become a grove
As Kate this chamber with her princely gait?
O, be thou Dian, and let her be Kate;
And then let Kate be chaste and Dian sportful!
Sweet Katharine, setting all this chat aside,
20   Thus in plain terms: your father hath consented
That you shall be my wife; your dowry 'greed on;
And, will you, nill you, I will marry you.
Now, Kate, I am a husband for your turn;
For, by this light, whereby I see thy beauty—
25   Thy beauty that doth make me like thee well—
Thou must be married to no man but me;
For I am he am born to tame you, Kate,
And bring you from a wild Kate to a Kate
Conformable as other household Kates.
30   Here comes your father. Never make denial;
I must and will have Katharine to my wife.

**1 coy** distant, disdainful  **3 gamesome** gay, playful  **passing** exceedingly
**4 But slow** only gentle and deliberate  **yet** now as always  **5 askance**
scornfully  **9 conference** conversation  **14 halt** limp  **15 Dian** Diana, the
moon goddess and goddess of chastity  **18 sportful** wanton  **20 Thus** here
it is  **22 will you, nill you** whether you will or will not (consent to this
marriage)  **23 husband . . . turn** suitable husband for a woman of your
character and inclination  **29 Conformable** obedient, submissive
**household** domesticated

(2)                          PETRUCHIO                    [III.ii.184]

SCENE: Baptista's house

*{With the conclusion of Kate and Petruchio's wedding ceremony comes the
beginning of the gamesmanship. In an attempt to establish who wears the
pantaloons in the family, Petruchio brushes off protests from his bride and his
friends, and abruptly whisks Katharina off to her new home.}*

1   Gentlemen and friends, I thank you for your pains.
I know you think to dine with me today,
And have prepar'd great store of wedding cheer,
But so it is, my haste doth call me hence,

And therefore here I mean to take my leave.                                    5
Make it no wonder; if you knew my business,
You would entreat me rather go than stay.
And, honest company, I thank you all
That have beheld me give away myself
To this most patient, sweet, and virtuous wife.                               10
Dine with my father, drink a health to me,
Go to the feast, revel and domineer,
Carouse full measure to her maidenhead;
Be mad and merry—or go hang yourselves.
But for my bonny Kate, she must with me.                                       15
Nay, look not big, nor stamp, nor stare, nor fret;
I will be master of what is mine own.
She is my goods, my chattels; she is my house,
My household stuff, my field, my barn,
My horse, my ox, my ass, my any thing;                                        20
And here she stands, touch her whoever dare.
I'll bring mine action on the proudest he
That stops my way in Padua. Grumio,
Draw forth thy weapon, we are beset with thieves.
Rescue thy mistress, if thou be a man.                                         25
Fear not, sweet wench, they shall not touch thee, Kate!
I'll buckler thee against a million.

**1 pains** trouble, efforts   **6 Make...wonder** do not wonder at (my sudden
exit)   **8 honest** honorable, worthy   **11 father** (referring to Baptista, who is
now his father-in-law)   **12 domineer** indulge yourselves   **13 her
maidenhead** i.e., to Kate and the end of her virginity   **16 big** imposing,
threatening (Though directed toward the wedding party, it's almost certainly
his wife's conduct that Petruchio is actually describing.)   **22 mine action** an
attack   **proudest he** most vigorous man   **23 stops** blocks   **24 Draw...
weapon** (Though Petruchio and his manservant Grumio may actually
unsheath their swords here, there's little doubt that Petruchio only pretends
to perceive a threat; it's all part of the act to dramatically "rescue" his bride.)
**27 buckler** defend

(3)                              PETRUCHIO                       [IV.i.188]

SCENE: Petruchio's country house

*{Petruchio figures to rein in his unruly bride with the same method he employs
to tame his falcons, i.e., deprivation of food and sleep. The brainwashing begins
when Kate is denied her supper and sent off to the bedchamber. Before joining
her there, Petruchio tarries a moment to reflect upon his strategy.}*

1    Thus have I politicly begun my reign,
And 'tis my hope to end successfully.
My falcon now is sharp and passing empty,
And till she stoop, she must not be full-gorg'd,
5    For then she never looks upon her lure.
Another way I have to man my haggard,
To make her come and know her keeper's call:
That is, to watch her, as we watch these kites
That bate and beat and will not be obedient.
10    She eat no meat today, nor none shall eat;
Last night she slept not, nor tonight she shall not;
As with the meat, some undeserved fault
I'll find about the making of the bed,
And here I'll fling the pillow, there the bolster,
15    This way the coverlet, another way the sheets.
Ay, and amid this hurly I intend
That all is done in reverend care of her.
And in conclusion she shall watch all night,
And if she chance to nod I'll rail and brawl
20    And with the clamor keep her still awake.
This is a way to kill a wife with kindness;
And thus I'll curb her mad and headstrong humor.
He that knows better how to tame a shrew,
Now let him speak; 'tis charity to shew.

**1 politicly** shrewdly  **3 sharp** famished  **passing** extremely  **4 stoop** swoop down to the lure, i.e., submit to authority (Here as elsewhere in the piece, Petruchio is drawing a parallel between falconry and wife-taming.) **full-gorg'd** filled with food  **5 lure** dummy bird used to entice the falcon back to its master  **6 Another** (there is) another  **man** tame  **haggard** wild female hawk  **8 watch her** keep her awake  **kites** falcons  **9 bate and beat** furiously beat their wings in an attempt to escape the falconer's control  **10 She eat** she ate (here eat is pronounced "et")  **16 hurly** commotion **I intend** I'll pretend  **18 watch** remain sleepless  **19 brawl** i.e., disturb the peace  **20 still** constantly  **24 shew** show, i.e., reveal one's method

**ALTERNATES**
Lord      [Induction.i.31–73]
Petruchio  [II.i.290–324]

# THE TEMPEST

Twelve years ago, Prospero was ousted as the Duke of Milan by his brother Antonio, and set adrift at sea along with his baby daughter Miranda. The two castaways eventually washed up on a remote island inhabited only by a cantankerous creature named Caliban. It is there that Prospero, as possessor of strange and supernatural powers, now prepares to exact his revenge.

A storm worked up by Prospero has shipwrecked the King of Naples and his company (including Prospero's brother Antonio) on the island. With the assistance of Ariel, his indentured spirit, Prospero proceeds to conjure a series of wondrous spectacles, all of which serve to thoroughly confound Antonio and the others. Once he's made his point, Prospero takes pity on his bewildered guests, provides them with safe passage to Naples, renounces his magic, and grants Ariel his freedom.

**ALONSO,** King of Naples
**SEBASTIAN,** brother to Alonso
**PROSPERO,** the rightful Duke of Milan
**ANTONIO,** brother to Prospero, the usurping Duke of Milan
**CALIBAN,** a savage, slave to Prospero
**TRINCULO,** a jester

**MIRANDA,** daughter to Prospero
**ARIEL,** an airy spirit

(1)                          CALIBAN                          [II.ii.1]

SCENE: Somewhere on Prospero's island

*{Per Prospero's orders, Caliban is out rummaging around the island for firewood. The poor savage has been less than happy of late, and the way he sees things, his wretched condition is all Prospero's doing.}*

1    All the infections that the sun sucks up
     From bogs, fens, flats, on Prosper fall, and make him
     By inch-meal a disease! His spirits hear me,
     And yet I needs must curse. But they'll nor pinch,
5    Fright me with urchin-shows, pitch me i' th' mire,
     Nor lead me, like a firebrand, in the dark
     Out of my way, unless he bid 'em; but
     For every trifle are they set upon me;
     Sometime like apes that mow and chatter at me,
10   And after bite me; then like hedgehogs which
     Lie tumbling in my barefoot way and mount
     Their pricks at my footfall. Sometime am I
     All wound with adders, who with cloven tongues
     Do hiss me into madness. [*Enter Trinculo.*] Lo, now, lo!
15   Here comes a spirit of his, and to torment me
     For bringing wood in slowly. I'll fall flat;
     Perchance he will not mind me.

**3 By inch-meal** little by little   **4 nor** neither   **5 urchin-shows** goblins and other ghostly characters   **9 mow** grimace, make faces   **10 hedgehogs** small porcupine-like animals that roll up into a ball as a means of self-defense   **11 mount** set up   **12 pricks** needles, spines   **13 wound** wrapped around   **17 mind** notice

(2)                         TRINCULO                         [II.ii.18]

SCENE: Somewhere on Prospero's island

*{Swept overboard by Prospero's tempest, Trinculo was separated from his companions and washed ashore. Now, with another storm in the offing, he's more than ready to settle for whatever shelter he can find.}*

1    Here's neither bush nor shrub to bear off any weather at all, and another
     storm brewing; I hear it sing i' th' wind. Yond same black cloud, yond huge

one, looks like a foul bombard that would shed his liquor. If it should thunder
as it did before, I know not where to hide my head. Yond same cloud cannot
choose but fall by pailfuls. [*He sees the motionless Caliban.*] What have we here?    5
A man or a fish? Dead or alive? A fish, he smells like a fish; a very ancient and
fish-like smell; a kind of not-of-the-newest Poor-John. A strange fish! Were I
in England now, as once I was, and had but this fish painted, not a holiday fool
there but would give a piece of silver. There would this monster make a man;
any strange beast there makes a man. When they will not give a doit to relieve    10
a lame beggar, they will lay out ten to see a dead Indian. Legg'd like a man!
And his fins like arms! Warm, o' my troth! I do now let loose my opinion,
hold it no longer: this is no fish, but an islander, that hath lately suffer'd by a
thunderbolt. [*Thunder is heard.*] Alas, the storm is come again! My best way
is to creep under his gaberdine; there is no other shelter hereabout. Misery    15
acquaints a man with strange bedfellows. I will here shroud till the dregs of the
storm be past.

**I bear off** ward off, repel   **3 bombard** large leather jug   **5 fall** let fall (rain)
**What . . . here?** (For an account of how Caliban ended up this way, see
preceding entry.)   **7 Poor-John** a cheap, lower-quality variety of fish
**8 painted** publicized by means of a painted sign (which would be displayed
outside a booth at some local fair to attract the curious)   **holiday** idle,
trifling   **9 make a man** make one's fortune   **10 doit** half a farthing, i.e., a
trifling sum   **11 dead Indian** (American Indians were featured exhibits in
London in the early 1600s.)   **12 o' my troth** by my faith (a mild oath of the
day)   **13 hold it** hold it back   **15 gaberdine** a long, loose-fitting upper
garment   **16 shroud** take shelter   **dregs** last remains

(3)                           PROSPERO                    [V.i.33]

SCENE: The island, before Prospero's cell

*{Having accomplished his mission, Prospero prepares to put an end to the mayhem he has created.}*

Ye elves of hills, brooks, standing lakes and groves,    1
And ye that on the sands with printless foot
Do chase the ebbing Neptune, and do fly him
When he comes back; you demi-puppets that
By moonshine do the green sour ringlets make,    5
Whereof the ewe not bites; and you whose pastime
Is to make midnight mushrooms, that rejoice
To hear the solemn curfew: by whose aid,
Weak masters though ye be, I have bedimm'd

10    The noontide sun, call'd forth the mutinous winds,
      And 'twixt the green sea and the azur'd vault
      Set roaring war; to the dread rattling thunder
      Have I given fire, and rifted Jove's stout oak
      With his own bolt; the strong-bas'd promontory
15    Have I made shake, and by the spurs pluck'd up
      The pine and cedar; graves at my command
      Have wak'd their sleepers, op'd, and let 'em forth
      By my so potent art. But this rough magic
      I here abjure, and, when I have requir'd
20    Some heavenly music, which even now I do,
      To work mine end upon their senses that
      This airy charm is for, I'll break my staff,
      Bury it certain fathoms in the earth,
      And deeper than did ever plummet sound
25    I'll drown my book.

**3 fly** fly from    **4 demi-puppets** half-sized puppets, i.e., tiny creatures
**5 green sour ringlets** fairy rings (Fairy rings were circular bands found in
dew-covered grass that, according to superstition, were the handiwork of
elves and fairies.)    **7 midnight mushrooms** (It was believed that
mushrooms, because they often popped up overnight, were created by
elves.)    **9 Weak** (weak, that is, compared to the powerful demons conjured
up by black magic)    **10 noontide** noontime    **11 azur'd vault** blue sky
**13 given fire** added lightning    **rifted** split    **oak** oak tree    **15 spurs** roots
**17 op'd** opened    **18 rough** harsh, violent    **19 requir'd** requested    **21 end**
purpose    **22 airy charm** enchantment


(4)                          PROSPERO                    [EPILOGUE]

*{His work done, Prospero steps forward to offer the audience some final
thoughts.}*

1     Now my charms are all o'erthrown,
      And what strength I have's mine own;
      Which is most faint. Now, 'tis true,
      I must be here confin'd by you,
5     Or sent to Naples. Let me not,
      Since I have my dukedom got
      And pardon'd the deceiver, dwell
      In this bare island by your spell,
      But release me from my bands

With the help of your good hands.                                    10
Gentle breath of yours my sails
Must fill, or else my project fails,
Which was to please. Now I want
Spirits to enforce, art to enchant,
And my ending is despair,                                            15
Unless I be reliev'd by prayer,
Which pierces so that it assaults
Mercy itself and frees all faults.
As you from crimes would pardon'd be,
Let your indulgence set me free.                                     20

**1 charms** magic spells   **9 bands** bonds   **10 hands** applause   **11 Gentle
breath** favorable breeze (as produced by applause)   **13 want** lack
**16 prayer** (referring to this plea of his to the audience)   **17 assaults** woos
**18 frees** remits, obtains forgiveness of   **19 crimes** sins


**Alternates**
Caliban    [I.ii.321–344]
Prospero   [V.i.33–57]

# TIMON OF ATHENS

Through years of misguided largess and a lavish lifestyle, Timon has managed to squander his entire personal fortune. When creditors come calling, Timon turns for help to his friends—and promptly discovers that the same folk who for so long wallowed in his generosity now offer him nothing but empty sympathy and the bum's rush.

An embittered and vengeful Timon decides to regale his fair-weather pals with one final mock-banquet in their dishonor, and then turns his back on Athens for the life of a cave-dwelling recluse.

Some time later, two senators come crawling before Timon's cave to enlist his help in defending Athens against an impending attack by the banished Athenian captain, Alcibiades. Timon's reply is to offer them a tree upon which to hang themselves.

As Alcibiades stands before Athens' walls negotiating a peace with the city's leaders, word arrives that Timon, "who, alive, all living men did hate," is dead.

**TIMON,** a wealthy Athenian
**APEMANTUS,** a cynical philosopher
**ALCIBIADES,** an Athenian captain

(1)                          **ALCIBIADES**                          [III.v.7]

SCENE: The Senate House in Athens

*{Alcibiades has come before the Senate to plead for the life of a fellow soldier who, in defense of his honor, has killed a man.}*

I am an humble suitor to your virtues;                                    1
For pity is the virtue of the law,
And none but tyrants use it cruelly.
It pleases time and fortune to lie heavy
Upon a friend of mine, who, in hot blood,                                5
Hath stepp'd into the law, which is past depth
To those that, without heed, do plunge into 't.
He is a man, setting his fate aside,
Of comely virtues;
Nor did he soil the fact with cowardice—                                10
An honor in him which buys out his fault—
But with a noble fury and fair spirit,
Seeing his reputation touch'd to death,
He did oppose his foe;
And with such sober and unnoted passion                                 15
He did behave his anger, ere 'twas spent,
As if he had but prov'd an argument.
[You say] to revenge is no valor, but to bear;
My lords, then, under favor, pardon me
If I speak like a captain.                                              20
Why do fond men expose themselves to battle,
And not endure all threats? Sleep upon 't,
And let the foes quietly cut their throats
Without repugnancy? If there be
Such valor in the bearing, what make we                                 25
Abroad? Why then, women are more valiant
That stay at home, if bearing carry it;
And the ass more captain than the lion, the felon
Loaden with irons wiser than the judge,
If wisdom be in suffering. O my lords,                                  30
As you are great, be pitifully good.
Who cannot condemn rashness in cold blood?
To kill, I grant, is sin's extremest gust;
But, in defense, by mercy, 'tis most just.
To be in anger is impiety;                                              35
But who is man that is not angry?
Weigh but the crime with this.

**1 your virtues** those who personify virtue   **2 virtue** merit, distinction
**4 heavy** grievous, severe   **6 into** i.e., into conflict with   **6–7 past depth
To** over the heads of   **8 fate** ill-fated action   **10 fact** deed   **11 buys out**
redeems   **13 touch'd to death** threatened with a fatal wound
**15 unnoted** so well controlled as to be unnoticed or imperceptible
**16 behave** control   **17 prov'd** put forth, tried   **18 to . . . bear** there is no
honor in seeking revenge; to bear wrongs without reply is true valor
**19 under favor** by your leave, with your permission   **21 fond** foolish
**22 Sleep** (why not just) sleep   **24 repugnancy** opposition   **25 bearing**
(of insults)   **make we** are we doing   **26 Abroad** in other countries
**27 carry it** is proper conduct   **29 Loaden** laden   **31 pitifully good** good
in your show of compassion   **33 sin's extremest gust** indulgence in the
most extreme form of sin   **34 But . . . mercy** but to kill in defense (of one's
honor), if one mercifully interprets the law   **36 man** the man   **not** never

(2)                                           TIMON                              [III.vi.58]

SCENE: A banquet room in Timon's home

*{In his hour of need, not a one of Timon's friends would deign to lend him a
hand. Their betrayal has inspired Timon to delay his departure from Athens
just long enough to prepare a final banquet in their, uhm, honor. With table
set and all players in attendance, Timon's show begins.}*

1    My worthy friends, will you draw near? Each man to his stool, with that spur
as he would to the lip of his mistress. Your diet shall be in all places alike.
Make not a city feast of it, to let the meat cool ere we can agree upon the first
place. Sit, sit; the gods require our thanks. [*All but Timon take their seat at the*
5    *table.*] You great benefactors, sprinkle our society with thankfulness. For your
own gifts, make yourselves prais'd; but reserve still to give, lest your deities
be despis'd. Lend to each man enough, that one need not lend to another; for,
were your godheads to borrow of men, men would forsake the gods. Make the
meat be belov'd more than the man that gives it. Let no assembly of twenty be
10    without a score of villains. If there sit twelve women at the table, let a dozen of
them be—as they are. The rest of your fees, O gods—the senators of Athens,
together with the common lag of people—what is amiss in them, you gods,
make suitable for destruction. For these my present friends, as they are to me
nothing, so in nothing bless them, and to nothing they are welcome. Uncover,
15    dogs, and lap!
[*They uncover their dishes, which are full of warm water.*]
May you a better feast never behold,
You knot of mouth-friends! Smoke and luke-warm water
Is your perfection. This is Timon's last,

Who, stuck and spangled with your flatteries,                                20
Washes it off, and sprinkles in your faces
Your reeking villainy.
[*Throwing the water in their faces.*]
Live loath'd and long,
Most smiling, smooth, detested parasites;                                     25
Courteous destroyers, affable wolves, meek bears;
You fools of fortune, trencher-friends, time's flies,
Cap-and-knee slaves, vapors, and minute-jacks!
Of man and beast the infinite malady
Crust you quite o'er! What, dost thou go?                                     30
Soft! Take thy physic first—thou too—and thou;
Stay, I will lend thee money, borrow none.
[*Throws the dishes at them, and drives them out.*]
What, all in motion? Henceforth be no feast
Whereat a villain's not a welcome guest.                                      35
Burn, house! Sink, Athens! Henceforth hated be
Of Timon, man, and all humanity!

**1 that spur** such speed, such sense of purpose   **2 diet** meal   **3 city feast**
formal affair (with seating according to rank)   **3–4 the first place** (who
shall occupy) the place of honor   **6 reserve still** always hold back
(something) **your deities** you gods   **11 The** (as for) the **your fees** those
who owe you homage and allegiance (?)   **12 lag** dregs   **13 make suitable
for** regard as sufficient cause for (their)   **For** as for   **18 knot** company, band
**mouth-friends** those who profess friendship with words (rather than with
deeds)   **Smoke** steam   **19 Is your perfection** is the ultimate reward for
you, is perfectly suited to you   **Timon's last** the end of Timon, Timon's last
appearance   **20 stuck and spangled** plastered and adorned   **25 smooth**
slick   **27 fools** dupes, playthings   **trencher-friends** parasites   **time's flies**
creatures who seem to show up only during the bountiful times (like flies in
summer)   **28 Cap-and-knee** obsequious (as demonstrated by those who
continually tip their caps and bow)   **slaves** base creatures   **vapors**
insubstantial nothings   **minute-jacks** those who change their minds merely
to suit the moment   **29 the infinite malady** every conceivable disease and
disorder   **30 Crust** encrust   **31 Soft** wait, hold on   **physic** medicine
**37 Of** by

(3)                          TIMON                          [IV.i.1]

SCENE: Outside the walls of Athens

*{Bound for his new life in the forest, Timon pauses outside the city walls to
deliver a few parting sentiments.}*

1   Let me look back upon thee. O thou wall
    That girdles in those wolves, dive in the earth,
    And fence not Athens! Matrons, turn incontinent!
    Obedience fail in children! Slaves and fools,
5   Pluck the grave wrinkled Senate from the bench,
    And minister in their steads! To general filths
    Convert o' th' instant, green virginity!
    Do 't in your parents' eyes! Bankrupts, hold fast;
    Rather than render back, out with your knives,
10  And cut your trusters' throats! Bound servants, steal;
    Large-handed robbers your grave masters are,
    And pill by law. Maid, to thy master's bed;
    Thy mistress is o' th' brothel! Son of sixteen,
    Pluck the lin'd crutch from thy old limping sire;
15  With it beat out his brains! Piety, and fear,
    Religion to the gods, peace, justice, truth,
    Domestic awe, night-rest, and neighborhood,
    Instruction, manners, mysteries, and trades,
    Degrees, observances, customs, and laws,
20  Decline to your confounding contraries,
    And yet confusion live! Plagues incident to men,
    Your potent and infectious fevers heap
    On Athens, ripe for stroke! Thou cold sciatica,
    Cripple our senators, that their limbs may halt
25  As lamely as their manners! Lust and liberty
    Creep in the minds and marrows of our youth,
    That 'gainst the stream of virtue they may strive,
    And drown themselves in riot! Itches, blains,
    Sow all th' Athenian blossoms, and their crop
30  Be general leprosy! Breath infect breath,
    That their society, as their friendship, may
    Be merely poison! Nothing I'll bear from thee
    But nakedness, thou detestable town!
    [*Taking off his outer garments.*]
35  Take thou that too, with multiplying bans!
    Timon will to the woods, where he shall find
    Th' unkindest beast more kinder than mankind.
    The gods confound—hear me, you good gods all—
    Th' Athenians both within and out that wall!
40  And grant, as Timon grows, his hate may grow
    To the whole race of mankind, high and low!
    Amen.

**3 fence** defend **incontinent** unchaste, promiscuous   **6 steads** places
**general filths** common prostitutes   **7 o' th' instant** immediately   **green**

**virginity** young virgins  **9 render back** pay back what is owed (to lenders)
**10 trusters'** creditors'  **Bound** indentured  **11 Large-handed** grasping,
covetous  **12 pill** plunder, pillage  **14 lin'd** padded  **15 fear** religious awe
**16 Religion to** reverence of  **17 Domestic awe** respect for one's parents
and elders  **neighborhood** neighborliness  **18 mysteries** crafts
**19 Degrees** ranks  **20 confounding contraries** chaos-inducing opposites
**21 And yet** and still (through all of the destruction) may  **incident to**
preying upon  **24 halt** limp  **25 liberty** lechery  **27 strive** flail, struggle
**28 riot** wanton living  **blains** sores, blisters  **31 their** (referring to the
Athenian citizens)  **society** association with one another  **32 merely**
utterly, entirely  **35 bans** curses

(4)             **TIMON**           **[IV.III.321]**

SCENE: Before Timon's cave

*{Now living a solitary life out in the woods, Timon sees an unexpected (and unappreciated) visit by Apemantus as an opportunity to dispense his beastly philosophy.}*

What wouldst thou do with the world, Apemantus, if it lay in thy power?    1
Wouldst thou have thyself fall in the confusion of men, and remain a beast
with the beasts? A beastly ambition, which the gods grant thee t' attain to!
If thou wert the lion, the fox would beguile thee; if thou wert the lamb, the
fox would eat thee; if thou wert the fox, the lion would suspect thee, when   5
peradventure thou wert accus'd by the ass; if thou wert the ass, thy dullness
would torment thee, and still thou liv'dst but as a breakfast to the wolf; if thou
wert the wolf, thy greediness would afflict thee, and oft thou shouldst hazard
thy life for thy dinner; wert thou the unicorn, pride and wrath would confound
thee and make thine own self the conquest of thy fury; wert thou a bear, thou   10
wouldst be kill'd by the horse; wert thou a horse, thou wouldst be seiz'd by the
leopard; wert thou a leopard, thou wert germane to the lion and the spots of
thy kindred were jurors on thy life; all thy safety were remotion and thy defense
absence. What beast couldst thou be, that were not subject to a beast? And
what a beast art thou already, that seest not thy loss in transformation!   15

**2 confusion of men** destruction of mankind (Timon is replying to
Apemantus' assertion that he would give over the world to "the beasts, to be
rid of men.")  **6 peradventure** by chance  **dullness** stupidity, obtuseness
**7 liv'dst** would live  **9 confound** destroy (According to legend, unicorns
could be captured by goading them into charging a stout tree, whereupon
they would be unable to dislodge their horns.)  **12 germane** closely related

**12–13 the spots…life** the crimes and disgraces ("spots") of your relatives (the lions) would be reason enough for condemning you to death
**13–14 all…absence** your only chance for safety and self-preservation would lie in a solitary and nomadic lifestyle **14 to a beast** to some other beast **15 beast** contemptible creature **thy…transformation** what you would lose by being changed (into a beast)

(5)                    TIMON                    [V.i.156]

SCENE: Before Timon's cave

*{Two senators have arrived at Timon's hovel to beg that he help defend Athens against Alcibiades's imminent attack. After they assure Timon that everyone regrets their mistreatment of him, and that wealth and honors will once more be his if only he will come to their rescue, they pause for his response.}*

1      [You] surprise me to the very brink of tears.
       Lend me a fool's heart and a woman's eyes,
       And I'll beweep these comforts, worthy senators.
       If Alcibiades kill my countrymen,
5      Let Alcibiades know this of Timon,
       That Timon cares not. But if he sack fair Athens,
       And take our goodly aged men by th' beards,
       Giving our holy virgins to the stain
       Of contumelious, beastly, mad-brain'd war,
10     Then let him know, and tell him Timon speaks it,
       In pity of our aged and our youth,
       I cannot choose but tell him that I care not,
       And let him take 't at worst—for their knives care not,
       While you have throats to answer. For myself,
15     There's not a whittle in th' unruly camp
       But I do prize it at my love before
       The reverend'st throat in Athens. So I leave you
       To the protection of the prosperous gods,
       As thieves to keepers.
20     Why, I was writing of my epitaph;
       It will be seen tomorrow. My long sickness
       Of health and living now begins to mend,
       And nothing brings me all things. Go, live still;
       Be Alcibiades your plague, you his,
25     And last so long enough!

But yet, I love my country, and am not
One that rejoices in the common wrack,
As common bruit doth put it.
Commend me to my loving countrymen,
And tell them that, to ease them of their griefs,                    30
Their fears of hostile strokes, their aches, losses,
Their pangs of love, with other incident throes
That nature's fragile vessel doth sustain
In life's uncertain voyage, I will some kindness do them:
I'll teach them to prevent wild Alcibiades' wrath.                    35
I have a tree, which grows here in my close,
That mine own use invites me to cut down,
And shortly must I fell it. Tell my friends,
Tell Athens, in the sequence of degree
From high to low throughout, that whoso please                       40
To stop affliction, let him take his haste,
Come hither, ere my tree hath felt the axe,
And hang himself. I pray you, do my greeting,
And come not to me again. But say to Athens,
Timon hath made his everlasting mansion                              45
Upon the beached verge of the salt flood,
Who once a day with his embossed froth
The turbulent surge shall cover. Thither come,
And let my grave-stone be your oracle.
Lips, let four words go by and language end!                         50
What is amiss, plague and infection mend!
Graves only be men's works and death their gain!
Sun, hide thy beams! Timon hath done his reign!

**1 surprise** overwhelm   **4 kill** should kill   **8 stain** disgrace, corruption
**9 contumelious** insolent, abusive   **13 take...worst** interpret my meaning
in the most severe way possible   **their** (referring to Alcibiades and his
troops)   **care not** will exercise no restraint or compassion   **14 answer**
answer for (your misdeeds)   **For** as for   **15 whittle** pocketknife **unruly**
rebel   **16 prize** value   **at** in   **18 prosperous** favorable   **19 keepers** jailors
**22 mend** subside (Timon employs irony here in his reference to what had
been his long-standing good health and what now appears to be his imminent
demise.)   **23 nothing** i.e., death   **27 the common wrack** general
destruction, devastation   **28 bruit** rumor   **31 strokes** blows   **32 incident**
incidental   **33 nature's fragile vessel** the human body   **35 to prevent**
how to avoid by timely action   **36 close** garden, yard   **37 invites** induces
**39 degree** rank, status   **45 everlasting mansion** grave   **46 beached...**
**flood** land at the edge of the ocean's beach   **47 Who** (1) whom (if the
object of the statement is taken to be Timon himself) (2) which (if the object

is seen as Timon's "everlasting mansion")  **embossed** foaming   **49 oracle** source of wisdom   **50 four** (used to indicate some indefinite number, either large or small)

## Alternates
Timon    [I.ii.88–108]
Timon    [IV.iii.1–48]
Timon    [IV.iii.424–449]

# TITUS ANDRONICUS

Titus has returned to Rome from a successful military campaign against the Goths. With him are Tamora, Queen of the Goths, and her three sons, one of whom Titus sacrifices in retribution for his own two sons lost in battle. Though he is clearly the people's choice as Rome's next emperor, Titus defers in favor of the late Emperor's eldest son, Saturninus. In turn, Saturninus agrees to marry Titus's daughter Lavinia—a plan that does not sit well with Saturninus's brother Bassianus, who claims Lavinia as his own betrothed.

A struggle ensues and Bassianus escapes with Lavinia, after which Saturninus opts for the beguiling Tamora as his new bride. Though Saturninus holds Titus responsible for this embarrassing turn of events, he is persuaded by Tamora to feign forgiveness for the time being, so that she might later "find a day to massacre them all."

Tamora's plot of revenge quickly takes shape. She and her sons Chiron and Demetrius encounter Bassianus and Lavinia out in the forest, where the former is murdered and the latter is raped and mutilated. When false evidence fabricated by Tamora's lover Aaron implicates Titus's sons Martius and Quintus in the murder of Bassianus, the two are quickly executed.

Things then turn from bad to worse for Titus when he discovers the pitiful Lavinia, mangled and mute. With Marcus and Lucius by his side, Titus plots his revenge.

The climactic carnage unfolds as everyone gathers for a banquet at Titus's home. A pie featuring the remains of Chiron and Demetrius (freshly butchered by Titus a bit earlier in the day) is served to Tamora, and for dessert she is stabbed to death. Titus slays poor Lavinia as well (the idea being that her shame dies with her), after which he is slain by Saturninus, who then is killed by Lucius. Since Lucius is the last one standing, he is proclaimed Rome's new Emperor, and promptly condemns Aaron to death by burial and starvation.

**SATURNINUS,** Emperor of Rome
**BASSIANUS,** brother to Saturninus
**TITUS ANDRONICUS,** a Roman noble and general
**MARCUS ANDRONICUS,** brother to Titus Andronicus
**LUCIUS,** son to Titus Andronicus
**DEMETRIUS,** son to Tamora

**CHIRON,** son to Tamora
**AARON,** a Moor, beloved of Tamora

**TAMORA,** Queen of the Goths, wife to Saturninus
**LAVINIA,** daughter to Titus Andronicus, in love with Bassianus

(1)                    **MARCUS ANDRONICUS**                    [II.iv.13]

SCENE: A forest near Rome

*{While out hunting in the woods, Marcus happens upon a most pitiful sight;
his niece Lavinia, "her hands cut off, and her tongue cut out, and ravish'd."}*

| | |
|---|---|
| 1 | If I do dream, would all my wealth would wake me! |
| | If I do wake, some planet strike me down, |
| | That I may slumber an eternal sleep! |
| | Speak, gentle niece, what stern ungentle hands |
| 5 | Hath lopp'd and hew'd and made thy body bare |
| | Of her two branches, those sweet ornaments |
| | Whose circling shadows kings have sought to sleep in, |
| | And might not gain so great a happiness |
| | As have thy love? Why dost not speak to me? |
| 10 | Alas, a crimson river of warm blood, |
| | Like to a bubbling fountain stirr'd with wind, |
| | Doth rise and fall between thy rosed lips, |
| | Coming and going with thy honey breath. |
| | But sure, some Tereus hath deflow'red thee, |
| 15 | And, lest thou shouldst detect him, cut thy tongue. |
| | Ah, now thou turn'st away thy face for shame! |
| | And notwithstanding all this loss of blood, |
| | As from a conduit with three issuing spouts, |
| | Yet do thy cheeks look red as Titan's face |
| 20 | Blushing to be encount'red with a cloud. |
| | Shall I speak for thee? Shall I say 'tis so? |
| | O, that I knew thy heart, and knew the beast, |
| | That I might rail at him to ease my mind! |
| | Sorrow concealed, like an oven stopp'd, |
| 25 | Doth burn the heart to cinders where it is. |
| | Fair Philomela, why, she but lost her tongue, |
| | And in a tedious sampler sew'd her mind; |
| | But, lovely niece, that mean is cut from thee. |
| | A craftier Tereus, cousin, hast thou met, |
| 30 | And he hath cut those pretty fingers off |

That could have better sew'd than Philomel.
O, had the monster seen those lily hands
Tremble, like aspen-leaves, upon a lute,
And make the silken strings delight to kiss them,
He would not then have touch'd them for his life!                    35
Or, had he heard the heavenly harmony
Which that sweet tongue hath made,
He would have dropp'd his knife, and fell asleep
As Cerberus at the Thracian poet's feet.
Come, let us go, and make thy father blind;                          40
For such a sight will blind a father's eye.
One hour's storm will drown the fragrant meads;
What will whole months of tears thy father's eyes?
Do not draw back, for we will mourn with thee.
O, could our mourning ease thy misery!                               45

**4 stern** cruel, pitiless   **8 And** and yet   **9 As** as to   **14 Tereus** (Marcus refers here and subsequently to the story of Tereus and Philomela. Philomela was raped by Tereus, who then cut out her tongue so that she could not identify him. She nonetheless succeeded in implicating him by weaving in a tapestry an account of his brutality.)   **15 detect** expose   **19 Titan** the sun-god   **24 stopp'd** plugged up   **27 tedious** taxing, laboriously constructed   **sampler** embroidered cloth or tapestry   **28 mean** means **39 Cerberus...feet** (According to legend, Orpheus (the "Thracian poet") was able, with his sweet-sounding music, to pacify Cerberus, the beast guarding the entrance to Hades.)   **42 meads** meadows   **43 thy** do to thy

(2)                      TITUS ANDRONICUS                  [III.i.93]

SCENE: A street in Rome

*{As Marcus and Lucius stand nearby, a devastated Titus confronts the horrific spectacle of his mutilated daughter.}*

Now I stand as one upon a rock                                        1
Environ'd with a wilderness of sea,
Who marks the waxing tide grow wave by wave,
Expecting ever when some envious surge
Will in his brinish bowels swallow him.                               5
This way to death my wretched sons are gone;
Here stands my other son, a banish'd man,
And here my brother, weeping at my woes.
But that which gives my soul the greatest spurn
Is dear Lavinia, dearer than my soul.                                10

Had I but seen thy picture in this plight,
It would have madded me; what shall I do
Now I behold thy lively body so?
Thou hast no hands to wipe away thy tears,
15    Nor tongue to tell me who hath martyr'd thee.
Thy husband he is dead, and for his death
Thy brothers are condemn'd, and dead by this.
Look, Marcus! Ah, son Lucius, look on her!
When I did name her brothers, then fresh tears
20    Stood on her cheeks, as doth the honey-dew
Upon a gath'red lily almost withered.
Gentle Lavinia, let me kiss thy lips,
Or make some sign how I may do thee ease.
Shall thy good uncle, and thy brother Lucius,
25    And thou, and I, sit round about some fountain,
Looking all downwards, to behold our cheeks
How they are stain'd, like meadows yet not dry,
With miry slime left on them by a flood?
And in the fountain shall we gaze so long
30    Till the fresh taste be taken from that clearness,
And made a brine-pit with our bitter tears?
Or shall we cut away our hands, like thine?
Or shall we bite our tongues, and in dumb shows
Pass the remainder of our hateful days?
35    What shall we do? Let us, that have our tongues,
Plot some device of further misery,
To make us wonder'd at in time to come.

**2 Environ'd** surrounded   **3 waxing** mounting, increasing   **4 envious**
malicious   **5 his** its   **9 spurn** kick, shove (or some similar contemptuous
treatment)   **11 picture** portrait   **12 madded me** driven me mad
**13 lively** living   **15 martyr'd** mutilated   **17 by this** by now   **20 honey-
dew** a sweet sticky fluid found on the leaves and stems of many plants
**21 gath'red** picked   **23 do thee ease** bring you relief   **25 fountain** spring
**30 that clearness** i.e., the clear and pure water of the spring

(3)                                    **AARON**                                    [V.i.91]

SCENE: The fields near Rome

*{Having been taken prisoner, Aaron proudly confesses to Lucius an inventory of
his villainous deeds.}* [For a shorter take on this piece, line 11 can also serve
as a starting point.]

'Twas [Tamora's] sons that murder'd Bassianus;                                    1
They cut thy sister's tongue and ravish'd her
And cut her hands and trimm'd her as thou sawest.
Why, she was wash'd and cut and trimm'd, and 'twas
Trim sport for them which had the doing of it.                                    5
Indeed, I was their tutor to instruct them.
That codding spirit had they from their mother,
As sure a card as ever won the set;
That bloody mind, I think, they learn'd of me,
As true a dog as ever fought at head.                                            10
Well, let my deeds be witness of my worth.
I train'd thy brethren to that guileful hole
Where the dead corpse of Bassianus lay;
I wrote the letter that thy father found
And hid the gold within that letter mention'd,                                   15
Confederate with the Queen and her two sons;
And what not done, that thou hast cause to rue,
Wherein I had no stroke of mischief in it?
I play'd the cheater for thy father's hand,
And when I had it, drew myself apart                                             20
And almost broke my heart with extreme laughter.
I pried me through the crevice of a wall
When, for his hand, he had his two sons' heads,
Beheld his tears, and laugh'd so heartily
That both mine eyes were rainy like to his;                                      25
And when I told the Empress of this sport,
She swounded almost at my pleasing tale,
And for my tidings gave me twenty kisses.
Even now I curse the day—and yet, I think,
Few come within the compass of my curse—                                        30
Wherein I did not some notorious ill,
As kill a man, or else devise his death,
Ravish a maid, or plot the way to do it,
Accuse some innocent and forswear myself,
Set deadly enmity between two friends,                                          35
Make poor men's cattle break their necks,
Set fire on barns and haystalks in the night,
And bid the owners quench them with their tears.
Oft have I digg'd up dead men from their graves
And set them upright at their dear friends' door,                               40
Even when their sorrows almost was forgot,
And on their skins, as on the bark of trees,
Have with my knife carved in Roman letters,
"Let not your sorrow die, though I am dead."
Tut, I have done a thousand dreadful things                                     45

As willingly as one would kill a fly,
And nothing grieves me heartily indeed
But that I cannot do ten thousand more.

**3 trimm'd** (used here in the sense that one trims a cut of meat)  **5 trim** fine, nice  **7 codding** lecherous  **8 sure** winning  **set** game  **10 fought at head** went for the bear's head (in reference to bearbaiting, a popular activity of the day)  **12 train'd** lured  **guileful** deceptive  **17 not** was not  **19 cheater** escheater, one who oversees properties forfeited to the king (playing as well on the word's more familiar "deceiver" sense)  **hand** (see III.i.150)  **21 broke my heart** died  **22 pried me** peered  **26 Empress** i.e., Tamora  **27 swounded** fainted  **30 compass** reach, sphere  **31 ill** wickedness  **37 haystalks** haystacks

(4)                    TITUS ANDRONICUS                    [V.II.169]

SCENE: The courtyard of Titus's house

*{After outfoxing Tamora and her sons, Chiron and Demetrius, Titus now has the latter two at his mercy. But mercy is far from what Titus has in mind for this pair of villains. With Lavinia at his side, he begins preparations for a most ghoulish feast of revenge.}*

1    O villains, Chiron and Demetrius!
     Here stands the spring whom you have stain'd with mud,
     This goodly summer with your winter mix'd.
     You kill'd her husband, and for that vile fault
5    Two of her brothers were condemn'd to death;
     My hand cut off and made a merry jest;
     Both her sweet hands, her tongue, and that more dear
     Than hands or tongue, her spotless chastity,
     Inhuman traitors, you constrain'd and forc'd.
10   What would you say, if I should let you speak?
     Villains, for shame you could not beg for grace.
     Hark, wretches, how I mean to martyr you.
     This one hand yet is left to cut your throats,
     Whiles that Lavinia 'tween her stumps doth hold
15   The basin that receives your guilty blood.
     You know your mother means to feast with me,
     And calls herself Revenge, and thinks me mad.
     Hark, villains, I will grind your bones to dust
     And with your blood and it I'll make a paste,

And of the paste a coffin I will rear                                    20
And make two pasties of your shameful heads,
And bid that strumpet, your unhallowed dam,
Like to the earth swallow her own increase.
This is the feast that I have bid her to,
And this the banquet she shall surfeit on;                              25
For worse than Philomel you us'd my daughter,
And worse than Progne I will be reveng'd.
And now prepare your throats. Lavinia, come,
Receive the blood, and when that they are dead,
Let me go grind their bones to powder small                             30
And with this hateful liquor temper it;
And in that paste let their vile heads be bak'd.
Come, come, be everyone officious
To make this banquet, which I wish may prove
More stern and bloody than the Centaurs' feast.                         35

**2 the spring** i.e., Lavinia   **4 fault** offense   **9 constrain'd** violated   **forc'd**
took by force   **11 for shame** because of (your) shame   **grace** mercy
**12 martyr** mutilate   **17 Revenge** (see V.ii.1–8)   **20 coffin** pie crust   **rear**
build, erect   **21 pasties** meat pies   **22 dam** mother   **23 increase** offspring
**24 bid** invited   **25 surfeit** feed   **26–27 Philomel, Progne** (Philomela was
raped and mutilated by Tereus. Progne, wife to Tereus and sister to
Philomela, took revenge on her husband by serving him a meal that consisted
of their own son's flesh.)   **31 this hateful liquor** (referring to their blood)
**temper** moisten, mix   **33 officious** busy with activity   **35 stern** cruel,
pitiless   **Centaur's feast** (This refers to a mythical feast at which
centaurs—fabled creatures of half man and half horse—were slaughtered by
their hosts after they attempted to abduct the women that were present.)

**ALTERNATES**

Aaron   [II.i.1–25]
Aaron   [II.i.45–131]
Aaron   [IV.ii.88–111]

# TROILUS AND CRESSIDA

With the Trojan War raging in the background, Troilus and Cressida have managed to fall deeply in love with each other. Things go swimmingly between the two until Cressida is shipped over to the Grecian side as part of a prisoner exchange. Once there, Cressida quickly proves unfaithful to Troilus by taking up with a Greek commander named Diomedes.

Upon learning of Cressida's infidelity, an irate and embittered Troilus exacts his revenge on the Greeks by wreaking considerable havoc on the battlefield. But it would appear that Troilus's heroics may be all for naught, as the story ends with his beloved Troy teetering on the brink of defeat.

**PRIAM,** King of Troy
**TROILUS,** son to Priam
**PANDARUS,** uncle to Cressida
**DIOMEDES,** a Greek commander

**HELEN,** wife to the King of Sparta
**CRESSIDA,** a Trojan maiden

(1)                       PANDARUS                      [I.ii.177]

SCENE: A street in Troy

*{As the men of Troy file home from a hard day at the war, Pandarus and his niece Cressida scramble for a decent view of the impromptu parade.}*

Hark, they are coming from the field. Shall we stand up here, and see them       1
as they pass toward Illium? Good niece, do, sweet niece Cressida. Here, here,
here's an excellent place; here we may see most bravely. I'll tell you them all by
their names as they pass by, but mark Troilus above the rest. [*The soldiers begin
to file past.*] That's Aeneas; is not that a brave man? He's one of the flowers of       5
Troy, I can tell you. But mark Troilus; you shall see anon. [*Antenor passes by.*]
That's Antenor. He has a shrewd wit, I can tell you, and he's man good enough.
He's one o' th' soundest judgments in Troy, whosoever, and a proper man of
person. When comes Troilus? I'll show you Troilus anon. If he see me, you
shall see him nod at me. [*Hector passes by.*] That's Hector, that, that, look you,       10
that; there's a fellow! Go thy way, Hector! There's a brave man, niece. O brave
Hector! Look how he looks! There's a countenance! Is 't not a brave man? Is
'a not? It does a man's heart good. Look you what hacks are on his helmet!
Look you yonder, do you see? Look you there. There's no jesting; there's laying
on, take 't off who will, as they say. There be hacks! By God's lid, it does one's       15
heart good. Yonder comes Paris, yonder comes Paris. [*Paris passes by.*] Look
ye yonder, niece; is 't not a gallant man too, is 't not? Why, this is brave now.
Who said he came hurt home today? He's not hurt. Why, this will do Helen's
heart good now, ha! Would I could see Troilus now! You shall see Troilus anon.
[*Helenus passes by.*] That's Helenus. I marvel where Troilus is. That's Helenus.       20
I think he went not forth today. That's Helenus. I marvel where Troilus is.
Hark, do you not hear the people cry "Troilus?" Helenus is a priest. [*Troilus
passes by.*] 'Tis Troilus! There's a man, niece! Hem! Brave Troilus! The prince
of chivalry! Mark him, note him. O brave Troilus! Look well upon him, niece.
Look you how his sword is bloodied, and his helm more hack'd than Hector's,       25
and how he looks, and how he goes! O admirable youth! He ne'er saw three
and twenty. Go thy way, Troilus, go thy way! Had I a sister were a grace, or
a daughter a goddess, he should take his choice. O admirable man! [*Common
soldiers pass by.*] Here comes more. Asses, fools, dolts! Chaff and bran, chaff
and bran! Porridge after meat! I could live and die in the eyes of Troilus. Ne'er       30
look, ne'er look. The eagles are gone; crows and daws, crows and daws! I had
rather be such a man as Troilus than Agamemnon and all Greece.

**1 up here** (Pandarus refers to some unspecified vantage point, perhaps a
balcony or other elevated spot.)   **3 bravely** excellently   **6 anon** soon
**8 judgments** pundits   **whosoever** bar none   **8–9 proper...person**
good-looking man   **11 Go thy way** (an exclamation similar to "on your
way" or "off you go")   **13 'a** he   **hacks** hack-marks, dents   **14–15 laying**

**on** (evidence of) strong blows   **15 take … will** despite what someone may say to the contrary   **By God's lid** by God's eyelid (a mild oath of the day)   **21 he** (referring to Troilus)   **25 helm** helmet   **26 goes** walks   **26–27 three and twenty** (years of age)   **27 grace** one of the sister-goddesses, who were portrayed as women of unmatched beauty and charm   **30 in … Troilus** merely looking at or being looked at by Troilus   **31 daws** jackdaws (Jackdaws were crow-like birds thought to be stupid and of no use.)   **32 Agamemnon** general of the Greek army

(2)                           TROILUS                        [II.ii.61]

SCENE: Priam's palace

*{The Greeks have offered to end their siege of Troy if the Trojans will surrender fair Helen, who was abducted from Greece some time ago. When Priam asks his sons for their thoughts on the proposal, Troilus takes a firm stand for honor and integrity.}*

| | |
|---|---|
| 1 | I take today a wife, and my election |
| | Is led on in the conduct of my will; |
| | My will enkindled by mine eyes and ears, |
| | Two traded pilots 'twixt the dangerous shores |
| 5 | Of will and judgment. How may I avoid, |
| | Although my will distaste what it elected, |
| | The wife I chose? There can be no evasion |
| | To blench from this and to stand firm by honor. |
| | We turn not back the silks upon the merchant |
| 10 | When we have soil'd them, nor the remainder viands |
| | We do not throw in unrespective sieve |
| | Because we now are full. It was thought meet |
| | Paris should do some vengeance on the Greeks. |
| | Your breath with full consent bellied his sails; |
| 15 | The seas and winds, old wranglers, took a truce |
| | And did him service. He touch'd the ports desir'd, |
| | And for an old aunt whom the Greeks held captive, |
| | He brought a Grecian queen, whose youth and freshness |
| | Wrinkles Apollo's, and makes pale the morning. |
| 20 | Why keep we her? The Grecians kept our aunt. |
| | Is she worth keeping? Why, she is a pearl |
| | Whose price hath launch'd above a thousand ships, |
| | And turn'd crown'd kings to merchants. |
| | If you'll avouch 'twas wisdom Paris went— |

As you must needs, for you all cried "Go, go"— 25
If you'll confess he brought home worthy prize—
As you must needs, for you all clapp'd your hands
And cried "Inestimable!"—why do you now
The issue of your proper wisdoms rate,
And do a deed that never Fortune did; 30
Beggar the estimation which you priz'd
Richer than sea and land? O, theft most base,
That we have stol'n what we do fear to keep!
But thieves unworthy of a thing so stol'n,
That in their country did them that disgrace 35
We fear to warrant in our native place!

1 **I take today** (suppose that) today I take  **election** choice  **2 led...of**
guided by  **3 enkindled** incited  **4 traded** experienced  **5 avoid** rid myself
of  **6 distaste** (comes to) dislike  **7 evasion** contrived excuse  **8 blench**
shrink, turn aside  **and to** and yet to  still  **10 remainder viands** left-over
food  **11 in** into (an)  **unrespective sieve** a garbage can (into which only
unregarded or "unrespective" items are thrown)  **12 meet** proper
**14 bellied** filled  **15 old wranglers** longtime adversaries (usually at odds
with each other)  **16 touch'd** arrived safely (in)  **17 old aunt** (referring to
Hesione, Priam's sister)  **19 Wrinkles Apollo's** makes Apollo's youthful
appearance seem old and withered by comparison  **22 above** more than
**23 turn'd...merchants** made kings seems like merchants in search of a
rare pearl (an allusion to Matthew 13:45)  **25 must needs** necessarily must
**29 The...rate** find fault with the fruits of your own wise judgments
**31 Beggar the estimation** deem worthless the thing of value  **priz'd**
(once) valued  **33 That** in that  **34 But thieves** (we are) but thieves
**35–36 That...place** who disgraced the Greeks in their own country with
actions that we are now afraid to justify and defend here in our own land

# TWELFTH NIGHT

After being shipwrecked on the coast of Illyria, Viola adopts the guise of a young man named Cesario, and finds employment as a page to Duke Orsino. Since the Duke has made no headway of late in his attempts to woo the rich widow Olivia, he instructs Cesario to act as emissary between himself and the lady. Unfortunately, because Cesario does such a bang-up job of arguing Orsino's cause, Olivia falls for the messenger instead of the message. What's more, Olivia's beloved Cesario finds he/she has fallen in love with the Duke.

Further complicating matters is the sudden appearance in town of Viola's twin brother Sebastian, who was assumed to have been lost at sea.

Predictably enough, mistaken identities and misplaced affections soon become the order of the day. Though confusion reigns for a time, things eventually sort themselves out: Sebastian marries Olivia, while Viola drops her disguise and professes her love for her husband-to-be, the Duke.

At the same time all of the above is unfolding, Olivia's gentlewoman Maria is spearheading a plot to exact revenge on Olivia's tiresome and fussy steward, Malvolio. Their conspiracy pays off with Malvolio's imprisonment as a madman—a fate from which he is rescued only when Olivia discovers Maria & company's scheme.

**ORSINO,** Duke of Illyria
**SEBASTIAN,** brother to Viola
**SIR TOBY BELCH,** uncle to Olivia
**SIR ANDREW AGUECHEEK,** companion to Sir Toby
**MALVOLIO,** steward to Olivia
**FESTE,** a jester, servant to Olivia

**OLIVIA,** a rich countess
**VIOLA,** servant to Duke Orsino
**MARIA,** Olivia's gentlewoman

(1)                    Malvolio                    [II.v.23]

SCENE: Olivia's garden

*{While fantasizing about Olivia during the course of an afternoon stroll, Malvolio stumbles upon a letter. And so his troubles begin.}* [There are a number of ways to whittle down this piece. Alternate starting points to consider include lines 17, 43, and 54.]

'Tis but fortune; all is fortune. Maria once told me she did affect me; and I have          1
heard herself come thus near; that, should she fancy, it should be one of my
complexion. Besides, she uses me with a more exalted respect than any one
else that follows her. What should I think on 't? To be Count Malvolio. There
is example for 't: the lady of the Strachy married the yeoman of the wardrobe.          5
Having been three months married to her, sitting in my state, calling my officers
about me, in my branch'd velvet gown; having come from a daybed where I have
left Olivia sleeping, and then to have the humor of state; and after a demure
travel of regard, telling them I know my place as I would they should do theirs,
to ask for my kinsman, Toby. Seven of my people, with an obedient start, make          10
out for him. I frown the while; and perchance wind up my watch, or play
with my—some rich jewel. Toby approaches; curtsies there to me. I extend
my hand to him thus, quenching my familiar smile with an austere regard of
control, saying, "Cousin Toby, my fortunes having cast me on your niece give
me this prerogative of speech. You must amend your drunkenness. Besides,          15
you waste the treasure of your time with a foolish knight, one Sir Andrew."
What employment have we here? [*Picking up the letter.*] By my life, this is my
lady's hand. These be her very c's, her u's and her t's; and thus makes she her
great P's. It is, in contempt of question, her hand. [*Reads.*] "To the unknown
belov'd, this, and my good wishes."—Her very phrases! By your leave, wax.          20
Soft! And the impressure her Lucrece, with which she uses to seal. 'Tis my
lady. To whom should this be? [*Opens the letter and reads.*]
          "Jove knows I love,
          But who?
          Lips, do not move;          25
          No man must know."
"No man must know." What follows? The numbers alter'd! "No man must
know." If this should be thee, Malvolio? [*Reads.*]
          "I may command where I adore,
          But silence, like a Lucrece knife,          30
          With bloodless stroke my heart doth gore;
          M.O.A.I. doth sway my life."
"M.O.A.I. doth sway my life." Nay, but first, let me see, let me see, let me see.
"I may command where I adore." Why, she may command me; I serve her, she
is my lady. Why, this is evident to any formal capacity; there is no obstruction          35

in this. And the end—what should that alphabetical position portend? If I could make that resemble something in me! Softly! M.O.A.I. M—Malvolio; M—why, that begins my name. M—but then there is no consonancy in the sequel that suffers under probation: A should follow, but O does. And then I comes behind.

40    M.O.A.I. This simulation is not as the former. And yet, to crush this a little, it would bow to me, for every one of these letters are in my name. Soft! Here follows prose.

[*Reads.*] "If this fall into thy hand, revolve. In my stars I am above thee, but be not afraid of greatness. Some are born great, some achieve greatness,

45    and some have greatness thrust upon 'em. Thy Fates open their hands; let thy blood and spirit embrace them; and, to inure thyself to what thou art like to be, cast thy humble slough and appear fresh. Be opposite with a kinsman, surly with servants. Let thy tongue tang arguments of state; put thyself into the trick of singularity. She thus advises thee that sighs for thee. Remember

50    who commended thy yellow stockings, and wish'd to see thee ever cross-garter'd. I say, remember. Go to, thou art made, if thou desir'st to be so. If not, let me see thee a steward still, the fellow of servants, and not worthy to touch Fortune's fingers. Farewell. She that would alter services with thee, The Fortunate-Unhappy." Daylight and champain discovers not more. This is

55    open. I will be proud, I will read politic authors, I will baffle Sir Toby, I will wash off gross acquaintance, I will be point-devise the very man. I do not now fool myself, to let imagination jade me; for every reason excites to this, that my lady loves me. She did commend my yellow stockings of late, she did praise my leg being cross-garter'd; and in this she manifests herself to my love, and with

60    a kind of injunction drives me to these habits of her liking. I thank my stars, I am happy! I will be strange, stout, in yellow stockings, and cross-garter'd, even with the swiftness of putting on. Jove and my stars be prais'd! Here is yet a postscript. [*Reads.*] "Thou canst not choose but know who I am. If thou entertain'st my love, let it appear in thy smiling; thy smiles become thee well.

65    Therefore in my presence still smile, dear my sweet, I prithee."

Jove, I thank thee. I will smile; I will do everything that thou wilt have me.

**1 she ... me** that (Olivia) was fond of me    **2 fancy** fall in love    **3 uses** treats, behaves toward    **4 follows her** is one of her entourage    **5 example** precedent    **the ... wardrobe** (Malvolio refers to an otherwise unidentified couple who he evidently feels paved the way for his own ambitions.)
**6 state** chair of state, throne    **7 branch'd** embroidered with a decorative pattern of branches or leaves    **8 humor ... state** imperious attitude of authority    **9 travel of regard** inspection of the troops    **11–12 play with my** (Malvolio seems about to refer to his steward's chain—a symbol of his actual station in life—but catches himself in time.)    **13 familiar** friendly
**17 employment** business, matter (For an account of the letter's significance, see II.iii.131.)    **18 c's, u's, t's** ("cut" was a slang word for the female genitalia)    **19 in contempt of** beyond    **20 By ... wax** (Malvolio is addressing the letter's wax seal as he breaks it.)    **21 Soft** wait    **impressure**

**her Lucrece** impression on the wax seal is of Lucrece (Lucrece committed suicide after being raped by Tarquin.)   **27 numbers** meter (of the verse) **35 any formal capacity** anyone of normal intelligence  **obstruction** obstacle, difficulty   **36 position** arrangement   **36–37 If . . . me** (Malvolio never quite deduces that "M.O.A.I." refers to the first, last, second and second to last letters of his own name, respectively.)   **37 Softly** slowly **38 consonancy . . . sequel** similar pattern among the rest of the letters **39 suffers under probation** stands up under scrutiny   **40 simulation** disguised meaning  **crush** force   **41 bow** yield, (i.e., pertain)   **43 revolve** consider   **46 inure** accustom   **47 slough** discarded skin of a snake, i.e., former appearance (Malvolio's point here is that he should cast off his old, casual demeanor in favor of a more haughty attitude.)  **opposite** hostile, quarrelsome   **48 tang** sound loud (with)  **of state** political   **49 trick of singularity** habit of being eccentric   **50–51 cross-garter'd** a method of wearing one's garters that featured crossing them behind the knees   **51 Go to** (an exclamation of impatience on the order of "Come on")  **made** assured of success   **53 alter services** exchange places (i.e., make you the master and myself a servant)   **54 champain** flat and open country **discovers** reveals   **55 open** obvious  **politic authors** writers of political theory  **baffle** treat with contempt   **55–56 wash off** rid myself of **56 gross acquaintance** lowly friends  **point-devise** precisely   **57 jade** trick   **59 manifests** shows   **60 injunction** command, order  **these habits** this attire   **61 strange** reserved, aloof  **stout** proud, haughty   **62 putting on** a command   **65 still** continually  **prithee** pray thee, beg you

---

(2)                         MALVOLIO                         [III.iv.64]

SCENE: Olivia's garden

*{Malvolio is mad with love for Olivia, while Olivia wonders if he might be going mad—which is to say that Maria's scheme (see II.iii.131) is playing out precisely as intended. Alone with his delusions of love, Malvolio is in a mood to rejoice.}*

O, ho, do you come near me now? No worse man than Sir Toby to look to   1
me! This concurs directly with the letter. She sends him on purpose, that I
may appear stubborn to him; for she incites me to that in the letter. "Cast thy
humble slough," says she; "be opposite with a kinsman, surly with servants; let
thy tongue tang with arguments of state; put thyself into the trick of singular-   5
ity." And consequently sets down the manner how: as, a sad face, a reverend
carriage, a slow tongue, in the habit of some sir of note, and so forth. I have
lim'd her; but it is Jove's doing, and Jove make me thankful! And when she

went away now, "Let this fellow be look'd to." "Fellow!" Not "Malvolio," nor
10     after my degree, but "fellow." Why, everything adheres together, that no dram
of a scruple, no scruple of a scruple, no obstacle, no incredulous or unsafe
circumstance—What can be said? Nothing that can be can come between me
and the full prospect of my hopes. Well, Jove, not I, is the doer of this, and he
is to be thank'd.

**1 come near** begin to comprehend (Malvolio addresses Olivia, who's just
exited in a state of bewilderment.)   **1–2 Sir . . . me** (Prior to leaving, Olivia
saw to it that Sir Toby looked after Malvolio.)   **2 letter** (see preceding
entry)   **4 slough** discarded skin of a snake, i.e., former appearance
**opposite** hostile, quarrelsome   **5 tang** sound loud (with)   **of state** political
**5–6 trick of singularity** habit of being eccentric   **6 sad** grave, serious
**7 slow** sober, serious   **habit** apparel   **8 lim'd** ensnared   **9 now** just now
**10 after my degree** according to my rank (as merely her steward)
**adheres together** hangs together, fits   **dram** one-eighth of a fluid ounce
(hence, a very small amount)   **11 scruple** one-third of a dram   **incredulous**
incredible   **unsafe** uncertain

(3)                    SIR TOBY BELCH                    [III.iv.218]

SCENE: Olivia's garden

*{Up to his usual mischief, Sir Toby attempts to convince Cesario (i.e., Viola)
that Sir Andrew Aguecheek is champing at the bit to do battle with him. In fact,
nothing could be further from the truth . . . but that doesn't stop Sir Toby from
amusing himself with this grossly inaccurate account of the timid Sir Andrew.}*

1     Gentleman, God save thee! That defense thou hast, betake thee to 't. Of what
nature the wrongs are thou hast done him, I know not; but thy intercepter, full
of despite, bloody as the hunter, attends thee at the orchard-end. Dismount
thy tuck, be yare in thy preparation; for thy assailant is quick, skillful, and deadly.
5     Therefore, if you hold your life at any price, betake you to your guard; for your
opposite hath in him what youth, strength, skill, and wrath can furnish man
withal. He is knight, dubb'd with unhatch'd rapier and on carpet consideration,
but he is a devil in private brawl. Souls and bodies hath he divorc'd three; and
his incensement at this moment is so implacable, that satisfaction can be none
10     but by pangs of death and sepulcher. Hob, nob, is his word; give 't or take 't. His
indignation derives itself out of a very competent injury; therefore, get you on
and give him his desire. Back you shall not to the house, unless you undertake
that with me which with as much safety you might answer him. Therefore,

on, or strip your sword stark naked; for meddle you must, that's certain, or
forswear to wear iron about you.                                                      15

**1 That defense** whatever ability to defend yourself   **2 intercepter** one
who ambushes another   **3 despite** ill-will, hatred **bloody** intent on
bloodshed   **hunter** hunting dog (tracking down its prey)   **attends** awaits
**3–4 Dismount thy tuck** unsheath your rapier   **4 yare** brisk and ready
**7 withal** with   **unhatch'd** unused (in battle)   **on carpet consideration**
i.e., his title was obtained through his connections with the royal court
rather than as a reward for valor on the battlefield   **8 divorc'd** separated
**9 incensement** rage   **10 Hob, nob** have it or have it not, give it or take it
(such being the sentiments of a man who means business)   **11 competent**
sufficient (to justify action)   **13 that** i.e., a duel   **14 strip...naked** draw
your sword (and fight)   **meddle** engage (in combat)   **15 forswear...you**
give up your right to wear a sword

**ALTERNATES**

| | |
|---|---|
| Orsino | [I.i.1–40] |
| Sir Toby Belch | [III.iv.147–196] |
| Sebastian | [IV.iii.1–21] |

# THE TWO GENTLEMEN OF VERONA

Valentine and Proteus arrive at the court of the Duke of Milan intending to acquire a bit of worldly experience. In almost no time both gentlemen of Verona fall in love with the Duke's daughter, Silvia. Silvia takes a shine to Valentine as well, so she and Valentine make plans to run away together. But their plans fall apart when the Duke hears from Proteus of his daughter's intentions, and promptly banishes Valentine.

Proteus's subsequent attempt to win Silvia for himself is a dismal failure. Silvia rebuffs his advances and sets off for the woods in search of her beloved Valentine.

Meanwhile Julia, Proteus's girlfriend back in Verona, has decided to adopt the guise of a page and pursue Proteus to Milan. Once there, Julia discovers her beau's infatuation with Silvia. Undeterred (and still in disguise), Julia then joins Proteus as he seeks out Silvia—a mission that culminates in Proteus rescuing Silvia from a band of outlaws.

Things begin to settle a bit when Valentine appears on the scene and Julia reveals her true identity. Eventually, Proteus realizes that it is Julia he truly loves, and Valentine is granted Silvia's hand in marriage.

Appearing from time to time as a playful adjunct to the main story are Proteus's servant Launce and his indelicate dog, Crab.

**DUKE OF MILAN**
**VALENTINE,** a gentleman of Verona
**PROTEUS,** a gentleman of Verona
**LAUNCE,** servant to Proteus

**JULIA,** a lady of Verona, beloved of Proteus
**SILVIA,** daughter to the Duke of Milan, beloved of Valentine
**LUCETTA,** a young woman attending on Julia

(1)                         LAUNCE                         [II.iii.1]

SCENE: A street in Venice

*{The time has come for Launce to leave the nest, and as a result, almost everyone at home is overcome with grief.}*

Nay, 'twill be this hour ere I have done weeping; All the kind of the Launces    1
have this very fault. I have receiv'd my proportion, like the prodigious son, and
am going with Sir Proteus to the Imperial's court. I think Crab my dog be the
sourest-natur'd dog that lives: my mother weeping, my father wailing, my sister
crying, our maid howling, our cat wringing her hands, and all our house in a    5
great perplexity, yet did not this cruel-hearted cur shed one tear. He is a stone,
a very pebblestone, and has no more pity in him than a dog. A Jew would have
wept to have seen our parting. Why, my grandam, having no eyes, look you,
wept herself blind at my parting—nay, I'll show you the manner of it. This shoe
is my father—no, this left shoe is my father—no, no, this left shoe is my mother.    10
Nay, that cannot be neither. Yes, it is so, it is so—it hath the worser sole. This
shoe, with the hole in it, is my mother, and this my father. A vengeance on 't!
There 'tis. Now, sir, this staff is my sister; for, look you, she is as white as a lily
and as small as a wand. This hat is Nan, our maid. I am the dog—no, the dog is
himself, and I am the dog—oh, the dog is me, and I am myself; ay, so, so. Now    15
come I to my father: "Father, your blessing." Now should not the shoe speak a
word for weeping. Now should I kiss my father; well, he weeps on. Now come
I to my mother. O, that she could speak now like a wood woman! Well, I kiss
her; why, there 'tis; here's my mother's breath up and down. Now come I to
my sister; mark the moan she makes. Now the dog all this while sheds not a    20
tear nor speaks a word; but see how I lay the dust with my tears! Well, I will go.

**I kind** family, kindred  **2 proportion** (Launce means "portion," i.e., his
rightful share of the family wealth.) **prodigious** (Launce's malapropism for
"prodigal") **3 Imperial's** (Launce means "Emperor's")  **8 grandam**
grandmother **9 the manner of it** i.e., the way it went  **This shoe** (At this
point Launce proceeds to demonstrate with his own shoes, staff, etc.)
**II sole** (with a play on "soul")  **18 wood** frenzied, distraught (playing as
well on the image of a wooden shoe)  **19 up and down** exactly  **21 lay**
keep down

(2)                          **PROTEUS**                    [II.vi.i]

SCENE: The Duke of Milan's palace

*{Having fallen in love with his best friend's girl, Proteus must now deal with a sticky situation: Should he remain faithful to his pal Valentine and to his girl back home, Julia . . . or should he instead listen to his libido and pursue the fair Silvia?}* [Line 30 works well as the end point for an abbreviated version of this piece.]

| | |
|---|---|
| 1 | To leave my Julia, shall I be forsworn; |
| | To love fair Silvia, shall I be forsworn; |
| | To wrong my friend, I shall be much forsworn. |
| | And ev'n that pow'r which gave me first my oath |
| 5 | Provokes me to this threefold perjury. |
| | Love bade me swear and Love bids me forswear. |
| | O sweet-suggesting Love, if thou hast sinn'd, |
| | Teach me, thy tempted subject, to excuse it! |
| | At first I did adore a twinkling star, |
| 10 | But now I worship a celestial sun. |
| | Unheedful vows may heedfully be broken, |
| | And he wants wit that wants resolved will |
| | To learn his with t' exchange the bad for better. |
| | Fie, fie, unreverend tongue! To call her bad, |
| 15 | Whose sovereignty so oft thou has preferr'd |
| | With twenty thousand soul-confirming oaths. |
| | I cannot leave to love, and yet I do; |
| | But there I leave to love where I should love. |
| | Julia I lose and Valentine I lose: |
| 20 | If I keep them, I needs must lose myself; |
| | If I lose them, thus I find by their loss |
| | For Valentine, myself; for Julia, Silvia. |
| | I to myself am dearer than a friend, |
| | For love is still most precious in itself; |
| 25 | And Silvia—witness Heaven, that made her fair!— |
| | Shows Julia but a swarthy Ethiope. |
| | I will forget that Julia is alive, |
| | Rememb'ring that my love to her is dead; |
| | And Valentine I'll hold an enemy, |
| 30 | Aiming at Silvia as a sweeter friend. |
| | I cannot now prove constant to myself |
| | Without some treachery us'd to Valentine. |
| | This night he meaneth with a corded ladder |
| | To climb celestial Silvia's chamber-window; |

Myself in counsel, his competitor.                                              35
Now presently I'll give her father notice
Of their disguising and pretended flight;
Who, all enrag'd, will banish Valentine;
For Thurio, he intends, shall wed his daughter.
But, Valentine being gone, I'll quickly cross                                    40
By some sly trick blunt Thurio's dull proceeding.
Love, lend me wings to make my purpose swift,
As thou hast lent me wit to plot this drift!

**I shall I** I shall   **3 friend** i.e., Valentine   **7 sweet-suggesting** sweetly
seductive   **7–8 if…it** i.e., if even you have committed transgressions in the
name of romance, teach me—in that I am now under your influence—how
to excuse myself   **11 Unheedful** rash   **heedfully** with careful consideration
**12 wants** lacks   **13 learn** teach   **15 sovereignty** excellence   **preferr'd**
praised   **16 soul-confirming** sworn on my soul   **17 leave** cease
**20–22 If…Silvia** if I keep their friendship, then I must lose myself; if I
abandon them, then I will find in exchange for Valentine's friendship, myself;
and in place of Julia's love, Silvia   **24 still** always   **26 Shows Julia** by
comparison, shows Julia to be   **Ethiope** Ethiopian (or any person of black
complexion)   **30 Aiming at** considering, intending   **32 us'd** done
**33 corded ladder** rope ladder   **35 Myself in counsel** having taken me
into his confidence   **37 disguising** concealing   **pretended** intended
**40 cross** thwart   **41 blunt** stupid   **dull** listless   **43 drift** scheme

(3)                                  LAUNCE                              [IV.IV.1]

SCENE: Outside the Duke of Milan's palace

*{Life with Crab the dog, part two. (For Launce's previous ruminations on the
subject, see entry (1), above.)}*

When a man's servant shall play the cur with him, look you, it goes hard—     1
one that I brought up of a puppy, one that I sav'd from drowning when three
or four of his blind brothers and sisters went to it. I have taught him, even as
one would say precisely, "Thus I would teach a dog." I was sent to deliver him
as a present to Mistress Silvia from my master, and I came no sooner into the   5
dining-chamber, but he steps me to her trencher and steals her capon's leg. O,
'tis a foul thing when a cur cannot keep himself in all companies! I would have,
as one should say, one that takes upon him to be a dog indeed, to be, as it
were, a dog at all things. If I had not more wit than he, to take a fault upon me
that he did, I think verily he had been hang'd for 't; sure as I live, he had suffer'd   10

for 't. You shall judge: he thrusts me himself into the company of three or four gentlemanlike dogs, under the Duke's table. He had not been there—bless the mark!—a pissing-while, but all the chamber smelt him. "Out with the dog!" says one. "What cur is that?" says another. "Whip him out," says the third.

15 "Hang him up," says the Duke. I, having been acquainted with the smell before, knew it was Crab, and goes me to the fellow that whips the dogs. "Friend," quoth I, "you mean to whip the dog?" "Ay, marry do I," quoth he. "You do him the more wrong," quoth I; "'twas I did the thing you wot of." He makes me no more ado, but whips me out of the chamber. How many masters would

20 do this for his servant? Nay, I'll be sworn, I have sat in the stocks for puddings he hath stol'n, otherwise he had been executed. I have stood on the pillory for geese he hath kill'd, otherwise he had suffer'd for 't. Thou think'st not of this now. Nay, I remember the trick you serv'd me when I took my leave of Madam Silvia. Did not I bid thee still mark me and do as I do? When didst thou

25 see me heave up my leg and make water against a gentlewoman's farthingale? Didst thou ever see me do such a trick?

**1 it goes hard** it's extremely trying   **2 of** from   **6 trencher** wooden platter   **7 keep** restrain, behave   **9 a dog at** adept at   **10 verily** in fact **had** would have   **12–13 bless the mark** (an expression that in effect begs forgiveness if any offense is taken over what is about to be uttered) **13 pissing-while** very short time (Naturally, Launce is exploiting the term's more literal sense as well.)   **17 marry** indeed   **18 more** greater   **wot of** know of, are aware of   **20 puddings** sausages   **22 Thou** (he addresses Crab)   **23 serv'd** played (on)   **25 farthingale** hooped petticoat

**ALTERNATES**

| | |
|---|---|
| Speed | [II.i.18–32] |
| Proteus | [II.iv.191–214] |
| Duke of Milan | [III.i.136–169] |

# THE WINTER'S TALE

For no particularly good reason, Leontes, the King of Sicilia, accuses his wife, Hermione, of stepping out on him with his friend, Polixenes. Though Polixenes manages to escape the wrath of Leontes by returning to his home in Bohemia, Hermione is not so fortunate.

Shortly after being thrown in prison by her husband, Hermione gives birth to a daughter, who Leontes declares is "a bastard by Polixenes," and so orders it abandoned in some remote place. Although Hermione is cleared at her trial of any wrongdoing, it's only when word arrives that she has suddenly taken ill and died that a repentant Leontes finally sees the error of his ways.

Hermione's babe, meanwhile, is abandoned on the coast of Bohemia. But fortunately, the tot is soon discovered by a kindly shepherd, who proceeds to raise her as his own daughter, Perdita.

At the age of sixteen, Perdita falls in love with Florizel, the son of Polixenes. Since Polixenes deems a poor shepherd's daughter unworthy of his son, he thwarts their plans for marriage. The two lovers thus sail off to Sicilia, where Leontes soon figures out that Perdita is his long-lost daughter. Eventually, Polixenes and Leontes are reconciled, and arrangements are made for the marriage of Florizel and Perdita. Adding to the happy proceedings is a surprise appearance by Hermione; evidently, news of the Queen's death was greatly exaggerated.

**LEONTES,** King of Sicilia
**ANTIGONUS,** a lord of Sicilia
**POLIXENES,** King of Bohemia
**FLORIZEL,** son to Polixenes
**SHEPHERD,** guardian to Perdita
**CLOWN,** son to the shepherd
**AUTOLYCUS,** a rogue

**HERMIONE,** queen to Leontes
**PERDITA,** daughter to Leontes and Hermione
**PAULINA,** wife to Antigonus

(1)                        **ANTIGONUS**                [III.iii.15]

SCENE: A deserted area near the Bohemian seacoast

*{Antigonus was commanded by Leontes to take Hermione's newborn and leave it in a far-off and barren locale. Though overwhelmed by compassion and sorrow, Antigonus's sense of duty compels him to abandon the poor babe he clutches here on the shores of Bohemia.}*

1      Come, poor babe.
       I have heard, but not believ'd, the spirits o' th' dead
       May walk again. If such thing be, thy mother
       Appear'd to me last night, for ne'er was dream
5      So like a waking. To me comes a creature,
       Sometimes her head on one side, some another;
       I never saw a vessel of like sorrow,
       So fill'd and so becoming. In pure white robes,
       Like very sanctity, she did approach
10     My cabin where I lay; thrice bow'd before me,
       And, gasping to begin some speech, her eyes
       Became two spouts. The fury spent, anon
       Did this break from her: "Good Antigonus,
       Since fate, against thy better disposition,
15     Hath made thy person for the thrower-out
       Of my poor babe, according to thine oath,
       Places remote enough are in Bohemia;
       There weep and leave it crying. And, for the babe
       Is counted lost forever, Perdita,
20     I prithee, call 't. For this ungentle business,
       Put on thee by my lord, thou ne'er shalt see
       Thy wife Paulina more." And so, with shrieks,
       She melted into air. Affrighted much,
       I did in time collect myself and thought
25     This was so and no slumber. Dreams are toys;
       Yet for this once, yea, superstitiously,
       I will be squar'd by this. I do believe
       Hermione hath suffer'd death, and that
       Apollo would, this being indeed the issue
30     Of King Polixenes, it should be here laid,
       Either for life or death, upon the earth
       Of its right father. Blossom, speed thee well!
       [*He lays down the baby, as thunder is heard.*]
       The storm begins. Poor wretch,
35     That for thy mother's fault art thus expos'd

To loss and what may follow. Weep I cannot,
But my heart bleeds; and most accurs'd am I
To be by oath enjoin'd to this. Farewell!

**6 on one side** to one side (of me)  **7 vessel** person  **8 fill'd and** filled
(with grief), and yet  **12 spouts** (of tears)  **anon** soon  **14 disposition**
inclination  **19 Perdita** (The literal meaning of which is "the lost girl.")
**20 prithee** pray thee, beg you  **For** on account of  **ungentle** ignoble,
disgraceful  **25 toys** nonsense, trifles  **27 squar'd** governed  **29 would**
would have, wills  **32 right** true  **speed thee** fare you  **36 loss** death
**Weep** (alludes to line 18)  **38 enjoin'd** bound

(2)                    SHEPHERD                    [III.iii.59]

SCENE: A deserted area near the Bohemian seacoast

*{After regretfully doing his duty (see preceding entry), Antigonus was chased
away by a bear, leaving the infant Perdita all alone amidst the rising storm.
But then, along comes this kindly old shepherd....}*

I would there were no age between ten and three-and-twenty, or that youth        1
would sleep out the rest; for there is nothing in the between but getting
wenches with child, wronging the ancientry, stealing, fighting—Hark you now!
Would any but these boil'd brains of nineteen and two-and-twenty hunt this
weather? They have scar'd away two of my best sheep, which I fear the wolf       5
will sooner find than the master. If anywhere I have them, 'tis by the seaside,
browsing of ivy. Good luck, an 't be thy will! [*Sees the infant.*] What have we
here? Mercy on 's, a barne, a very pretty barne! A boy or a child, I wonder? A
pretty one, a very pretty one. Sure, come scape. Though I am not bookish, yet
I can read waiting-gentlewoman in the scape. This has been some stair-work,      10
some trunk-work, some behind-door-work. They were warmer that got this
than the poor thing is here. I'll take it up for pity. Yet I'll tarry till my son come;
he halloo'd but even now. Whoa, ho, hoa!

**I would** wish that  **3 ancientry** elders  **4 boil'd brains** hot-headed
creatures  **nineteen...twenty** (Apparently two young hunters, ages
nineteen and twenty-two, have managed to frighten away a pair of the
shepherd's sheep.)  **this** in this  **7 browsing of** grazing on  **an...will** if it be
God's will  **8 barne** child  **child** female infant  **9 scape** transgression,
escapade (of a sexual nature)  **10–11 stair, trunk, behind-door** (Shepherd
is referring to a few of the more likely spots for an impromptu sexual liaison.)
**11 warmer** (with a play on hot-blooded, i.e., passionate)  **got** begot

(3)                              Clown                       [III.iii.83]

SCENE: A deserted area near the Bohemian seacoast

*{The kindly old Shepherd is not the only one to have made a startling discovery on this fateful day (see preceding entry). Breathless with excitement, his son Clown (literally, "rustic" or "country fellow") arrives on the scene to recount a fantastical tale of his own.}*

1  I have seen two such sights, by sea and by land! But I am not to say it is a sea, for it is now the sky; betwixt the firmament and it you cannot thrust a bodkin's point. I would you did but see how it chafes, how it rages, how it takes up the shore! But that's not to the point. O, the most piteous cries of the poor souls!
5  Sometimes to see 'em, and not to see 'em; now the ship boring the moon with her mainmast, and anon swallowed with yest and froth, as you'd thrust a cork into a hogshead. And then for the land-service, to see how the bear tore out his shoulder-bone; how he cried to me for help and said his name was Antigonus, a nobleman. But to make an end of the ship, to see how the sea
10  flap-dragon'd it; but, first, how the poor souls roar'd, and the sea mock'd them; and how the poor gentleman roar'd and the bear mock'd him, both roaring louder than the sea or weather.

**2 now the sky** i.e., rages so violently that it seems to touch the sky **bodkin's** needle's **3 takes up** contends with, rebukes **6 anon** soon thereafter **yest** foam **7 hogshead** large oak barrel **land-service** events on land **9 Antigonus** (For an account of Antigonus's presence in the area, see entry (1).) **make an end** i.e., conclude my tale **10 flap-dragon'd it** swallowed it as one would a "flapdragon" (which was a flaming raisin afloat in a glass of burning liquor)

(4)                            Polixenes                     [IV.iv.417]

SCENE: Shepherd's cottage

*{Sporting a disguise, Polixenes has arrived at the local sheep shearing festival aiming to check out something he's recently heard—namely, that his son Florizel is courting a shepherd's daughter named Perdita. Once he determines that the rumor is all too true, Polixenes embarks upon a royal rampage before his son, Perdita, and the rest of the festival crowd.}*

Mark your divorce, young sir, [*Unmasks himself.*]                    1
Whom son I dare not call. Thou art too base
To be acknowledg'd. Thou, a scepter's heir,
That thus affects a sheep-hook! Thou, old traitor,
I am sorry that by hanging thee I can                                 5
But shorten thy life one week. And thou, fresh piece
Of excellent witchcraft, who of force must know
The royal fool thou copest with,
I'll have thy beauty scratch'd with briers, and made
More homely than thy state. For thee, fond boy,                       10
If I may ever know thou dost but sigh
That thou no more shalt see this knack—as never
I mean thou shalt—we'll bar thee from succession,
Not hold thee of our blood, no, not our kin,
Farther than Deucalion off. Mark thou my words.                      15
Follow us to court. Thou, churl, for this time,
Though full of our displeasure, yet we free thee
From the dead blow of it. And you, enchantment—
Worthy enough a herdsman, yea, him too,
That makes himself, but for our honor therein,                       20
Unworthy thee—if ever henceforth thou
These rural latches to his entrance open,
Or hoop his body more with thy embraces,
I will devise a death as cruel for thee
As thou art tender to it.                                             25

**1 Mark your divorce** (Polixenes has jumped forth in response to Florizel's
request that Perdita's father "Mark our contract," i.e., intent to wed.)
**3 scepter's** i.e., king's   **4 affects** shows a desire for   **sheep-hook**
shepherd's staff   **Thou** (referring to Perdita's father, Shepherd)   **6 thou**
(referring to Perdita)   **7 of force** necessarily   **8 thou copest** you are
dealing   **10 state** situation in life   **fond** foolish   **12 knack** schemer
**13 we'll** (Polixenes is employing the royal plural)   **15 Farther . . . off** more
distantly related (to us) than Deucalian (who was a Noah-type figure of
classical mythology)   **16 churl** peasant (referring once again to Shepherd)
**18 dead** deadly   **enchantment** (referring to Perdita)   **19 enough** enough
of   **him** i.e., of Florizel   **20 but . . . therein** were it not for my royal blood
in him   **23 hoop** encircle

(5)                          **AUTOLYCUS**                      [IV.iv.595]

SCENE: Shepherd's cottage

*{Autolycus is a peddler, rogue, and small-time thief who is particularly delighted with himself at the moment. He's about to call it a day at the local festival, where he's met with considerable success doing what he does best.}*

1    Ha, ha, what a fool Honesty is! And Trust, his sworn brother, a very simple
     gentleman! I have sold all my trumpery; not a counterfeit stone, not a rib-
     bon, glass, pomander, brooch, table-book, ballad, knife, tape, glove, shoe-tie,
     bracelet, horn-ring, to keep my pack from fasting. They throng who should
5    buy first, as if my trinkets had been hallow'd and brought a benediction to the
     buyer; by which means I saw whose purse was best in picture, and what I saw,
     to my good use I rememb'red. My clown, who wants but something to be a
     reasonable man, grew so in love with the wenches' song, that he would not
     stir his pettitoes till he had both tune and words, which so drew the rest of
10   the herd to me that all their other senses stuck in ears. You might have pinch'd
     a placket, it was senseless; 'twas nothing to geld a codpiece of a purse; I could
     have fil'd keys off that hung in chains. No hearing, no feeling, but my sir's song,
     and admiring the nothing of it. So that in this time of lethargy I pick'd and cut
     most of their festival purses; and had not the old man come in with whoo-bub
15   against his daughter and the King's son and scar'd my choughs from the chaff,
     I had not left a purse alive in the whole army.

     **1 simple** naive, half-witted   **2 trumpery** useless articles, junk
     **3 pomander** perfumed ball   **table-book** notebook, tablet   **4 horn-ring**
     ring made of an animal's horn   **fasting** i.e., being empty   **4–5 They ... first**
     those who bought first crowded closely together   **6 was ... picture** looked
     most promising   **7 clown** (referring to Shepherd's son, Clown)   **wants but
     something** lacks only one thing (i.e., intelligence)   **8 wenches' song**
     (A song he and two country girls performed was the device Autolycus
     employed to capture everyone's attention; see IV.iv.297.)   **9 pettitoes** toes
     **10 stuck in ears** were preoccupied with listening   **11 placket** slit in a
     woman's petticoat (and in this case, a bawdy reference to that which lies
     within)   **senseless** without feeling or perception   **geld** cut   **codpiece**
     pouch-like flap on the front of a man's breeches   **of** from   **12 my sir's** i.e.,
     Clown's   **13 nothing** nonsense   **lethargy** stupor   **14 old man** (referring
     to Polixenes and his sudden eruption; see preceding entry)   **whoo-bub** a
     hubbub   **15 choughs** crows

**ALTERNATE**
Leontes   [I.ii.180–207]

# GUIDE TO PRONUNCIATION

Everything's going like clockwork. The pace feels right, you're focused, and your points are being made. This Shakespeare thing is a snap. And then just like that—something's wrong. Those same people at the table in front of you, who seconds earlier were hanging on every word of your monologue, now seem distracted. They're still listening—sort of—but their attention has been broken in two. What on earth could have happened?

In truth, almost anything. But when it comes to performing Shakespeare, an all-too-common culprit in this kind of disruption is faulty pronunciation. Perhaps nothing derails a smooth-running monologue quite so quickly as a botched moniker.

The bad news is that this sort of thing happens all the time. The good news is that it's entirely preventable. All you need is the resolve to get it right and a resource to help you do just that. The first part of the equation is your responsibility; the second is taken care of with this appendix.

The essentials of this pronunciation guide are as follows:

- Syllables are separated by a hyphen.
- Accented syllables are CAPITALIZED.
- Syllables or parts of syllables that are *italicized* indicate vowel sounds that are lightly articulated. For example, the sound of <*uh*> is identical to that of <uh>, but it's uttered for a shorter length of time: an eighth note versus a quarter, if you will.

In an attempt to strike a happy medium between ease of use and precision, a phonetic-based key to pronunciation has been adopted. The guide's basic sounds are as follows:

## Vowel Sounds

### A

**A, a** . . . as in MAN, ASK, FLAP
**AH, ah** . . . as in DOT, ODD, JOG
**AHR, ahr** . . . as in CAR, FAR, MARK

**AIR, air** . . . as in CARE, WEAR, FAIR
**AY, ay** . . . as in DAY, WEIGHT, THEY
**AW, aw** . . . as in RAW, BALL, TALK

279

E

**E, e** . . . as in PET, LESS, WRECK
**EE, ee** . . . as in EAT, WE, DEED

**EER, eer** . . . as in JEER, NEAR, PIER

I

**I, i** . . . as in TRIP, SIT, PIN

**Y, y** . . . as in ICE, TRY, NIGHT

O

**OH, oh** . . . as in TOE, DOUGH, OLD
**OO, oo** . . . as in OOZE, TWO, SOUP
**OR, or** . . . as in FOR, WAR, MORE

**OOR, oor** . . . as in TOUR, LURE
**OW, ow** . . . as in HOW, POUT, DOWN
**OY, oy** . . . as in TOY, OIL, COIN

U

**UH, uh** . . . as in DUMB, SON, UP
**UR, ur** . . . as in SPUR, STIR, EARN

**UU, uu** . . . as in HOOD, PULL, TOOK

## Consonant Sounds

**B, b** . . . as in BOB, CRAB
**CH, ch** . . . as in CHOP, DUTCH
**D, d** . . . as in DID, POD
**F, f** . . . as in FLUFF, LAUGH
**G, g** . . . as in GAG, RUG
**H, h** . . . as in HOT, HIP
**J, j** . . . as in JUICE, CAGE
**K, k** . . . as in CAKE, COOK
**L, l** . . . as in LULL, ALE
**M, m** . . . as in MOM, SOME
**N, n** . . . as in NUN, SOON

**NG, ng** . . . as in RING, BANG
**P, p** . . . as in POP, MAP
**R, r** . . . as in RIP, MORE
**S, s** . . . as in SASS, SIP
**T, t** . . . as in TOT, CAST
**TH, th** . . . as in PATH, THOUGHT
**V, v** . . . as in VERY, HIVE
**W, w** . . . as in WOW, QUIT
**Y, y** . . . as in YES, YAWN
**Z, z** . . . as in HAZE, ZOO
**ZH, zh** . . . as in BEIGE

Listed below are the most widely accepted pronunciations of character and location names appearing in *Shakespeare for One*. Commonly recognized words like *Henry* and *Verona* have been omitted, since most who use this book will know them already. For those who don't, any standard dictionary can fill in the gaps.

| | |
|---|---|
| **ACHERON** | (AK-*uh*-rahn) |
| **ACTAEON** | (ak-TEE-*uh*n) |
| **ADRIANA** | (ay-dree-AH-n*uh*) |
| **AENEAS** | (ee-NEE-*uh*s) |
| **AEOLUS** | (EE-*oh*-luhs) |
| **AGAMEMNON** | (ag-*uh*-MEM-nahn) |
| **AGINCOURT** | (AJ-in-kort) |
| **AGUECHEEK** | (AY-gyoo-cheek) |
| **ALBANY** | (AWL-b*uh*-nee) |
| **ALBION** | (AL-bee-ahn) |
| **ALCIBIADES** | (al-si-BY-*uh*-deez) |
| **AMIAMON** | (*uh*-MY-mahn) |
| **AMIENS** | (AY-mi-enz) |
| **ANCHISES** | (an-KY-seez) |
| **ANDRONICUS, MARCUS** | (MAR-kuhs an-DRON-i-kuhs) |
| **ANDRONICUS, TITUS** | (TY-tuhs an-DRON-i-kuhs) |
| **ANGIERS** | (AN-jeerz) |
| **ANJOU** | (AN-joo) |
| **ANTENOR** | (an-TEE-nur) |
| **ANTHROPOPHAGI** | (an-throh-PAHF-*uh*-jy) |
| **ANTIGONUS** | (an-TIG-*oh*-nuhs) |
| **ANTIOCHUS** | (an-TY-*oh*-kuhs) |
| **ANTIPHOLUS** | (an-TIF-oh-luhs) |
| **ANTIPODES** | (an-TIP-*oh*-deez) |
| **ANTONY** | (AN-t*oh*-nee) |
| **APEMANTUS** | (ap-e-MAN-tuhs) |
| **ARGUS** | (AHR-guhs) |
| **ARIEL** | (E-ree-*e*l or AIR-*ee*-el) |
| **ARMADO** | (ahr-MAH-doh) |
| **ARRAGON** | (AR-*uh*-gahn) |
| **ASCANIUS** | (as-KAY-n*ee*-uhs) |
| **ATE** | (AY-tee) |
| **AUTOLYCUS** | (aw-TAHL-i-kuhs) |
| | |
| **BACCHUS** | (BAK-*uh*s) |
| **BALTHAZAR** | (bal-tha-ZAHR or bal-TAH-zahr) |
| **BANQUO** | (BAN-kwoh) |
| **BAPTISTA** | (bap-TEES-t*ah*) |
| **BARBASON** | (BAHR-b*uh*-suhn) |
| **BARDOLPH** | (BAHR-dawlf) |
| **BASIMECU** | (baz-i-m*uh*-KOO) |

| | |
|---|---|
| **BASSANIO** | (ba-SAH-nee-oh) |
| **BEATRICE** | (BEE-*uh*-tris) |
| **BEAUFORT** | (BOH-furt) |
| **BELARIUS** | (bel-AH-ree-uhs or be-LAY-ree-uhs) |
| **BELLARIO** | (be-LAH-ree-oh) |
| **BENVOLIO** | (ben-VOH-l*ee*-oh) |
| **BEROWNE** | (be-ROON) |
| **BERTRAM** | (BUR-tr*uh*m) |
| **BLANCHE** | (BLAHNSH) |
| **BOHEMIA** | (boh-HEE-mee-*uh*) |
| **BOLINGBROKE** | (BO-ling-bruuk) |
| **BOYET** | (boy-ET) |
| **BRABANTIO** | (bra-BAN-shoh) |
| **BRITAINE** | (bre-TAN-y*uh*) |
| **BURGUNDY** | (BUR-guhn-dee) |
| **BURY ST. EDMUNDS** | (BE-ree SAYNT ED-muhndz) |
| | |
| **CAESAR, JULIUS** | (JOOL-yuhs SEE-zur) |
| **CAIUS MARCIUS** | (KAY-uhs or KAY-yuhs MAHR-shuhs) |
| **CALAIS** | (ka-LAY) |
| **CALIBAN** | (KAL-i-ban) |
| **CALPURNIA** | (kal-PUR-n*ee-uh*) |
| **CAMILLO** | (ka-MIL-oh) |
| **CAMPEIUS** | (kam-PAY-uhs) |
| **CAPULET** | (KAP-yoo-let) |
| **CARLISLE** | (kahr-LYL) |
| **CASCA** | (KAS-k*uh*) |
| **CASSIO** | (KAS-ee-oh) |
| **CASSIUS** | (KAS-ee-uhs) |
| **CATO** | (KAY-toh) |
| **CAWDOR** | (KAW-dur) |
| **CERBERUS** | (SUR-be-ruhs) |
| **CERIMON** | (SER-i-mahn) |
| **CESARIO** | (se-ZAH-ree-oh) |
| **CHAM** | (KAM) |
| **CHARMIAN** | (CHAHR-mee-*uh*n) |
| **CHIRON** | (KY-rahn) |
| **CICERO** | (SIS-*uh*-roh) |
| **CLEON** | (KLEE-ahn) |
| **CLOTEN** | (KLOH-t*uh*n) |
| **COLBRAND** | (KOHL-brand) |

| | |
|---|---|
| **COLOSSUS** | (ko-LAHS-*uh*s) |
| **COMINIUS** | (kah-MIN-ee-uhs) |
| **CORDELIA** | (kor-DEE-lyuh) |
| **CORIOLANUS** | (kor-ee-oh-LAY-nuhs) |
| **CRAB** | (KRAB) |
| **CRESSIDA** | (KRES-i-d*uh*) |
| **CRISPIAN** | (KRIS-pee-*a*n) |
| **CRISPIN** | (KRIS-pin) |
| **CROMER** | (KROH-mur) |
| **CYMBELINE** | (SIM-be-leen) |
| **CYTHEREA** | (sith-e-REE-*uh*) |
| | |
| **DE BURGH** | (D*UH* BURG) |
| **DE LA POLE** | (DE LAH POOL) |
| **DEMETRIUS** | (d*ee*-MEE-tri-uhs) |
| **DESDEMONA** | (dez-de-MOH-n*uh*) |
| **DEUCALION** | (dyoo-KAY-lee-*uh*n) |
| **DIAN** | (DY-an) |
| **DIONYZA** | (dy-oh-NY-z*uh*) |
| **DORSET** | (DOR-set) |
| **DROMIO** | (DROH-mee-oh) |
| **DUMAINE** | (dyoo-MAYN) |
| | |
| **ELSINORE** | (EL-si-nohr) |
| **ENOBARBUS** | (ee-noh-BAHR-buhs) |
| **EPHESUS** | (EF-e-suhs) |
| **EROS** | (EE-rahs) |
| **EXETER** | (EKS-*uh*-tur) |
| | |
| **FALCONBRIDGE** | (FAWL-k*uh*n-brij or FAW-k*uh*n-brij) |
| **FALSTAFF** | (FAWL-staf) |
| **FENTON** | (FEN-t*uh*n) |
| **FLORIZEL** | (FLAHR-i-zel) |
| **FORTINBRAS** | (FOR-tin-brahs) |
| **FULVIA** | (FUHL-vee-*uh*) |
| | |
| **GADSHILL** | (GADZ-hil) |
| **GAUNT** | (GAHNT) |
| **GIS** | (JIS) |
| **GLAMIS** | (GLAHM-is) |
| **GLOUCESTER** | (GLAHS-tur) |

| | |
|---|---|
| **GLOUCESTERSHIRE** | (GLAHS-tur-shir) |
| **GONERIL** | (GAHN-*uh*-ril) |
| **GRATIANO** | (grah-shee-AH-noh) |
| **GRUMIO** | (GROO-mee-oh or GROO-meeoh) |
| | |
| **HARFLEUR** | (HAHR-flur) |
| **HECATE** | (HEK-*uh*t or HEK-*uh*-tee) |
| **HECUBA** | (HEK-yoo-b*uh*) |
| **HELENUS** | (HEL-e-nuhs) |
| **HEREFORD** | (HUR-f*u*rd) |
| **HERMIA** | (HUR-mee-*uh*) |
| **HERMIONE** | (hur-MY-*oh*-n*ee*) |
| **HERNE** | (HURN) |
| **HERO** | (HE-roh) |
| **HESPERIDES** | (hes-PER-i-deez) |
| **HESPERUS** | (HES-p*uh*-ruhs) |
| **HOLOFERNES** | (hahl-*oh*-FUR-neez) |
| **HORATIO** | (hoh-RAY-shoh) |
| **HOTSPUR** | (HAHT-spur) |
| **HYPERION** | (hy-PEER-ee-*uh*n) |
| **HYRCANIA** | (hur-KAY-nee-*uh*) |
| | |
| **IACHIMO** | (EEAH-k*i*-moh or EEAH-kee-moh) |
| **IAGO** | (EEAH-goh) |
| **IMOGEN** | (IM-oh-jen) |
| **IRAS** | (EYE-rahs) |
| **ISABELLA** | (iz-*uh*-BEL-*uh*) |
| | |
| **JAQUENETTA** | (jak-*e*-NET-*uh*) |
| **JAQUES** | (JAY-kweez) |
| **JULIA** | (JYOOL-i-*uh*) |
| **JULIET** | (JYOOL-yet or JYOO-lee-et) |
| | |
| **KATHARINA** | (kat-*uh*-REE-n*uh*) |
| | |
| **LA PUCELLE** | (LAH puu-SEL) |
| **LAERTES** | (lay-UR-teez) |
| **LAUNCE** | (LAHNS or LAWNS) |
| **LAUNCELOT GOBBO** | (LAHN-s*e*-laht GAHB-boh) |
| **LAVINIA** | (l*uh*-VIN-ee-*uh*) |
| **LE BON** | (LE BAHN) |

| | |
|---|---|
| **LEDA** | (LEE-d*uh*) |
| **LEONATO** | (lee-oh-NAH-toh |
| | or lay-oh-NAH-toh) |
| **LEONINE** | (LEE-*oh*-nyn) |
| **LEONTES** | (lee-AHN-teez) |
| **LICHAS** | (LY-kas) |
| **LONGAVILLE** | (LAHNG-g*uh*-vil) |
| **LUCENTIO** | (loo-CHEN-seeoh) |
| **LUCIANA** | (loo-shee-AH-n*uh*) |
| **LUCIUS** | (LOO-shuhs) |
| **LUCRECE** | (loo-KREES or LOO-krees) |
| **LYMOGES** | (li-MOHZH) |
| **LYSANDER** | (ly-SAN-dur) |
| | |
| **MAB** | (MAB) |
| **MACBETH** | (mak-BETH) |
| **MACDUFF** | (mak-DUHF) |
| **MACHIAVEL** | (mak-ee-*uh*-VEL) |
| **MALVOLIO** | (mal-VOH-lee-oh) |
| **MARIA** [From *Love's Labor's Lost*] | (mah-REE-*uh*) |
| **MARIA** [From *Twelfth Night*] | (ma-RY-*uh*) |
| **MARINA** | (mah-REE-n*uh*) |
| **MARULLUS** | (ma-RUHL-uhs) |
| **MENENIUS AGRIPPA** | (me-NEE-nee-uhs *uh*-GRIP-*uh*) |
| **MERCUTIO** | (mer-KYOO-sheeoh) |
| **MESSINA** | (me-SEE-n*uh*) |
| **MILAN** | (mi-LAN) |
| **MONMOUTH** | (MAHN-muhth) |
| **MONTAGUE** | (MAHN-t*uh*-gyoo) |
| | |
| **NAVARRE** | (nah-VAHR) |
| **NERISSA** | (ne-RIS-*uh*) |
| **NESSUS** | (NES-uhs) |
| **NESTOR** | (NES-tur) |
| **NIOBE** | (NY-*oh*-bee) |
| **NORTHUMBERLAND** | (nor-THUHM-bur-l*uh*nd) |
| **NYM** | (NIM) |
| | |
| **OBERON** | (OH-be-rahn) |
| **OCTAVIUS** | (ahk-TAY-vee-uhs) |
| **OPHELIA** | (oh-FEEL-y*uh*) |

| | |
|---|---|
| **ORLEANS** | (OR-lee-*uh*nz) |
| **OSWALD** | (AHZ-w*uh*ld) |
| **OTHELLO** | (oh-THEL-oh) |
| | |
| **PADUA** | (PAD-yoo-*uh*) |
| **PALATINE** | (PAL-*uh*-tyn or PAL-*uh*-tin) |
| **PANDARUS** | (PAN-d*uh*-ruhs) |
| **PANDULPH** | (PAN-duhlf) |
| **PARIS** | (PA-ris) |
| **PAROLLES** | (pah-RAHL-es or pay-ROHL-es) |
| **PATAY** | (pah-TAY) |
| **PAULINA** | (paw-LEE-n*uh*) |
| **PEDRO** | (PAY-droh) |
| **PERDITA** | (PUR-di-t*uh*) |
| **PERICLES** | (PER-i-kleez) |
| **PETO** | (PEE-toh) |
| **PETRUCHIO** | (pe-TROOCH-eeoh or pe-TROO-keeoh) |
| **PHAETHON** | (FAY-e-th*uh*n) |
| **PHEBE** | (FEE-bee) |
| **PHILOMEL** | (FIL-*oh*-mel) |
| **PHILOMELA** | (fil-*oh*-MEE-l*uh*) |
| **PHOEBUS** | (FEE-buhs) |
| **PISANIO** | (pee-ZAH-neeoh) |
| **PISTOL** | (PIS-t*uh*l) |
| **PLANTAGENET** | (plan-TAJ-*uh*-net) |
| **POINS** | (POYNZ) |
| **POLIXENES** | (poh-LIKS-*uh*-neez) |
| **POLONIUS** | (p*oh*-LOH-nee-uhs) |
| **POMFRET** | (PAHM-fret) |
| **POMPEY** | (PAHM-pee) |
| **PORTIA** | (POR-sh*uh*) |
| **POSTHUMUS** | (PAHS-tyoo-muhs) |
| **PRIAM** | (PRY-am) |
| **PROGNE** | (PRAHG-nee) |
| **PROSPERO** | (PRAHS-pe-roh) |
| **PROTEUS** | (PROH-tee-uhs) |
| **PYRAMUS** | (PIR-*uh*-muhs) |
| | |
| **QUINCE** | (KWINS) |
| | |
| **REGAN** | (RAY-g*uh*n) |
| **REYNALDO** | (ray-NAWL-doh) |

| | |
|---|---|
| **RODERIGO** | (rahd-*uh*-REE-goh) |
| **ROMEO** | (ROH-meeoh) |
| **ROSALIND** | (RAHZ-*uh*-lind) |
| **ROSALINE** | (ROHZ-*uh*-lyn) |
| **ROSSILLION** | (roo-SIL-y*uh*n) |
| **ROUEN** | (roo-AHN or rohn) |
| **RUTLAND** | (RUHT-l*uh*nd) |
| | |
| **SAINT ALBANS** | (saynt AWL-b*uh*nz) |
| **SALISBURY** | (SAWLZ-b*uh*-ree) |
| **SATURNINUS** | (sat-ur-NY-nuhs) |
| **SAXONY** | (SAK-s*oh*-nee) |
| **SEACOLE** | (SEE-kohl) |
| **SEBASTIAN** | (se-BAS-ti*uh*n) |
| **SHREWSBURY** | (SHROOZ-b*uh*-ree) |
| **SHYLOCK** | (SHY-lahk) |
| **SICILIA** | (si-SIL-i-*uh*) |
| **SICILS** | (SIS-ilz) |
| **SILVIA** | (SIL-vee-*uh*) |
| **SILVIUS** | (SIL-vee-uhs) |
| **SINON** | (SY-n*ah*n) |
| **SOMERSET** | (SUHM-ur-set) |
| **STARVELING** | (STAHRV-ling) |
| **STRACHY** | (STRACH-ee or STRAHK-ee) |
| **SUFFOLK** | (SUHF-*uh*k) |
| | |
| **TAMORA** | (TAM-oh-r*uh*) |
| **TAMWORTH** | (TAM-wurth) |
| **TARQUIN** | (TAHR-kwin) |
| **TEARSHEET** | (TAIR-sheet) |
| **TEREUS** | (TEE-roos or TEE-r*ee*-uhs) |
| **TERMAGANT** | (TUR-mah-g*uh*nt) |
| **TEWKESBURY** | (TYOOKS-b*uh*-ree) |
| **THAISA** | (thay-IS-*uh* or thay-IZ-*uh*) |
| **THARSUS** | (TAHR-suhs) |
| **THERSITES** | (thur-SY-teez) |
| **THESEUS** | (THEE-see-uhs) |
| **THISBY** | (THIZ-b*ee*) |
| **THRACIAN** | (THRAY-sh*uh*n) |
| **TIMON** | (TY-m*uh*n) |
| **TITANIA** | (ti-TAHN-y*uh*) |
| **TITINIUS** | (ti-TIN-*ee*-uhs or ti-TIN-yuhs) |

| | |
|---|---|
| **TRINCULO** | (TRING-kyoo-loh) |
| **TROILUS** | (TROY-luhs) |
| **TULLUS AUFIDIUS** | (TUHL-uhs aw-FID-ee-uhs) |
| **TYBALT** | (TIB-*uh*lt) |
| **TYRREL** | (TIR-*e*l) |
| | |
| **ULYSSES** | (yoo-LIS-eez) |
| **URSULA** | (UR-syoo-l*uh*) |
| | |
| **VALENTINE** | (VAL-*uh*n-tyn) |
| **VINCENTIO** | (veen-CHEN-seeoh) |
| **VIOLA** | (VEE-oh-lah or VY-oh-lah) |
| **VOLUMNIA** | (voh-LUHM-nee-*uh*) |
| | |
| **WARWICK** | (WOR-ik) |
| **WESTMINSTER** | (WEST-min-stur) |
| **WESTMORLAND** | (WEST-m*ur*-l*uh*nd) |
| **WOLSEY** | (WUUL-zee) |
| | |
| **YORICK** | (YOR-ik) |

# THE LONG AND SHORT OF IT

Time is usually of the essence when it comes to choosing a monologue. How long the piece should be almost always depends on how it's going to be used. At one end of the spectrum lies the typical audition: most likely a lickety-split affair allowing you no more than two or three minutes in which to display your Shakespearean wares. At the other extreme is the relatively indulgent pace of the classroom, where a more thorough exploration of lengthier pieces is often the order of the day.

Of the 175 monologues presented in this volume of *Shakespeare for One*, two-thirds run between 25 and 45 lines, and thus are suitable for most applications. Should the time come, however, when only a particularly brief or extended selection will do, one the following entries will likely fill the bill.

## Monologues of Fewer Than 25 Lines

AS YOU LIKE IT
- (2) Duke Senior
- (7) Touchstone

THE COMEDY OF ERRORS
- (1) Antipholus of Syracuse

HAMLET
- (11) Hamlet

HENRY IV, PART 1
- (1) Prince Henry
- (3) Falstaff
- (8) Falstaff

JULIUS CAESAR
- (3) Brutus

KING LEAR
  (1) Edmund
  (3) Earl of Kent
  (4) Lear

LOVE'S LABOR'S LOST
  (1) Don Armado
  (3) Berowne

THE MERCHANT OF VENICE
  (1) Shylock

THE MERRY WIVES OF WINDSOR
  (3) Ford
  (5) Ford

A MIDSUMMER NIGHT'S DREAM
  (2) Bottom

OTHELLO
  (3) Iago
  (8) Othello

PERICLES
  (1) Pericles

ROMEO AND JULIET
  (3) Mercutio

THE TAMING OF THE SHREW
  (3) Petruchio

THE TEMPEST
  (1) Caliban
  (4) Prospero

TWELFTH NIGHT
  (2) Malvolio
  (3) Sir Toby

THE WINTER'S TALE
  (2) Shepherd
  (3) Clown

## Monologues of More Than 45 Lines

AS YOU LIKE IT
- (4) Adam
- (5) Jaques

CORIOLANUS
- (1) Menenius

HAMLET
- (4) Polonius
- (5) Polonius
- (6) Hamlet

HENRY V
- (4) King Henry
- (5) King Henry

HENRY VI, PART 2
- (3) Richard

HENRY VI, PART 3
- (1) Richard
- (3) King Henry
- (4) Richard

HENRY VIII
- (1) Cardinal Wolsey

JULIUS CAESAR
- (1) Cassius
- (6) Mark Antony
- (7) Mark Antony

KING LEAR
- (6) Lear

LOVE'S LABOR'S LOST
- (5) Berowne

THE MERCHANT OF VENICE
- (3) Prince of Morocco

OTHELLO
- (1) Othello
- (2) Iago

RICHARD II
(5) Richard
(6) Richard

RICHARD III
(3) Clarence

ROMEO AND JULIET
(1) Mercutio
(5) Friar Laurence

TIMON OF ATHENS
(5) Timon

TITUS ANDRONICUS
(3) Aaron

TROILUS AND CRESSIDA
(1) Pandarus

TWELFTH NIGHT
(1) Malvolio

# STRAIGHT TALK AND RHYME

Essentially, the fruit of Shakespeare's genius comes in one of three varieties: blank verse, rhyming verse, or prose. Since blank verse is used in the majority of his plays, it follows that most of the entries in *Shakespeare for One* are of the same stripe. Monologues *not* written in blank verse are singled out below.

## Prose

ALL'S WELL THAT ENDS WELL
    (1) Parolles

AS YOU LIKE IT
    (1) Orlando
    (7) Touchstone
    (8) Touchstone

CYMBELINE
    (3) Cloten

HAMLET
    (8) Hamlet
    (9) Hamlet
    (14) Hamlet

HENRY IV, PART 1
    (3) Falstaff
    (4) Hotspur
    (5) Falstaff
    (7) Falstaff
    (8) Falstaff

HENRY IV, PART 2
    (2) Falstaff

HENRY V
    (3) Boy
    (5) King Henry

HENRY VI, PART 2
(4) Jack Cade

HENRY VIII
(2) Porter's Man

JULIUS CAESAR
(5) Brutus

KING LEAR
(3) Earl of Kent
(6) Lear

LOVE'S LABOR'S LOST
(1) Armado
(3) Berowne
(6) Armado

THE MERCHANT OF VENICE
(2) Launcelot Gobbo
(4) Shylock

THE MERRY WIVES OF WINDSOR
(1) Falstaff
(2) Ford
(3) Ford
(4) Falstaff
(5) Ford
(6) Falstaff

A MIDSUMMER NIGHT'S DREAM
(2) Bottom

MUCH ADO ABOUT NOTHING
(1) Benedick
(2) Benedick
(3) Benedick
(4) Dogberry

OTHELLO
(2) Iago
(4) Iago

ROMEO AND JULIET
(3) Mercutio

THE TEMPEST
(2) Trinculo

TIMON OF ATHENS
- (2) Timon
- (4) Timon

TROILUS AND CRESSIDA
- (1) Pandarus

TWELFTH NIGHT
- (1) Malvolio
- (2) Malvolio
- (3) Sir Toby Belch

THE TWO GENTLEMEN OF VERONA
- (1) Launce
- (3) Launce

THE WINTER'S TALE
- (2) Shepherd
- (3) Clown
- (5) Autolycus


**Rhyme**

THE COMEDY OF ERRORS
- (1) Antipholus of Syracuse

LOVE'S LABOR'S LOST
- (4) Berowne

A MIDSUMMER NIGHT'S DREAM
- (3) Bottom
- (4) Puck

THE TEMPEST
- (4) Prospero

# SHAKESPEARE'S GREATEST HITS

## *Suggestions for the Initiates*

A wide array of options is an asset in most cases. But it can sometimes leave a person feeling overwhelmed. Take, for example, the actor who's just beginning to delve into the daunting world of classical monologues. He or she faces enough challenges as it is without having to sift through dozens of speeches hoping to find one that's particularly suited to a newcomer's needs.

With that in mind, offered below is a not-to-be-taken-too-seriously collection of greatest hits from *Shakespeare for One*: a score of friendly monologues deemed especially suitable for the uncertain actor who could use a nudge in the right direction.

Among the criteria considered in drawing up this list were:

• **Freshness.** Underexposed speeches had a big leg up on the competition. All warhorses ("To be, or not to be . . . ") were left in the stable.
• **Pace.** The selection was expected to generate a sense of momentum and be active rather than primarily introspective in nature.
• **Structure.** The piece had to be relatively straightforward in form, with a minimum of obscure references and syntactic mazes.
• **Staging.** It was considered a plus if the monologue suggested interesting or amusing physical possibilities. It was the kiss of death if too many prop or business requirements threatened to be a distraction.
• ***Death scenes need not apply.***

Don't forget, the list that follows doesn't really claim to be the "best" of Shakespeare. But if you're in need of a monologue that is accessible, coherent, and hasn't already been worked to death, this Shakespearean top-twenty is a worthy place to start looking.

HENRY IV, PART 1
(4) Hotspur

HENRY VI, PART 1
(1) Lord Talbot

HENRY VI, PART 2
(4) Jack Cade

HENRY VI, PART 3
(5) Richard

JULIUS CAESAR
(2) Casca

KING JOHN
(4) Philip the Bastard

KING LEAR
(3) Earl of Kent

MACBETH
(3) Macbeth

MEASURE FOR MEASURE
(1) Angelo

THE MERCHANT OF VENICE
(2) Launcelot Gobbo

THE MERRY WIVES OF WINDSOR
(5) Ford

A MIDSUMMER NIGHT'S DREAM
(2) Bottom

MUCH ADO ABOUT NOTHING
(3) Benedick
(4) Dogberry

OTHELLO
(7) Iago

RICHARD III
(5) Richard

THE TAMING OF THE SHREW
(2) Petruchio

THE TEMPEST
  (2) Trinculo

THE TWO GENTLEMEN OF VERONA
  (1) Launce

THE WINTER'S TALE
  (3) Clown